Collins Road Atlas
Town and Country Series
BRITAIN

CONTENTS

2	Key to Symbols
3 - 49	Route Planning Maps
50 - 51	Motorway Services Information
52 - 53	Aberdeen
54 - 55	Bath
56 - 57	Birmingham
58 - 59	Blackpool
60 - 61	Bournemouth
62 - 63	Bradford
64 - 65	Brighton
66 - 67	Bristol
68 - 69	Cambridge
70 - 71	Canterbury
72 - 73	Cardiff
74 - 75	Cheltenham
76 - 77	Chester
78 - 79	Coventry
80 - 81	Derby
82 - 83	Dover
84 - 85	Dundee
86 - 87	Durham
88 - 89	Edinburgh
90 - 91	Exeter
92 - 93	Folkestone
94 - 95	Glasgow
96 - 97	Gloucester
98 - 99	Harrogate
100 - 101	Hereford
102 - 103	Inverness
104 - 105	Kingston upon Hull
106 - 107	Leeds
108 - 109	Leicester
110 - 111	Lincoln
112 - 113	Liverpool
114 - 115	Manchester
116 - 117	Middlesbrough
118 - 119	Newcastle upon Tyne
120 - 121	Norwich
122 - 123	Nottingham
124 - 125	Oxford
126 - 127	Perth
128 - 129	Plymouth
130 - 131	Portsmouth
132 - 133	Reading
134 - 135	Sheffield
136 - 137	Southampton
138 - 139	Stoke-on-Trent
140 - 141	Stratford-on-Avon
142 - 143	Swansea
144 - 145	Swindon
146 - 147	Torquay
148 - 149	Winchester
150 - 151	Windsor
152 - 153	Worcester
154 - 155	York
156 - 157	London M25 Map
158 - 159	Central London Map
160 - 162	Index to London Street Names
163 - 175	Index to Route Planning Maps
176	Distance Chart
177	Web-Site Guide

Published by Collins
An imprint of HarperCollins Publishers
77-85 Fulham Palace Road, Hammersmith, London W6 8JB

The HarperCollins website address is:
www.fireandwater.com

Copyright © HarperCollins Publishers Ltd 2001
Mapping © Bartholomew Ltd 2001

Collins® is a registered trademark of HarperCollins Publishers Limited

Mapping generated from Bartholomew digital data

Bartholomew website address is:
www.bartholomewmaps.com

All rights reserved. No part of this publication may be reproduced, stored in a retrieval system, or transmitted, in any form or by any means, electronic, mechanical, photocopying, recording or otherwise, without the prior written permission of the publisher and copyright owners.

The contents of this publication are believed correct at the time of printing. Nevertheless, the publisher can accept no responsibility for errors or omissions, changes in the detail given, or for any expense or loss thereby caused.

The representation of a road, track or footpath is no evidence of a right of way.

Printed in Hong Kong   ISBN 0 00 448858 X   NC10564   CDDD

2 Key to Map Symbols

Key to Route Planning Maps

SCALE: approx. 7 miles to 1 inch

M1 (under constr.)	Motorway
Motorway tunnel	Motorway tunnel
Junction number (restricted access)	Junction number
Service area (restricted access)	Service area
A1 (dual carriageway)	Primary route
A634 (dual carriageway, under constr.)	'A' Road
B1246 (dual carriageway, under constr.)	'B' Road
Other road	Other road
13	Distance in miles

Gradient	Gradient
Toll	Toll
Railway/tunnel	Railway/tunnel
Car ferry	Car ferry
✈ Airport	Airport
Built-up areas	Built-up areas
Settlement	Settlement
International boundary	International boundary
National boundary	National boundary

National/Regional park	National/Regional park
Forest park	Forest park
Woodland	Woodland
Beach	Beach
Marsh	Marsh
Canal	Canal
Lake, dam and river	Lake, dam and river
718 △	Height in metres
☆	Place of interest

land below	0	328	657	985	1640	2295	2950	feet
water	sea level	0	100	200	300	500	700	900	metres

Key to Approach Route Maps

SCALE: approx. 2.5 miles to 1 inch

M5	Motorway
30 (full access) 29 (limited access)	Motorway junction
Maidstone / Birch / Sarn	Motorway service area with full/limited access/off road
A48 (dual/single)	Primary route
Primary route with passing places	Primary route with passing places
A30 (dual/single)	'A' Road
'A' Road with passing places	'A' Road with passing places
B1403 (dual/single)	'B' Road
'B' Road with passing places	'B' Road with passing places
Minor road	Minor road
Restricted access	Restricted access
Road projected or under construction	Road projected or under construction
Multi-level junction	Multi-level junction
Roundabout	Roundabout
10	Road distance in miles

Road tunnel	Road tunnel
Steep hill (arrows point downhill)	Steep hill (arrows point downhill)
Level crossing	Level crossing
Toll	Toll
Poole 2½ hrs (3 hrs)	Car ferry route & journey times; daytime and (night-time)
Railway line and station	Railway line and station
Railway tunnel	Railway tunnel
✈ Airport with scheduled services	Airport with scheduled services
H Heliport	Heliport
Built up area	Built up area
□ □ □ Town/Village/Other settlement	Town/Village/Other settlement
National boundary	National boundary
County/Unitary Authority boundary	County/Unitary Authority boundary
National/Regional park	National/Regional park
Forest park boundary	Forest park boundary
Danger Zone	Military range
Woodland	Woodland
468 ▲941	Spot height/Summit height in metres
Beach	Beach
Lake/Dam/River/Waterfall	Lake/Dam/River/Waterfall
Canal/Dry canal/Canal tunnel	Canal/Dry canal/Canal tunnel

A selection of tourist detail is shown on the mapping. It is advisable to check with the local tourist information office regarding opening times and facilities available.

i i	Tourist information centre (all year/seasonal)
Preserved railway	Preserved railway
⚔ 1738	Battlefield
ᛗ	Ancient monument
✝	Ecclesiastical building
Castle	Castle
Historic house (with or without garden)	Historic house (with or without garden)
❀	Garden
🏛	Museum/Art gallery
£	Factory shop village
Theme park	Theme park
Major sports venue	Major sports venue
Motor racing circuit	Motor racing circuit
Racecourse	Racecourse
Country park	Country park
Nature reserve	Nature reserve
Wildlife park or Zoo	Wildlife park or Zoo
★	Other interesting feature
⚑	Golf course
(NT) (NTS)	National Trust property/National Trust for Scotland
(MNT)	Manx National Trust (Isle of Man)

Key to Town Plan Maps

Motorway	Motorway
Through route	Through route
Dual carriageway	Dual carriageway
Restricted access	Restricted access
Pedestrian street	Pedestrian street
Path/Footbridge	Path/Footbridge

Tourist building	Tourist building
Important building	Important building
Higher Education building	Higher Education building
Hospital	Hospital
Cemetery	Cemetery
Green area	Green area

P	One way street/Car park
i	Tourist information centre
✝	Ecclesiastical building
Railway line	Railway line
Railway/Light rail station	Railway/Light rail station
Metro station/Underground	Metro station/Underground

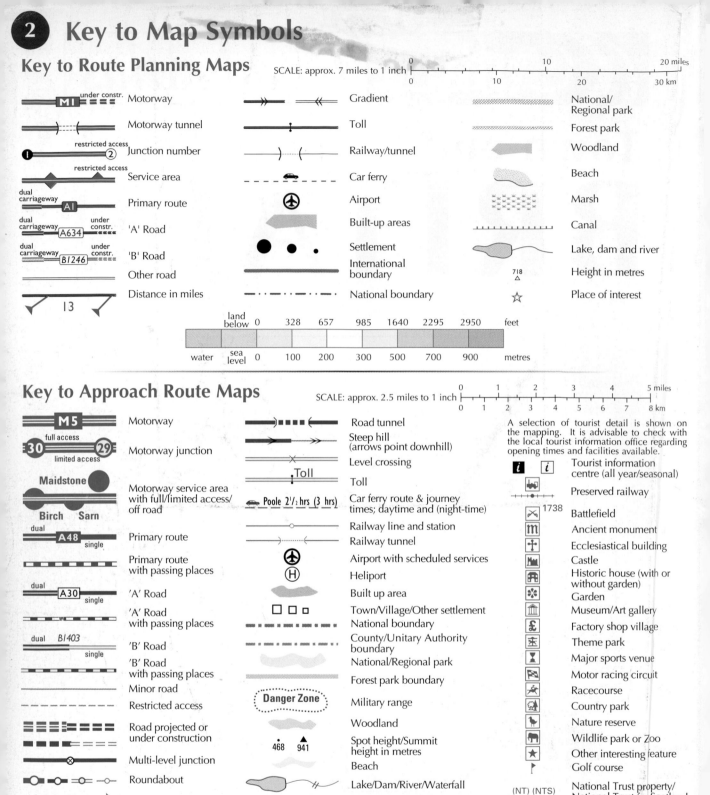

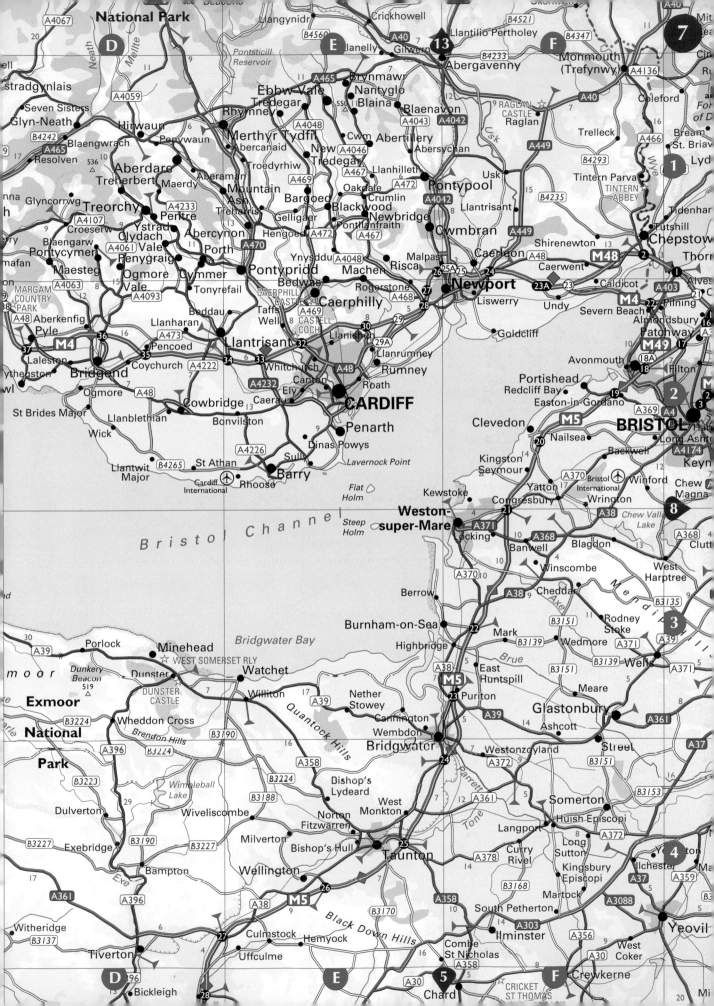

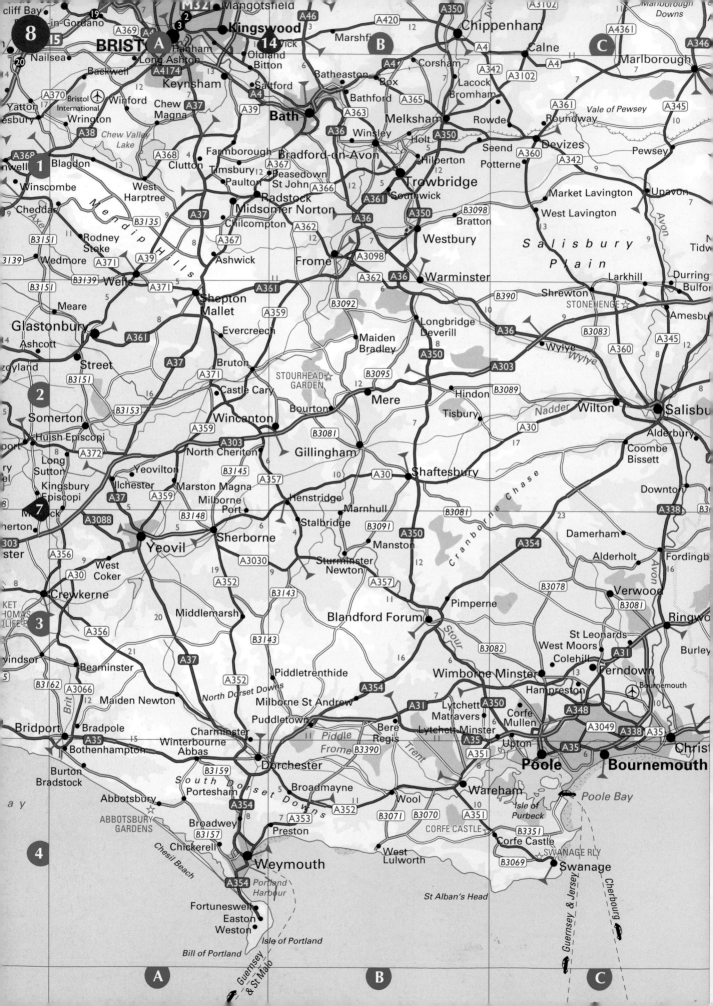

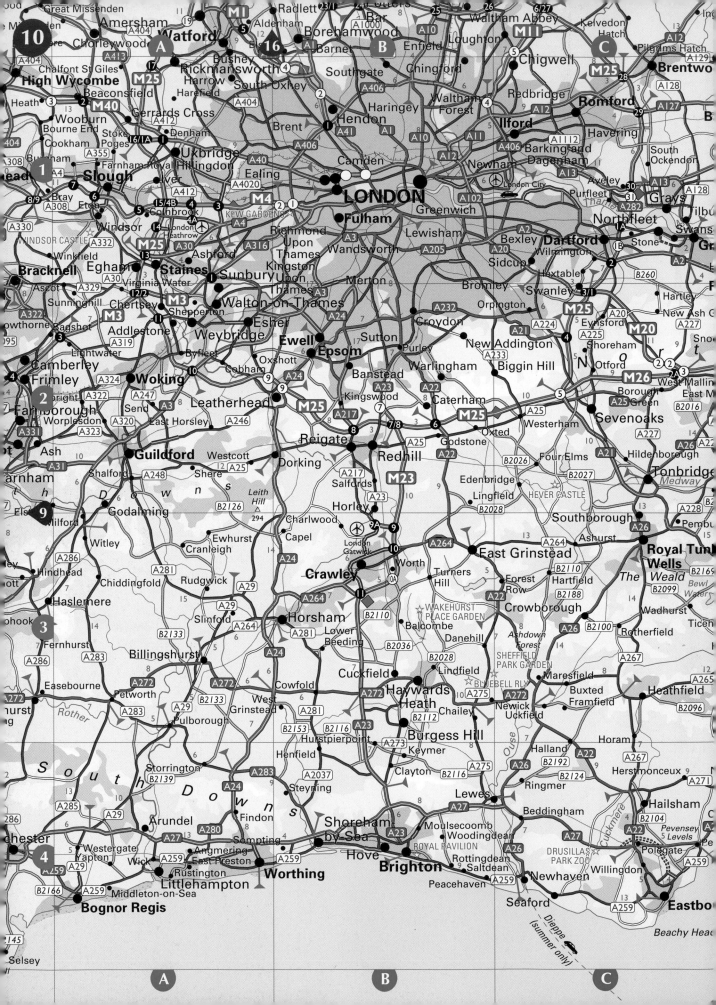

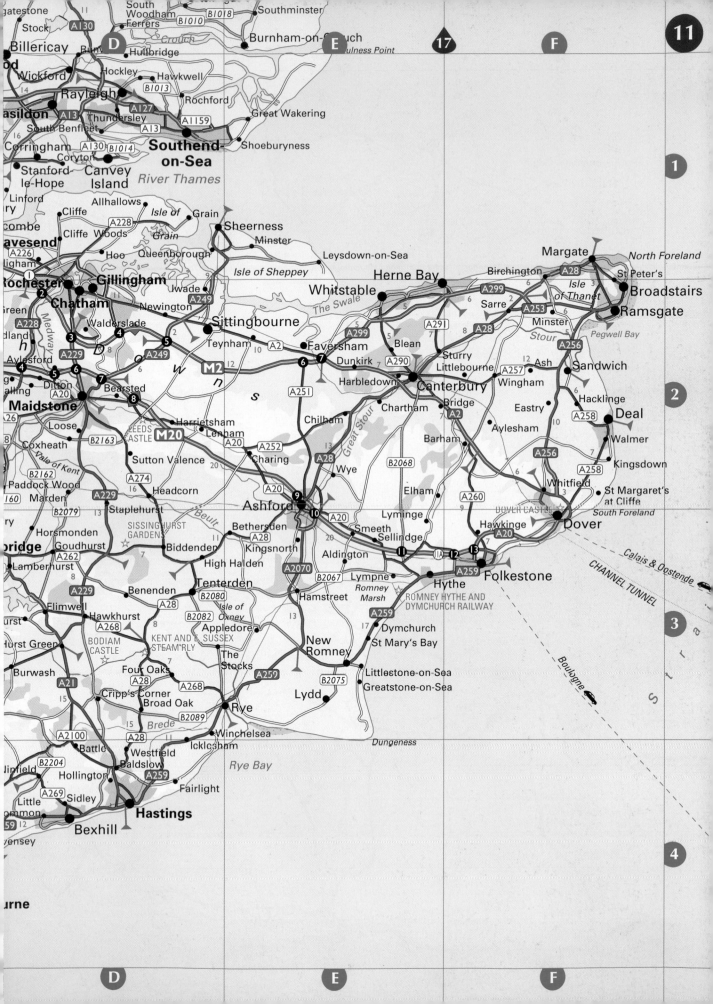

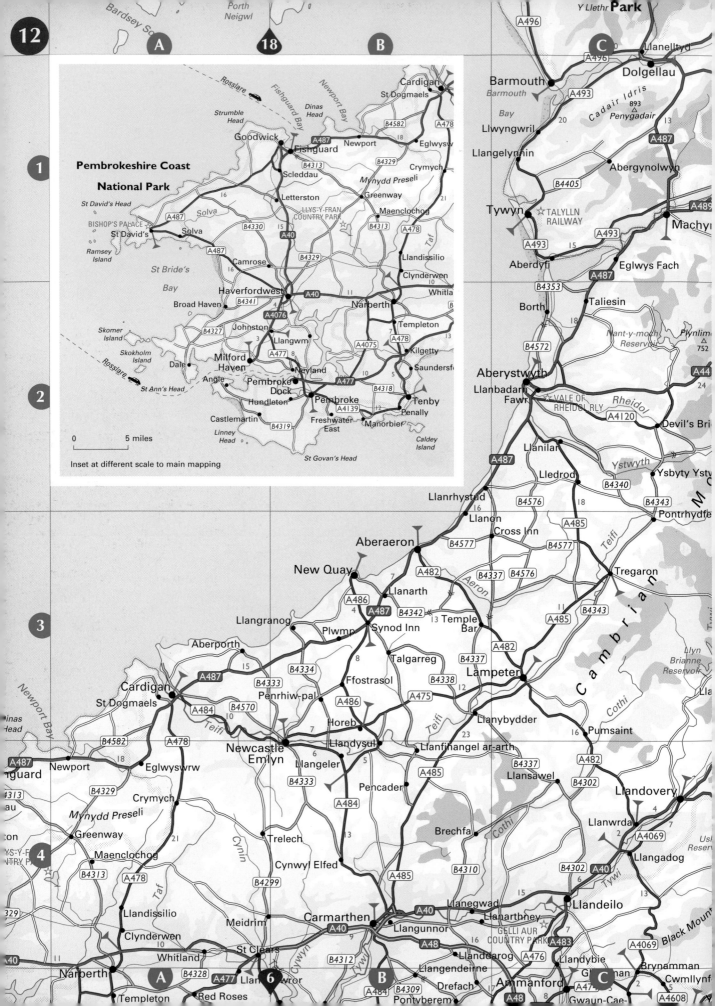

Inset map

Pembrokeshire Coast National Park

St David's Head
BISHOP'S PALACE
St David's
Ramsey Island
Solva
Camrose
Broad Haven
Haverfordwest
Johnston
Milford Haven
Dale
Angle
Pembroke Dock
Hundleton
Pembroke
Castlemartin
Linney Head
Freshwater East
St Ann's Head
St Bride's Bay
Skomer Island
Skokholm Island
Rosslare
St Govan's Head

Goodwick
Fishguard
Scleddau
Letterston
Llys-y-Fran Country Park
Newport
Crymych
Mynydd Preseli
Greenway
Maenclochog
Llandissilio
Clynderwen
Whitla
Narberth
Templeton
Kilgetty
Saundersf
Nayland
Llangwm
Tenby
Penally
Manorbier
Caldey Island

St Dogmaels
Cardigan

Rosslare

Strumble Head
Fishguard Bay
Dinas Head
Newport Bay
Eglwysw

Roads: A487, B4582, B4329, B4313, A478, B4330, A40, B4329, A4076, B4341, B4327, A477, A4139, B4319, A4075, A478, B4318, A4120

0   5 miles

Inset at different scale to main mapping

Main map

Bardsey So
Porth Neigwl
Porth Neigwl
Y Llethr Park

A496
Llanelltyd
Dolgellau
Barmouth
Barmouth Bay
A493
Cadair Idris
893 Penygadair
A487
Llwyngwril
Llangelynnin
B4405
Abergynolwyn
13
Tywyn
TALYLLN RAILWAY
A487
A489
Machy
A493
15
Aberdyfi
Eglwys Fach
A487
B4353
Borth
Taliesin
Nant-y-moch Reservoir
Plynlim
752
B4572
18
Aberystwyth
Llanbadarn Fawr
VALE OF RHEIDOL RLY
A44
24
A4120
Devil's Bri
Llanilar
Llanrhystud
A487
Ystwyth
Lledrod
Ysbyty Ystv
B4340
B4576
B4343
Pontrhydfe
Llanon
A485
18
Cross Inn
Aberaeron
B4577
A482
Aeron
B4337
B4576
B4577
Tregaron
New Quay
Llanarth
A486
A487
B4342
13
Temple Bar
11
B4343
A485
Llangranog
Plwmp
Synod Inn
4
Aberporth
B4334
Talgarreg
8
B4337
Lampeter
15
B4333
Ffostrasol
B4338
12
Cardigan
St Dogmaels
Penrhiw-pal
A486
A475
Llanybydder
16
Pumsaint
A484
B4570
10
Horeb
7
Cambrian
Teifi
Llyn Brianne Reservoir
Lla
Newport Bay
Dinas Head
Newcastle Emlyn
Llandysul
Llanfihangel ar-arth
A482
B4582
A478
Newport
18
Eglwyswrw
B4329
Crymych
Mynydd Preseli
Greenway
21
Maenclochog
B4313
A478
Llandissilio
Clynderwen
10
Whitland
Narberth
Templeton
B4328
A477
Llangeler
B4333
6
5
Pencader
A485
Llansawel
B4337
B4302
Llandovery
Brechfa
Cothi
Llanwrda
2
A4069
Llangadog
B4302
A40
Trelech
Cynin
13
Cynwyl Elfed
A485
B4310
Taf
Meidrim
Llanegwad
Llanarthney
A40
Carmarthen
Llangunnor
GELLI AUR COUNTRY PARK
A483
Llandeilo
B4299
Cynwyn
Cynin
St Clears
6
B4312
Tywi
A48
Llanddarog
A476
Llandybie
Brynamman
Cwmllyn
Narberth
B4328
A477
Llan wror
A484
B4309
Red Roses
Drefach
Ammanford
A47
Pontyberem
A48
Gwaun-Cae-
A4608
Templeton
Black Mount
Resen
Ust
Teifi
Cothi

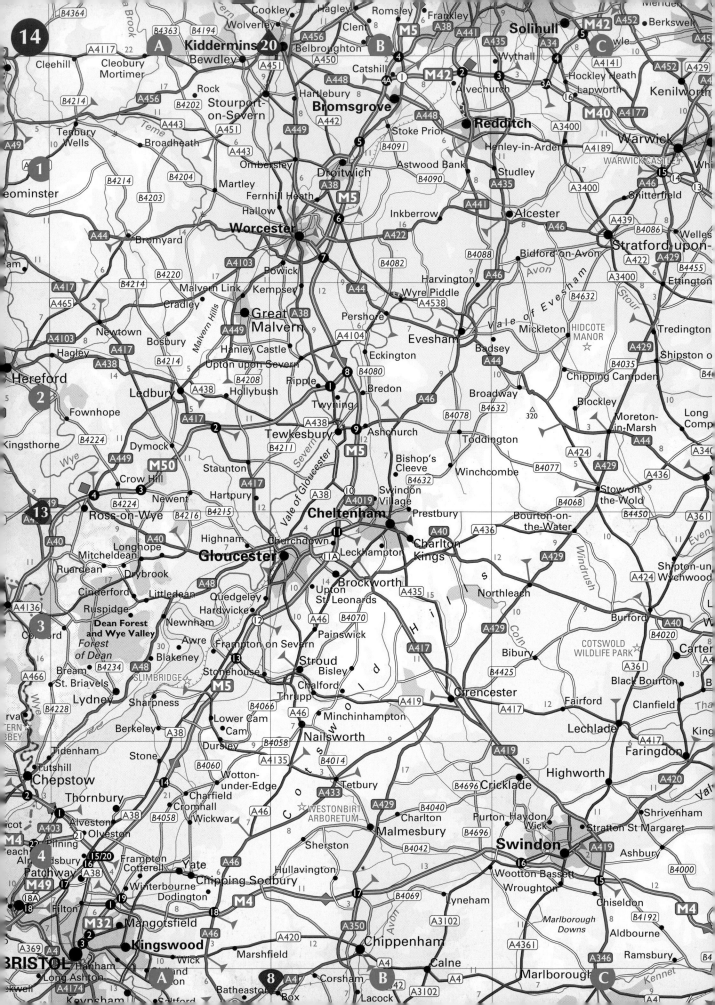

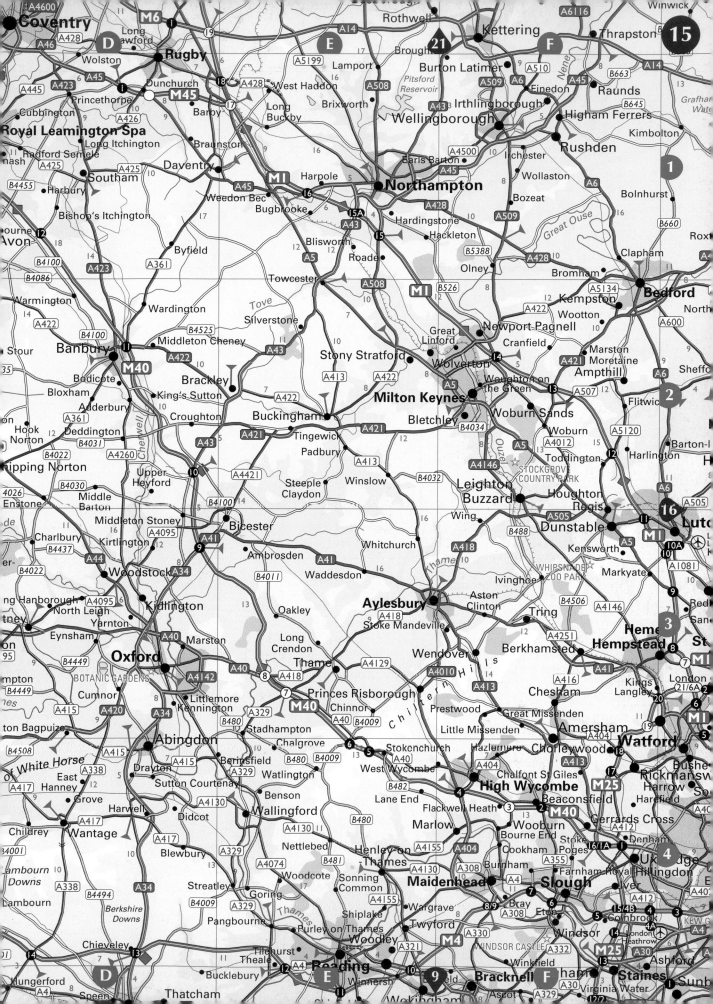

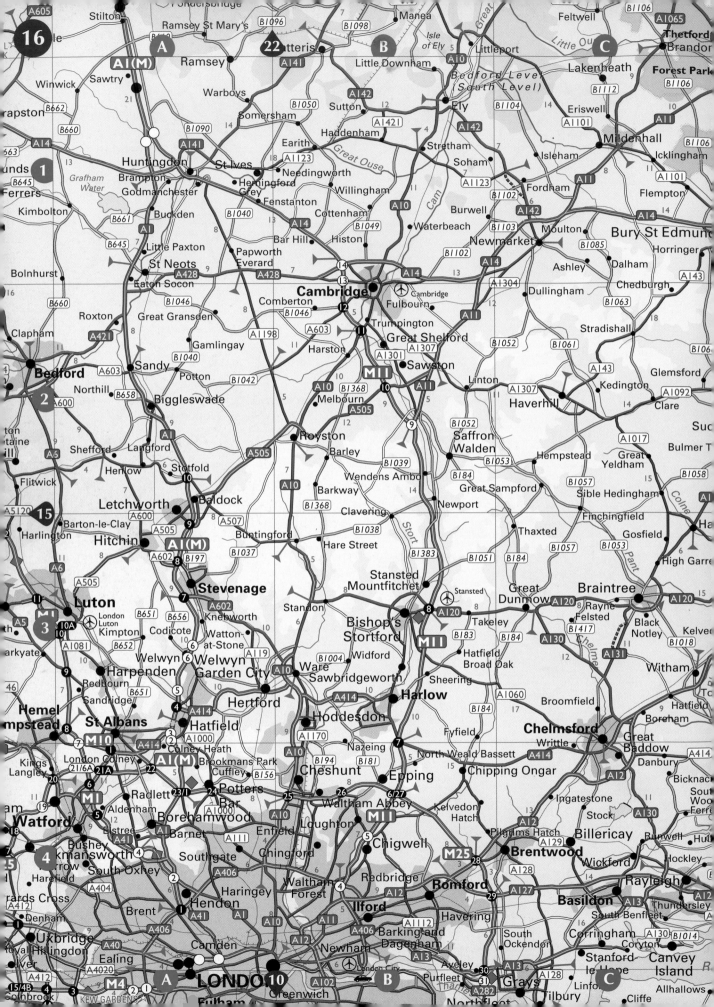

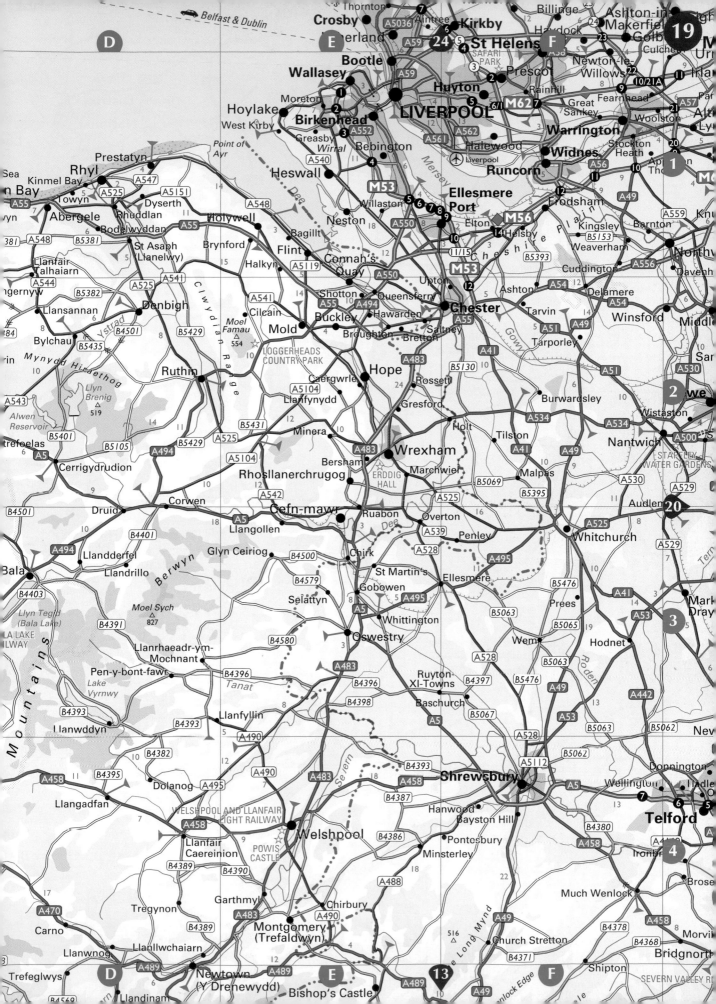

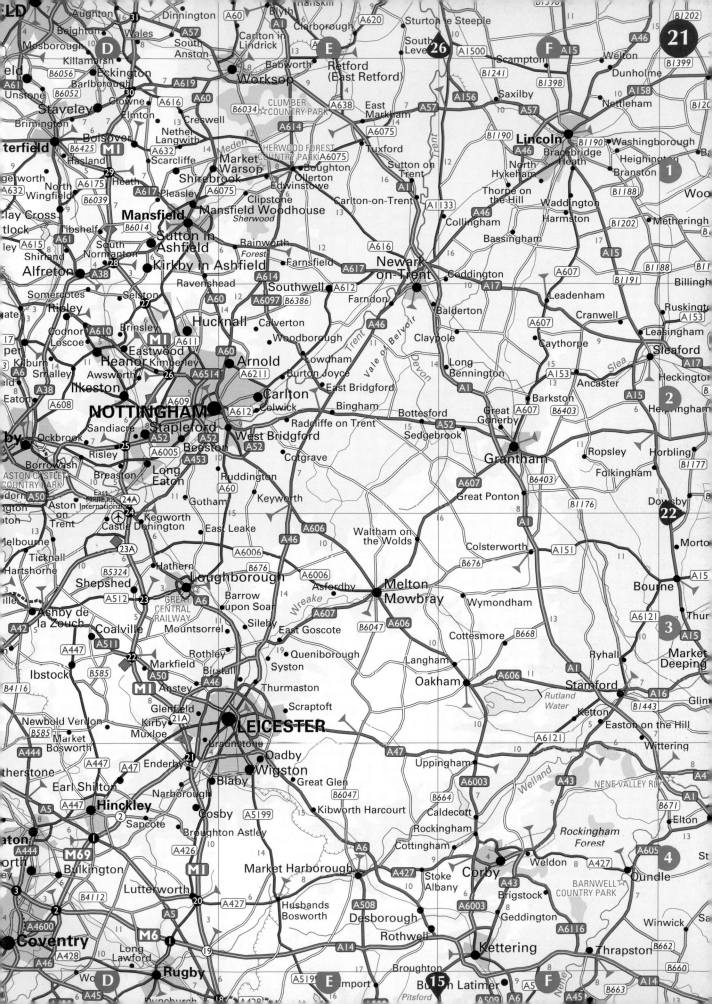

A   29   B   C

1

Bootle   Black Combe   600   Broughton in Furness   A5084   A593   A592   Newby Brid

Millom   Grizebeck   A5092   A5093   7   Greenodd   A590   Milnthorpe

Dalton-in-Furness   Ulverston   A595   Cartmel   Grange-over-S   B5278   B5277   Silverdale

Barrow-in-Furness   Bardsea   Warto   Carnforth

Vickerstown   A590   A5087   Baycliff   Aldingham   Bolton-le-Sands

Rampside   Morecambe Bay   Morecambe   A589

Isle of Walney   Hilpsford Point   Lancaster

🚗 Belfast (summer only)   Heysham   A683   A6

🚗 Douglas   A588   33A

Cockerham

2

Isle of Man

Point of Ayre   Ardrossan & Belfast (summer only)

A16   Fleetwood   Pilling   Garstang

Andreas   Freesall   A588

Sandygate   A17   A10   13   A585   Thornton   Hambleton   A586

A14   A9   Ramsey Bay   Cleveleys   Poulton-le-Fylde   Great Eccles

Ballaugh   A10   7   A3   5   Ramsey   Blackpool   Wyre   Elswick

Kirk Michael   7   Maughold   Great Marton   Fylde   Woodplumpte   A585

Snaefell   625   Maughold Head   A584   3   M55

9   A2   A15   ☆ MANX ELECTRIC RAILWAY   Blackpool   16   Kirkham

A4   A3   B10   Dhoon   SNAEFELL MOUNTAIN RAILWAY   A583   Wrea Green   Ba

Peel   A18   17   Laxey   Freckleton   17   Pre

Patrick   B22   8   Laxey Bay   Lytham   A584   12   Penwort

A1   10   A2   Clay Head   St Anne's   Ribble   Longton

Dalby   Foxdale   Glen Vine   Onchan   A11   Le

13   A24   Braaid   Douglas   Tarleton   B5248

A36   A27   A3   A5   ISLE OF MAN RAILWAY   A565   Croston

Ballabeg   A25   Southport   A570   Rufford   Eccl   A59

Port Erin   A27   Ballasalla   Heysham 🚗   Ainsdale   Scarisbrick   Burscough   A5209

Cregneash   A5   ⚓ Isle of Man   Burscough Bridge   Par   Appley B

Port St Mary   Castletown   18   A5147   A565

Calf of Man   🚗 Dublin (summer only)   Formby   Ormskirk   Skelmersdale

Aughton   3   4

Lydiate   M58   A570

Maghull   7   Rainford

🚗 Belfast & Dublin   Thornton   1

Crosby   A5036   Aintree   Kirkby

Litherland   A59   6   St Hele

🚗 Liverpool   5   SAFARI PARK

Bootle   17   3

4

Wallasey   A59   Huyton   2   Pre

Hoylake   Moreton   LIVERPOOL   5   6/1   M6

West Kirby   1   M62

Great Ormes Head   Birkenhead   2   A561   Halewood   Runco

Penrhyn Bay   Greasby   3   A552   A562   Liverpool

Llandudno   Rhôs-on-Sea   Prestatyn   Wirral   Bebington   4   ✈ Liverpool

Deganwy   Kinmel Bay   Point of Ayr   A540   11   M53

Colwyn Bay   Rhyl   Heswall   Willaston   7   8   Ellesmere Port

Conwy   A55   Old Colwyn   A525   A547   Dee   Neston   C

enmaenmawr   Abergele   19   Dyserth   A515   Holywell   A548

Towy   Rhuddlan

A165
Scarborough
Eastfield
Cayton
7
Staxton
Hunmanby
A1039 Filey
6
Wold
Newton
10
B1229 Bempton
Flamborough Head
Flamborough
B1253
A165
angtoft
Rudston
SEWERBY HALL
Bridlington
Kilham A614
Hilderthorpe
49
A165
Driffield
Bridlington
Bay
B1249 Skipsea
Hutton
Cranswick
Beeford
64
15
B1242
Brandesburton
B1244 Hornsea
2
Sigglesthorne
A1035
Leven
7
Molescroft B1243
A165 South
Beverley
Skirlaugh
Woodmansey
13 Aldbrough
m
10
B1238
Holderness
Sproatley
Bilton
B1242
A1079 A165
Preston Hedon
A1033
B1362
Withernsea
A1105 A63
5 KINGSTON
UPON HULL
Thorngumbald
A1033
21 Keyingham
A1033
by
Patrington
Easington
Barton-
upon-Humber
Goxhill
B1445
Barrow
upon Humber
15
B1206 A1077
10
Ulceby A160
Immingham
Spurn Head
6
B1211 A180
5 A18 Keelby Healing
9
Humberside
International
12
Grimsby Cleethorpes
A46 6
Laceby Humberston
rigg
A1084 A1173
A46
Waltham
13
6
A18
B1434
A16
Tetney
stow
Caistor
17
sey B1434
North Thoresby
B1225 B1203
North Somercotes
Binbrook
Rotterdam & Zeebrugge
A1031
A1103 Fotherby
A631
B1200
dle Rasen
Market Rasen
Grimoldby
A631 A157
elton B1202
Lincolnshire Wolds
Louth
Manby
Mablethorpe
15
15
A46
A153 A157
A1104 A52
15
Dunholme
B1399 gby
B1225
Maltby le Marsh
A1111 22
A158
Alford
Huttoft

1

2

3

4

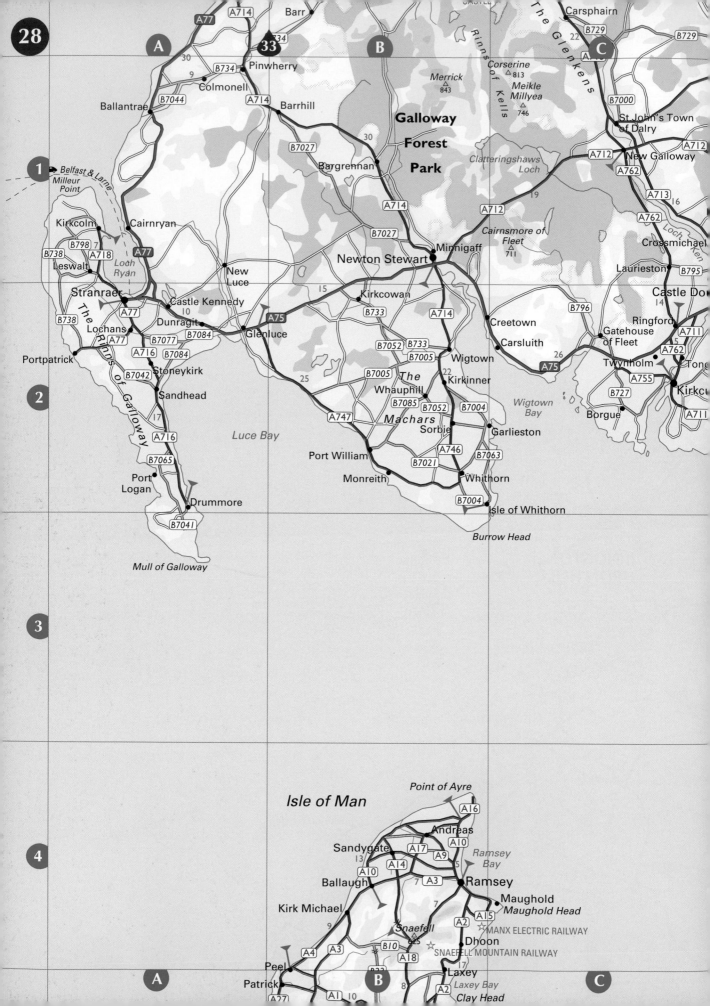

A77
A714
Barr
Carsphairn
B729
B729
28
A77
A714
33
B734
Pinwherry
B734
B
22
The Glenkens
C
A713

B7044
Colmonell
A712
St John's Town
of Dalry

Ballantrae
B7044
A714
Barrhill
Merrick
843
Corserine
813
Meikle
Millyea
746
Rinns of Kells
B7000
A712

B7027
Galloway
Forest
Park
A712
New Galloway
A712

1
Belfast & Larne
Milleur
Point
Bargrennan
B7027
Clatteringshaws
Loch
19
A762
A713
16
A762

Kirkcolm
Cairnryan
A714
Minnigaff
Cairnsmore of
Fleet
711
Crossmichael
Loch Ken

B738
B798 7
A718
B7027
Newton Stewart
A75

Leswalt
Loch
Ryan
A77
New
Luce
15
Kirkcowan
Creetown
B796
Laurieston
B795

Stranraer
A77
Castle Kennedy
B733
A714
Castle Do
14

B738
Dunragit
10
A75
Glenluce
B7052
B733
Carsluith
Ringford
Gatehouse
of Fleet
A711

Lochans
A77
B7077
B7084
B7052
B733
Wigtown
26
Twynholm
A755
Tong

Portpatrick
A716
B7084
B7005
22
Kirkinner
B727
Borgue
A711
Kirkc

2
B7042
Stoneykirk
25
B7005
The
Whauphill
Machars
B7085
B7052
B7004
Wigtown
Bay

Sandhead
A747
Sorbie
A746
Garlieston

A716
17
Luce Bay
Port William
B7021
B7063
Whithorn

B7065
Monreith
B7004
Isle of Whithorn

Port
Logan
Burrow Head

Drummore
B7041

Mull of Galloway

3

Point of Ayre
4
Isle of Man
A16

Andreas
A10
Sandygate
A17
A9
Ramsey
Bay

A14
5
Ballaugh
7
A3
Ramsey

Kirk Michael
7
Maughold
Maughold Head

9
A2
A15
Snaefell
625
MANX ELECTRIC RAILWAY

A4
A3
B10
Dhoon
SNAEFELL MOUNTAIN RAILWAY

Peel
A18
Laxey

A
Patrick
B
Laxey Bay
C
A1 10
A27
Clay Head

D · E · F

1 · 2 · 3 · 4

Ellington
Lynemouth
Newbiggin-by-the-Sea
Guide Post
Blyth
Cramlington
Seaton Sluice
Seghill
Seaton Delaval
Whitley Bay
Shiremoor
Tynemouth
ongbenton
North Shields
Wallsend
South Shields
Jarrow
Hebburn
Cleadon
elling
shead
Boldon
Sunderland
Washington
Chester-le-Street
Bournmoor
Houghton le Spring
Hetton-le-Hole
Seaham
Murton
South Hetton
Easington Colliery
Durham
Haswell
Easington
Sherburn
Horden
Thornley
Peterlee
Wheatley Hill
Blackhall Colliery
Bowburn
Wingate
Trimdon
Hartlepool
Ferryhill
Fishburn
Tees Bay
Chilton
Sedgefield
Newton Aycliffe
Billingham
South Bank
Redcar
Marske-by-the-Sea
Middlesbrough
Saltburn-by-the-Sea
Brotton
Stockton-on-Tees
Eston
Skelton
Loftus
Thornaby-on-Tees
Guisborough
Hinderwell
Eaglescliffe
Sandsend
Teesside International
Egglescliffe
Roseberry Topping
Whitby
Yarm
Great Ayton
Danby
Sleights
High Hawsker
urworth-on-Tees
Hutton Rudby
Stokesley
Castleton
Egton
Robin Hood's Bay
North Cowton
Great Broughton
NORTH YORKSHIRE MOORS RAILWAY
corton
Round Hill
North York Moors
Staintondale
terick
Brompton
Rosedale Abbey
Cloughton
Northallerton
North York Moors
Burnisto
National Park
Hackness
Leeming
Gillamoor
Lockton
Scalby
Knayton
North Riding Forest Park
hirsk
Boltby
Kirkbymoorside
Wrelton
Pickering
Seamer
Sowerby
Helmsley
Sproxton
Snainton
Wass
Thorn Dale

Stavanger, Haugesund & Bergen
Göteborg & Kristiansand
Amsterdam

Cleveland Hills
Hambleton Hills
North York Moors

A189 · A196 · A19 · A1058 · A194 · A183 · A1018 · A1231 · A183 · A690 · A1018 · A182 · A182 · A181 · A1086 · A179 · A19 · A1(M) · A177 · A689 · A689 · A178 · A1085 · A66 · A67 · A171 · A172 · A174 · A171 · B1416 · A167 · B1264 · A172 · B1257 · A167 · A684 · A168 · A167 · B1263 · B6267 · A61 · A170 · B1257 · A170 · A169 · A165 · A170 · B1269 · B1366

16 · 10 · 6 · 12 · 6 · 8 · 7 · 12 · 8 · 13 · 7 · 15 · 16 · 22 · 20 · 19 · 20 · 26

Bass Rock

North Berwick

A198

JOHN MUIR COUNTRY PARK

Dunbar

East nton

Tyne

ington

Stenton

B6370

Garvald

A1

Cockburnspath

Meikle Black Law

Ecclaw

St Abb's Head

3

A1107   13

St Abbs

Coldingham

rd

Grantshouse

B6355

Cranshaws

A6112

9

B6438

Eyemouth

Burnmouth

uir Hills

Meikle Says Law
535

Whiteadder Water

Auchencrow

Reston

B6438

B6437

B6355

A1

Preston

Chirnside

Foulden

Berwick-upon-Tweed

Dirrington Great Law

Duns

A6105

6

Tweed

Westruther

B6456

Polwarth

7

Blackadder Water

B6460

Paxton

15

B6437

B6461

Tweedmouth

Houndslow

8

A6105

12

Ladykirk

Norham

B6354

Scremerston

A6089

Greenlaw

B6460

12

Swinton

A6112

12

A698

Ancroft

B6525

A1

Gordon

B6364

Eccles

A697

Duddo

A6105

10

B6461

Coldstream

B6353

Fenwick

Holy Island or Lindisfarne

13

Stichill

A698

10

Cornhill-on-Tweed

Lowick

Burrows Hole

Earlston

A6089

Crookham

B6353

Ford

Farne Islands

A68

B6397

Smailholm

B6350

Flodden

B6525

28

Cockenheugh

Bamburgh

B1342

BAMBURGH CASTLE

B6356

FLOORS CASTLE

B6352

Milfield

B6349

14

211

Belford

Seahouses

lrose

B6404

Kelso

KELSO ABBEY

B6396

Kilham

Doddington

B6348

B1341

North Sunderland

ls

A699

B6352

B6351

Kirknewton

Chatton

Beadnell

DRYBURGH ABBEY

A698

B6436

Town Yetholm

Kirk Yetholm

Akeld

Wooler

Ellingham

B1340

Beadnell Bay

7

Nisbet

Eckford

B6401

Morebattle

Bowmont Water

The Cheviot
815

Cateran Hill

Christon Bank

Embleton

B6347

B1339

Craster

B6400

Ancrum

Bonjedward

Jedburgh

Kale Water

A697

Eglingham

B6346

A1

Rennington

JEDBURGH ABBEY

A698

B6358

Oxnam

Powburn

B1340

Longhoughton

Denholm

B6357

A68

Windy Gyle
619

Breamish

Glanton

Alnwick

38

13

Camptown

Cheviot Hills

Whittingham

B6341

Edlingham

A1068

Lesbury

Alnmouth

ster dge

14

Chesters

Netherton

30

Shilbottle

Warkworth

Southdean

A6088

Carter Bar

A68

13

National Park

Redesdale

Rochester

Thropton

Rothbury

B6341

Rothbury Forest

B6341

Longframlington

B6345

Felton

18

Coquet Island

Amble

Togston

A1068

57

Kielder

Kielder Forest Park

Otterburn

Elsdon

B6342

Longhorsley

A1

A697

Ulgham

23

Ellington

Lynemouth

istone

Kielder Water (Reservoir)

B6320

A696

B6343

Morpeth

rwood

A197

Ashington

A189

Guide

Newbigg

A196

A
40
B
C

Sound of Ca...

**Rum
(Rhum)**
Kinloch
Aird of Sleat
Ardvasar

Point of Sleat

Sound

Askival
△
812

Mora

Sound of Rum

A830

Cleadale

Rubha nam
Meirleach

Eigg

1
Castlebay

An Sgurr
△
393

Galmisdale

Sound of Arisai

Eilean
nan Each

Sound of Eigg

Loch na

Ro

Castlebay

Lochboisdale

Muck

Eilean
Shona

Ockle
Ardtoe

Point of
Ardnamurchan

Achosnich
Acharacle

B8044

Eilean Mor

A r d n a m u r c h a n

B8007

Ben Hiant
△
528

Glenbeg

B8007

B8072
Sorisdale

Kilchoan

Glenborrodale

Loch S

2
Clabhach
Coll
B8071

Ardmore Point

Drimnin

Mor

Arinagour

Tobermory

B8073

Loch
Arienas

12
Loch
Eatharna

Caliach
Point
Calgary

Killundine

B8070

Dervaig

Loch
Frisa

A848

B849
Fiunary

Gunna

Crossapol
Bay

Calgary Bay

Kilninian

Salen

Fis

Hough Bay
B8069
Caolas

Loch Tuath

B8035
A849

B8068

Treshnish Isles

Gometra
Lagganulva

B8073

Knock

23

Tiree
B8065
Scarinish

Ulva

Loch
Ba

Dun o
Ghaoit

76

Barrapoll

Hynish Bay

Little
Colonsay

Loch Na Keal

M u l l

Balephuil
Balemartine

Staffa

Balnahard

Ben More
△
966

B8035

Ben Buie
△
717

3

Glen More
A849

IONA ABBEY
Baile Mòr
Iona

Fionnphort

Loch Scridain

Pennyghael

Sound of Iona

A849
35

Loch Buie

Bunessan

Carsaig

Ross of Mull

Soa Island

Ardchiavaig

Malcolm's
Point

Firt

Garvellach

4

Scarba

Kiloran Bay
Rubh' a'Geodha

Colonsay
Kiloran

B8086
Scalasaig

Kilchattan

Loch Staosnaig

A
32
B
B8085
Garvard
C
einn Bhreac
△
467

I N N E R   H E B R I D E S

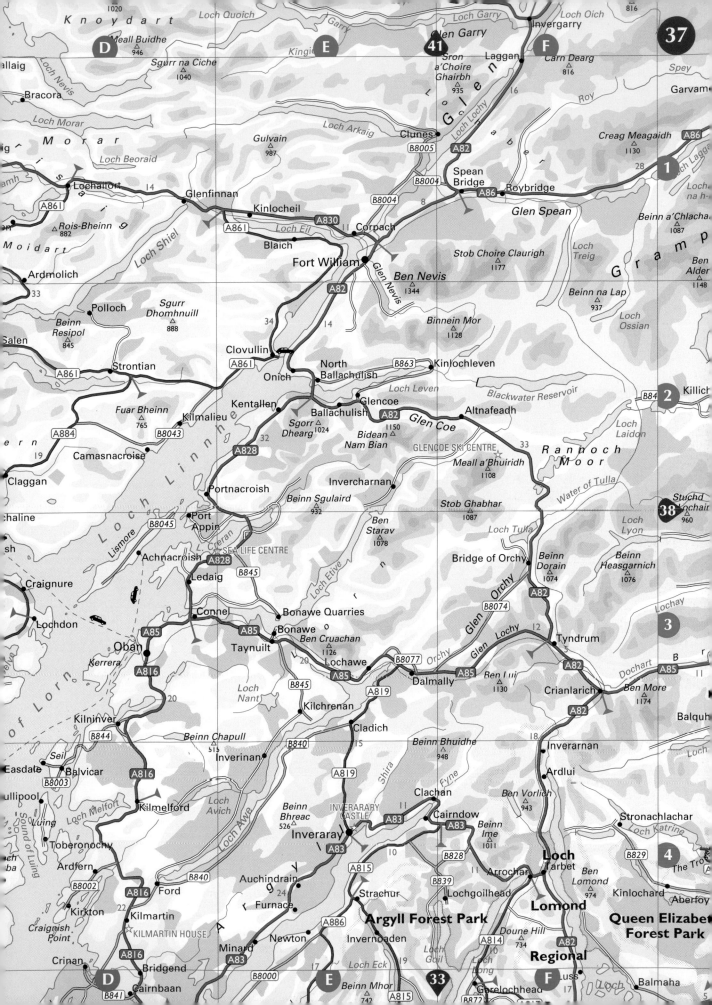

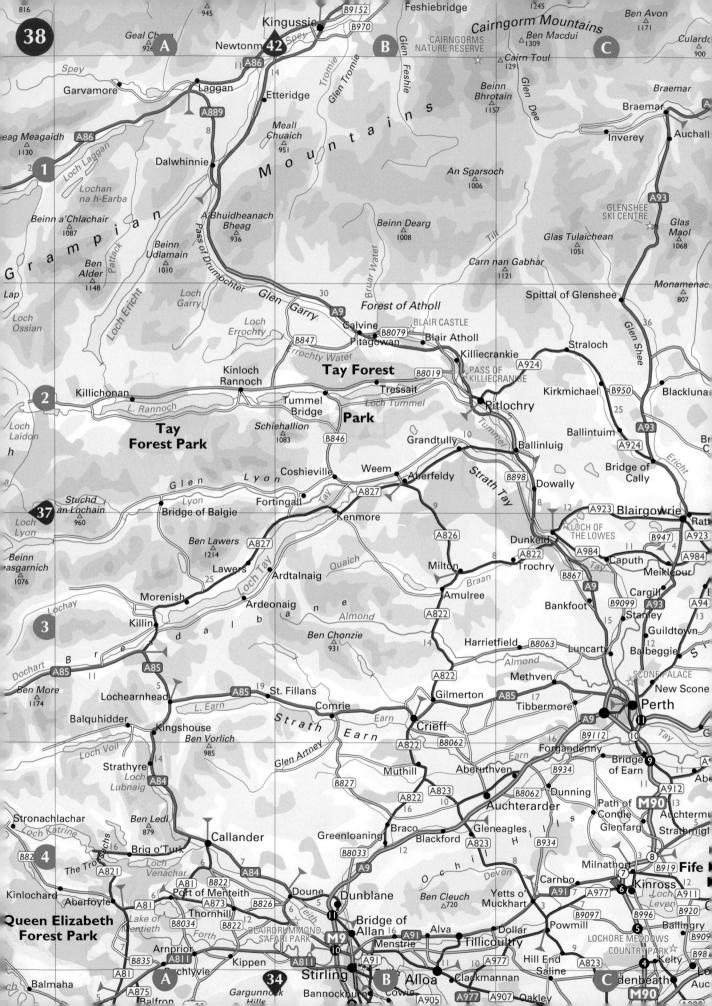

1

2

3

4

Findochty
Portknockie
Cullen
ckie
A942
26
A98
Portsoy
Whitehills
B990
Fordyce 199
Dun Hill
B9139
Macduff
Troup Head
Rosehearty
B9031
Fraserburgh
Inverallochy
Kirktown of Deskford
B9022
Banff
B9121
Gardenstown
New Aberdour
Mid Ardlaw
Memsie
A98
B9033
St Combs
016
B9018
A95
A97
Longmanhill
B9031
Ladysford
11
A981
A90
Loch of Strathbeg
Cornhill
B9025
15
New Pitsligo
Strichen
Crimond
Rattray Head
Knock Hill
B9023
B9121
A947
A98
B9105
New Byth
A950
B9093
New Leeds
A90
430
Finnygaud
Deveron
B9027
Cuminestown
Maud
Mintlaw
St Fergus
Newmill
B9022
B9025
Aberchirder
Turriff
B9170
B9170
Longside
A95
Keith
B9117
B9024
Darra
New Deer
B9029
ADEN COUNTRY PARK
A950
Peterhead
9014
A96
Milltown of Rothiemay
Bogniebrae
28
Stuartfield
B9030
Boddam
Isla
B9115
B9022
A97
B9001
B992
A947
B9170
A948
Hill of Dudwick
Auchnagatt
Hatton
A90
A920
Huntly
Kirkton of Auchterless
FYVIE CASTLE
B9005
Methlick
174
29
Toll of Birness
Cruden Ba
Deveron
18
A96
Badenscoth
Fyvie
HADDO COUNTRY PARK
Ythan
A948
16
A975
Bay of Cruden
STRATHBOGIE
B9001
Tarves
B9005
Ellon
21
Culdrain
Kirkton of Culsalmond
B992
A920
A947
B9170
A999
A920
9
Tap o' Noth
A97
23
B9001
A920
11
Pitmedden
Collieston
Kennethmont
B9002
Insch
A96
Oldmeldrum
A920
B9000
5
563
Bogie
B9002
Rhynie
A97
B9002
B9170
Whiterashes
Newburgh
B9002
Urie
Correen Hills
B992
Don
B993
Inverurie
A947
B999
A90
Mossat
A944
Newmachar
10
Kildrummy
Alford
B993
A96
B979
18
Balmedie
Glenkindie
A980
33
Kemnay
Kintore
B977
11
BALMEDIE COUNTRY PARK
ater
Muir of Fowlis
Tillyfourie
B993
16
B979
Aberdeen
Dyce
Blackburn
A97
Lyne of Skene
B979
Bucksburn
A997
Lumphanan
B9094
A944
Dunecht
Bridge of Don
B9119
Kirkton of Skene
Westhill
B9119
B9119
A980
Torphins
B977
Echt
B9125
B979
Cults
Aberdeen
B9119
Dinnet
B993
Kincardine O'Neil
B977
Peterculter
Charlestown
Cove Bay
7
A93
CRATHES CASTLE & GARDEN
18
A93
Dee
A90
Aboyne
B9077
Portlethen
lter
Glen Tanar
Carnferg
Marywell
Dee
Banchory
Kirkton of Durris
39

D

E

F

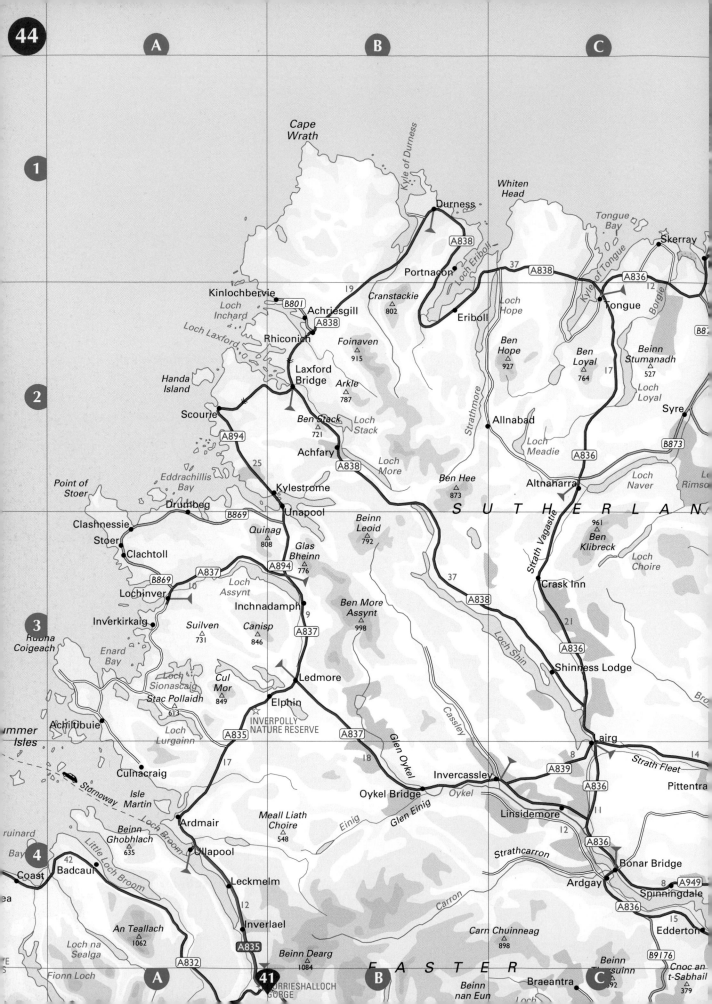

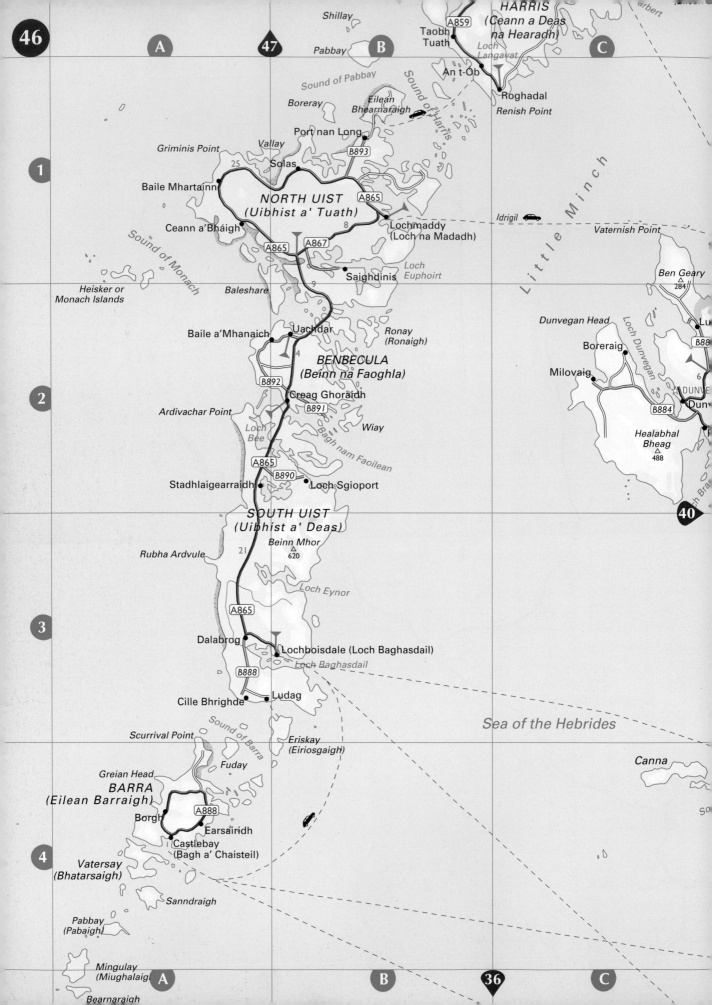

A   47   B   C

HARRIS
(Ceann a Deas
na Hearadh)

Shillay

Pabbay

Taobh
Tuath

A859

Loch
Langavat

An t-Ob

Sound of Pabbay

Roghadal

Renish Point

Sound of Harris

Boreray

Eilean
Bhearnaraigh

1

Griminis Point

Vallay

Port nan Long

Solas

B893

25

Baile Mhartainn

NORTH UIST
(Uibhist a' Tuath)

A865

Little Minch

Ceann a'Bháigh

8

Lochmaddy
(Loch na Madadh)

Idrigil

Vaternish Point

A865

A867

Saighdinis

Loch
Euphoirt

Ben Geary
284

Heisker or
Monach Islands

Baleshare

9

Dunvegan Head

Loch Dunvegan

Lu

B88

Baile a'Mhanaich

Uachdar

Ronay
(Ronaigh)

Boreraig

2

4

BENBECULA
(Beinn na Faoghla)

Milovaig

DUNVE

B892

Creag Ghoraidh

B884

Dun

Ardivachar Point

B891

Wiay

Loch
Bee

Bagh nam Faoilean

Healabhal
Bheag
488

Loch Brac

A865

B890

Stadhlaigearraidh

Loch Sgioport

40

SOUTH UIST
(Uibhist a' Deas)

Beinn Mhor
620

Rubha Ardvule

21

Loch Eynor

3

A865

Dalabrog

Lochboisdale (Loch Baghasdail)

B888

Loch Baghasdail

Sea of the Hebrides

Cille Bhrighde

Ludag

Scurrival Point

Sound of Barra

Eriskay
(Eiriosgaigh)

Canna

Greian Head

Fuday

BARRA
(Eilean Barraigh)

4

Borgh

A888

Earsairidh

Castlebay
(Bagh a' Chaisteil)

Vatersay
(Bhatarsaigh)

Sanndraigh

Pabbay
(Pabaigh)

Mingulay
(Miughalaigh)

A   B   36   C

Bearnaraigh

D

E

F

Rubha Robhanais

Eoropaidh
Tabost
Port Nis
Sgiogarstaigh

Dail Bho
Thuath

1

A857

15

Arnol

Barabhas

Siabost

Bragar

Muirneag
△ 248

Tolastadh Úr

Tolsta Head

West Loch Roag

East Loch Roag

A858

Carlabhagh

20

ISLE OF LEWIS
(Eilean Leodhais)

11

A857

Griais

B895

Great Bernera

Tolastadh
a'Chaolais

Beinn Mholach
△ 292

Tunga

Loch a' Tuath

Rubha an t-Siumpain

Miabhig

Breascleit
Calanais

B8059

Crulabhig

Newmarket

Port nan Giúran

Timsgearraidh

B8011

Gearraidh na h-Aibhne

Stornoway
(Steornabhagh)

Siulaisiadar

An Rubha

B8011

A858

A866

Breanais

Loch Suainaval

Mealisval
△ 574

Einacleit

13

Achadh
Mór

A859

B897

Crosbost

2

12

Mealasta Island

NORTH HARRIS
(Ceann a Tuath na Hearadh)

Baile Ailein

B8060

Cearsiadar

Loch Erisort

Ullapool

Scarp

Loch Langavat

21

Airidh
a'Bhruaich

Grabhair

B8060

Kebock Head

Huisinis

Tirga Mor
△ 679

A859

Beinn Mhór
△ 572

Loch Claidh

Leumrabhagh

Loch Shell

Abhainnsuidhe

B887

Clishham
△ 799

A859

Loch Seaforth

Loch Bhrollum

Sound of Taransay

Aird
Asaig

Tarbert
(An Tairbeart)

Shiant Islands

3

A859

East Loch Tarbert

Caolas Scalpaigh

Scalpay
(Eilean Scalpaigh)

Rubha Re

Toe Head

25

SOUTH HARRIS
(Ceann a Deas na Hearadh)

Mel

A859

Taobh
Tuath

Loch Langavat

An t-Ób

Roghadal

Renish Point

Sound of Harris

Rubha Hunish

Kilmaluag

4

rt Hen

A855

19

Staffin Bay

Redpoi

Little Minch

Lochmaddy
(Loch na Madadh)

Vaternish Point

Balgown

Staffin

nis
Loch Euphoirt

D

Ben Geary
△ 284

E

Idrigil

Uig

A87

40

F

Culnaknock

Trotternish

aasay

Rona

Fearnmore

Loch Snizort

13

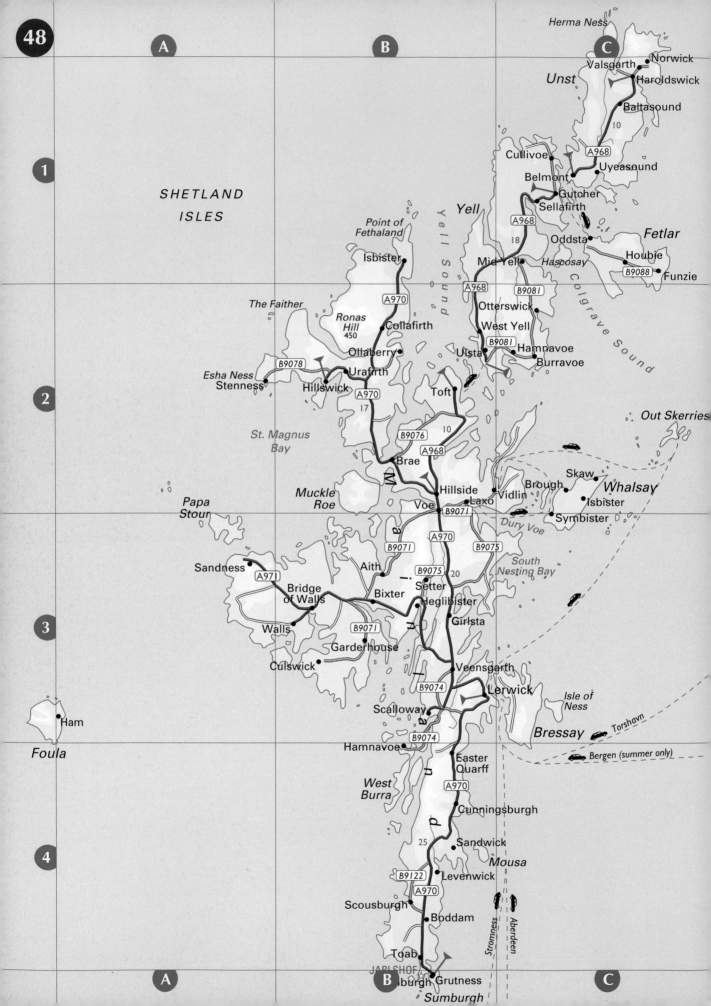

SHETLAND
ISLES

Herma Ness

C Valsgarth • Norwick
Haroldswick
Unst
Baltasound
10
A968

Cullivoe
Belmont Uyeasound
Gutcher
Yell Sellafirth
A968 *Fetlar*
Oddsta Houbie
Mid Yell *Hascosay* **B9088** Funzie
18

A968 **B9081**
Otterswick

Point of Fethaland
Isbister **A970**
West Yell
The Faither **B9081** Hamnavoe
Ronas Hill 450 Collafirth Ulsta Burravoe
Ollaberry
B9078 Urafirth
Esha Ness Stenness Hillswick **A970** Toft
17

Out Skerries
St. Magnus Bay **B9076**
10
A968
Brae
Papa Stour *Muckle Roe* Hillside Brough Skaw
Voe Laxo Vidlin *Whalsay*
B9071 Isbister
Symbister
Dury Voe
B9071 **A970** **B9075**
South Nesting Bay
Sandness Aith
A971 **B9075** 20
Bridge of Walls Bixter Setter
Heglibister
Walls Girlsta
B9071 Garderhouse
Culswick Veensgarth
B9074 Lerwick
Scalloway *Isle of Ness*
B9074 *Bressay* Torshavn
Hamnavoe Easter Quarff
Ham *West Burra* **A970** Bergen (summer only)
Foula Cunningsburgh

25 Sandwick *Mousa*
B9122 Levenwick
Scousburgh **A970** *Stromness* *Aberdeen*
Boddam
Toab
JARLSHOF
B burgh Grutness **C**
Sumburgh

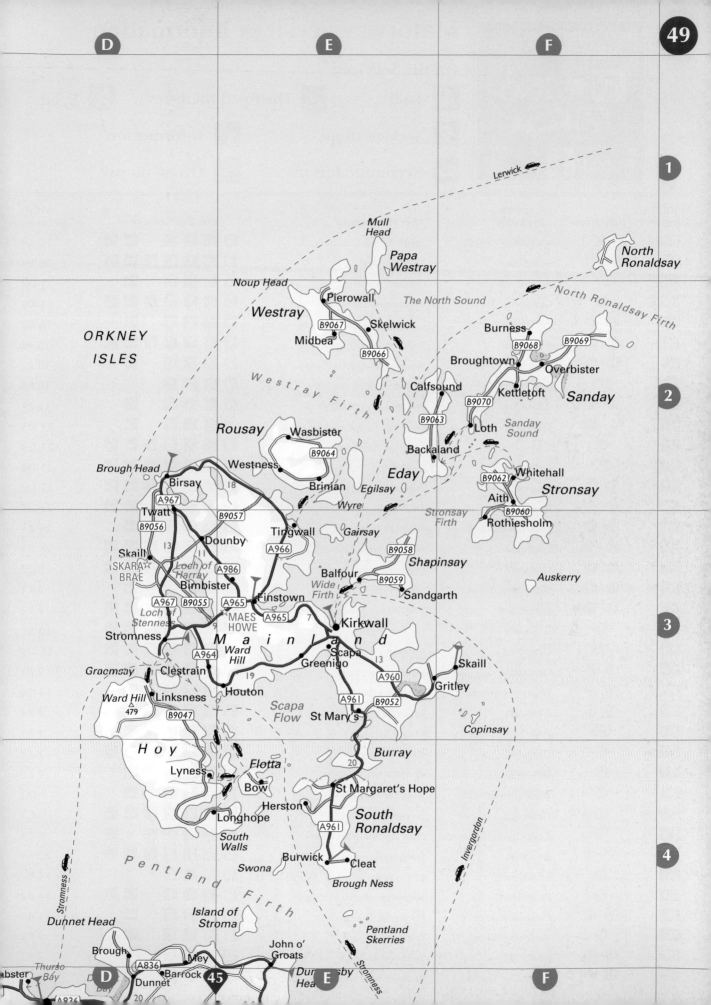

D   E   F

1

Lerwick

Mull
Head

Papa
Westray

North
Ronaldsay

Noup Head

Pierowall

The North Sound

Westray

Burness

B9068   B9069

B9067

Skelwick

Broughtown

Overbister

North Ronaldsay Firth

Midbea

B9066

ORKNEY
ISLES

Calfsound

Kettletoft

Sanday

B9070

W e s t r a y   F i r t h

B9063

Loth

Sanday Sound

2

Rousay

Wasbister

Backaland

B9064

Westness

Eday

Whitehall

B9062

Stronsay

Birnie

Egilsay

Aith

B9060

Brough Head

Birsay

18

Wyre

Rothiesholm

A967

Twatt

B9057

Tingwall

Gairsay

B9056

13

Dounby

A966

B9058

Shapinsay

Skaill

11

A986

Balfour

B9059

Auskerry

SKARA
BRAE

*Loch of
Harray*

Bimbister

Sandgarth

A967   B9055

A965

Finstown

*Wide
Firth*

*Loch of
Stenness*

MAES
HOWE

A965

7

Kirkwall

3

Stromness

M a i n l a n d

Scapa

Clestrain

A964

Ward
Hill

Greenigo

13

Skaill

Gracmsay

19

A960

Gritley

Ward Hill
△
479

Linksness

Houton

A961

B9052

B9047

*Scapa
Flow*

St Mary's

Copinsay

H o y

Burray

Lyness

Flotta

20

Bow

St Margaret's Hope

Herston

*South
Ronaldsay*

Longhope

*South
Walls*

A961

Burwick

Cleat

4

Swona

Brough Ness

P e n t l a n d

Dunnet Head

Island of
Stroma

*Pentland
Skerries*

F i r t h

Brough

Mey

John o'
Groats

45

A836

Barrock

Dunnet

sby
Hea

D   E   F

bster

*Thurso
Bay*

20

A936

Motorway Services Information

On-site Services:

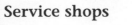

- Fuel
- Disabled facilities
- Food
- £ Service shops
- *i* Information
- Accommodation
- ₍£₎ Other shops

Motorway Number	Junction	Service Provider	Service Name	On-site Services	Map Reference
A1(M)	1	Welcome Break	South Mimms Services	Fuel · Disabled · Food · £ · Bed · ₍£₎	16 A4
A1(M)	34	Granada	Blyth Services	Fuel · Disabled · Food · £ · i · Bed · ₍£₎	26 B4
A1(M)	61	RoadChef	Durham Services	Fuel · Disabled · Food · £ · Bed	31 D2
A1(M)	64	Granada	Washington Services	Fuel · Disabled · Food · £ · i · Bed · ₍£₎	31 D2
M1	2–4	Welcome Break	London Gateway Services	Fuel · Disabled · Food · £ · Bed	16 A4
M1	11–12	Granada	Toddington Services	Fuel · Disabled · Food · £ · i · Bed · ₍£₎	15 F2
M1	14–15	Welcome Break	Newport Pagnell Services	Fuel · Disabled · Food · £ · Bed	15 F2
M1	15A	RoadChef	Rothersthorpe Services	Fuel · Disabled · Food · £	15 E1
M1	16–17	RoadChef	Watford Gap Services	Fuel · Disabled · Food · £ · Bed	15 E1
M1	21–21A	Welcome Break	Leicester Forest East Services	Fuel · Disabled · Food · £ · Bed	21 D3
M1	22	Granada	Leicester Services	Fuel · Disabled · Food · £ · i · Bed · ₍£₎	21 D3
M1	23A	Granada	Donington Park Services	Fuel · Disabled · Food · £ · i · ₍£₎	21 D3
M1	25–26	Granada	Trowell Services	Fuel · Disabled · Food · £ · i · Bed · ₍£₎	21 D2
M1	28–29	RoadChef	Tibshelf Services	Fuel · Disabled · Food · £ · Bed · ₍£₎	21 D1
M1	30–31	Welcome Break	Woodall Services	Fuel · Disabled · Food · £ · Bed	26 A4
M1	38–39	Granada	Woolley Edge Services	Fuel · Disabled · Food · £ · i · Bed	26 A3
M2	4–5	Granada	Medway Services	Fuel · Disabled · Food · £ · i · Bed · ₍£₎	11 D2
M3	4A–5	Welcome Break	Fleet Services	Fuel · Disabled · Food · £ · Bed	9 F1
M3	8–9	RoadChef	Winchester Services	Fuel · Disabled · Food · £ · Bed · ₍£₎	9 E2
M4	3	Granada	Heston Services	Fuel · Disabled · Food · £ · i · Bed · ₍£₎	10 A1
M4	13	Granada	Chieveley Services	Fuel · Disabled · Food · £ · i · Bed · ₍£₎	15 D4
M4	11–12	Granada	Reading Services	Fuel · Disabled · Food · £ · i · Bed · ₍£₎	9 E1
M4	14–15	Welcome Break	Membury Services	Fuel · Disabled · Food · £ · Bed	14 C4
M4	17–18	Granada	Leigh Delamere Services	Fuel · Disabled · Food · £ · i · Bed · ₍£₎	14 B4
M4	23A	First Motorway	Magor Services	Fuel · Disabled · Food · £ · i	7 F1
M4	33	Granada	Cardiff Services	Fuel · Disabled · Food · £ · i · Bed · ₍£₎	7 E2
M4	30	Granada	Cardiff Gate Services	Fuel · Disabled · Food · £ · Bed	7 E2
M4	36	Welcome Break	Sarn Park Services	Fuel · Disabled · Food · £ · Bed	7 D2
M4	47	Granada	Swansea Services	Fuel · Disabled · Food · £ · i · Bed · ₍£₎	6 C1
M4	49	RoadChef	Pont Abraham Services	Fuel · Disabled · Food · £ · i · ₍£₎	6 C1
M5	3–4	Granada	Frankley Services	Fuel · Disabled · Food · £ · i · Bed · ₍£₎	20 B4
M5	8	RoadChef	Strensham Services (South)	Fuel · Disabled · Food · £	14 B2
M5	8	RoadChef	Strensham Services (North)	Fuel · Disabled · Food · £ · Bed · ₍£₎	14 B2
M5	13–14	Welcome Break	Michaelwood Services	Fuel · Disabled · Food · £ · Bed	14 A4
M5	19	Welcome Break	Gordano Services	Fuel · Disabled · Food · £ · Bed	7 F2
M5	21–22	RoadChef	Sedgemoor Services (South)	Fuel · Disabled · Food · £	7 F3
M5	21–22	Welcome Break	Sedgemoor Services (North)	Fuel · Disabled · Food · £ · Bed	7 F3

Motorway	Junction	Operator	Services	Facilities	Grid Ref
M5	24	First Motorway	Bridgwater Services	⛽ ♿ 🍴 £ · 🛏	7 F4
M5	25–26	RoadChef	Taunton Deane Services	⛽ ♿ 🍴 £ · 🛏 £₤	7 E4
M5	28	Granada	Cullompton Services	⛽ ♿ 🍴 £	5 E1
M5	29–30	Granada	Exeter Services	⛽ ♿ 🍴 £ ℹ 🛏 £₤	5 D1
M6	3–4	Welcome Break	Corley Services	⛽ ♿ 🍴 £ · 🛏	20 C4
M6	10–11	Granada	Hilton Park Services	⛽ ♿ 🍴 £ ℹ 🛏 £₤	20 B3
M6	14–15	RoadChef	Stafford Services (South)	⛽ ♿ 🍴 £ · 🛏 £₤	20 B2
M6	14–15	Granada	Stafford Services (North)	⛽ ♿ 🍴 £ ℹ · £₤	20 B2
M6	15–16	Welcome Break	Keele Services	⛽ ♿ 🍴 £	20 A2
M6	16–17	RoadChef	Sandbach Services	⛽ ♿ 🍴 £	20 A1
M6	18–19	Granada	Knutsford Services	⛽ ♿ 🍴 £ ℹ · £₤	20 A1
M6	27–28	Welcome Break	Charnock Richard Services	⛽ ♿ 🍴 £ · 🛏	25 D3
M6	32–33	Granada	Lancaster Services	⛽ ♿ 🍴 £ ℹ 🛏 £₤	25 D2
M6	35A–36	Granada	Burton-in-Kendal Services	⛽ ♿ 🍴 £ ℹ 🛏 £₤	25 D1
M6	36–37	RoadChef	Killington Lake Services	⛽ ♿ 🍴 £ · 🛏	30 A4
M6	38–39	Westmorland	Tebay Services	⛽ ♿ 🍴 £ · 🛏	30 A4
M6	41–42	Granada	Southwaite Services	⛽ ♿ 🍴 £ ℹ 🛏 £₤	29 F2
M8	4–5	RoadChef	Harthill Services	⛽ ♿ 🍴 £	34 A2
M9	9	Granada	Stirling Services	⛽ ♿ 🍴 £ ℹ 🛏 £₤	34 A1
M11	8	Welcome Break	Birchanger Green Services	⛽ ♿ 🍴 £ · 🛏	16 B3
M18	5	Granada	Doncaster North Services	⛽ ♿ 🍴 £ ℹ 🛏 £₤	26 B3
M20	8	RoadChef	Maidstone Services	⛽ ♿ 🍴 £ ℹ 🛏	11 D2
M23	11	Granada	Pease Pottage Services	⛽ ♿ 🍴 £ ℹ 🛏 £₤	10 B3
M25	5–6	RoadChef	Clacket Lane Services	⛽ ♿ 🍴 £ · 🛏	10 C2
M25	30	Granada	Thurrock Services	⛽ ♿ 🍴 £ ℹ 🛏 £₤	10 C1
M27	3–4	RoadChef	Rownhams Services	⛽ ♿ 🍴 £ · 🛏	9 D3
M40	8	Welcome Break	Oxford Services	⛽ ♿ 🍴 £ · 🛏	15 E3
M40	10	Granada	Cherwell Valley Services	⛽ ♿ 🍴 £ ℹ 🛏 £₤	15 D2
M40	12–13	Welcome Break	Warwick Services	⛽ ♿ 🍴 £ · 🛏	15 D1
M42	2	Welcome Break	Hopwood Park Services	⛽ ♿ 🍴 £ · £₤	14 B1
M42	10	Granada	Tamworth Services	⛽ ♿ 🍴 £ ℹ 🛏 £₤	20 C3
M48	1	Granada	Severn View Services	⛽ ♿ 🍴 £ ℹ 🛏 £₤	14 A4
M50	4	Welcome Break	Ross Spur Services	⛽ ♿ 🍴 £	14 A2
M56	14	RoadChef	Chester Services	⛽ ♿ 🍴 £ ℹ 🛏	19 F1
M61	6–7	First Motorway	Bolton West Services	⛽ ♿ 🍴 £ · 🛏	25 D3
M62	7–9	Welcome Break	Burtonwood Services	⛽ ♿ 🍴 £ · 🛏	25 D4
M62	18–19	Granada	Birch Services	⛽ ♿ 🍴 £ ℹ 🛏 £₤	25 E3
M62	25–26	Welcome Break	Hartshead Moor Services	⛽ ♿ 🍴 £ · 🛏	25 F3
M62	33	Granada	Ferrybridge Services	⛽ ♿ 🍴 £ ℹ · £₤	26 A3
M74	4–5	RoadChef	Bothwell Services	⛽ ♿ 🍴 £	33 F2
M74	5–6	RoadChef	Hamilton Services	⛽ ♿ 🍴 £ ℹ 🛏	33 F2
M74	11–12	Cairn Lodge	Happendon Services	⛽ ♿ 🍴 £	34 A3
M74	12–13	Welcome Break	Abington Services	⛽ ♿ 🍴 £ · 🛏	34 A3
M74	16	RoadChef	Annandale Water Services	⛽ ♿ 🍴 £ · 🛏	34 B4
M74	22	Welcome Break	Gretna Green Services	⛽ ♿ 🍴 £ · 🛏	29 F1
M90	6	Granada	Kinross Sevices	⛽ ♿ 🍴 £ ℹ 🛏 £₤	38 C4

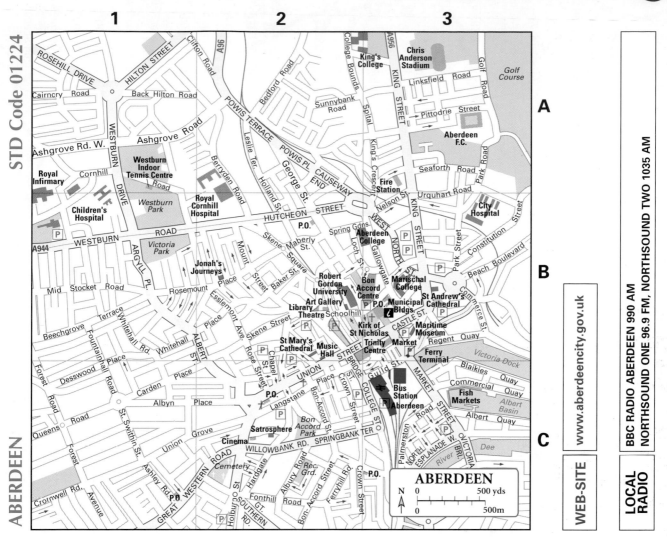

STD Code 01224

ABERDEEN

WEB-SITE www.aberdeencity.gov.uk

LOCAL RADIO BBC RADIO ABERDEEN 990 AM NORTHSOUND ONE 96.9 FM, NORTHSOUND TWO 1035 AM

ABERDEEN
N 0 — 500 yds
0 — 500m

INDEX TO STREET NAMES

Albert Quay	C3	Carden Place	C1	Fountainhall		Loch Street	B2	Schoolhill	B2
Albert Street	B2	Castle Street	B3	Road	B1	Maberly Street	B2	Seaforth Road	A3
Albury Road	C2	Causewayend	A2	Gallowgate	B3	Market Street	C3	Skene Square	B2
Albyn Place	C1	Chapel Street	B2	George Street	A2	Mid Stocket Road	B1	Skene Street	B2
Argyll Place	B1	Clifton Road	A1	Golf Road	A3	Mount Street	B2	Spital	A3
Ashgrove Road	A1	College Bounds	A2	Great Southern		Nelson Street	B3	Springbank	
Ashgrove Road	A1	College Street	C3	Road	C2	North Esplanade		Terrace	C2
West		Commerce Street	B3	Great Western		West	C3	Spring Gardens	B2
Ashley Road	C1	Commercial Quay	C3	Road	C1	Palmerston Road	C3	Sunnybank Road	A2
Back Hilton Road	A1	Constitution		Guild Street	C3	Park Road	A3	Union Grove	C1
Baker Street	B2	Street	B3	Hardgate	C2	Park Street	B3	Union Street	C2
Beach Boulevard	B3	Cornhill Road	A1	Holburn Street	C2	Pittodrie Street	A3	Urquhart Road	B3
Bedford Road	A2	Cromwell Road	C1	Holland Street	A2	Powis Place	A2	Victoria Bridge	C3
Beechgrove		Crown Street	C2	Hutcheon Street	B2	Powis Terrace	A2	Westburn Drive	A1
Terrace	B1	Desswood Place	C1	King's Crescent	A3	Queens Road	C1	Westburn Road	B1
Berryden Road	A2	Esslemont Avenue	B2	King Street	A3	Regent Quay	B3	West North	
Blaikie's Quay	C3	Ferryhill Road	C2	Langstane Place	C2	Rosehill Drive	A1	Street	B3
Bon-Accord Street	C2	Fonthill Road	C2	Leslie Terrace	A2	Rosemount Place	B1	Whitehall Place	B1
Bridge Street	B2	Forest Road	C1	Linkfield Road	A3	Rose Street	B2	Whitehall Road	B1
Cairncry Road	A1	Forest Avenue	C1			St Swithin Street	C1	Willowbank Road	C2

TOURIST INFORMATION ☎ 01224 632727 ST. NICHOLAS HOUSE, BROAD STREET, ABERDEEN, AB9 1DE

HOSPITAL A & E ☎ 01224 681818 ABERDEEN ROYAL INFIRMARY, FORESTERHILL, ABERDEEN, AB25 2ZN

COUNCIL OFFICE ☎ 01224 522000 TOWN HOUSE, BROAD STREET, ABERDEEN, AB10 1FY

Aberdeen Population: 189,707. City, cathedral and university city and commercial centre on E coast 57m/92km NE of Dundee. Known as 'The Granite City', local stone having been used in many of its buildings. By 13c, Aberdeen had become an important centre for trade and fishing and remains a major port and commercial base. In 19c shipbuilding brought great prosperity to the city. These industries had receded by mid 20c but the city's prospects were transformed when North Sea oil was discovered in 1970, turning it into a city of great wealth. St. Machar's Cathedral at Old Aberdeen. Many museums and art galleries. Extensive flower gardens. Airport at Dyce, 6m/9km NW of Aberdeen.

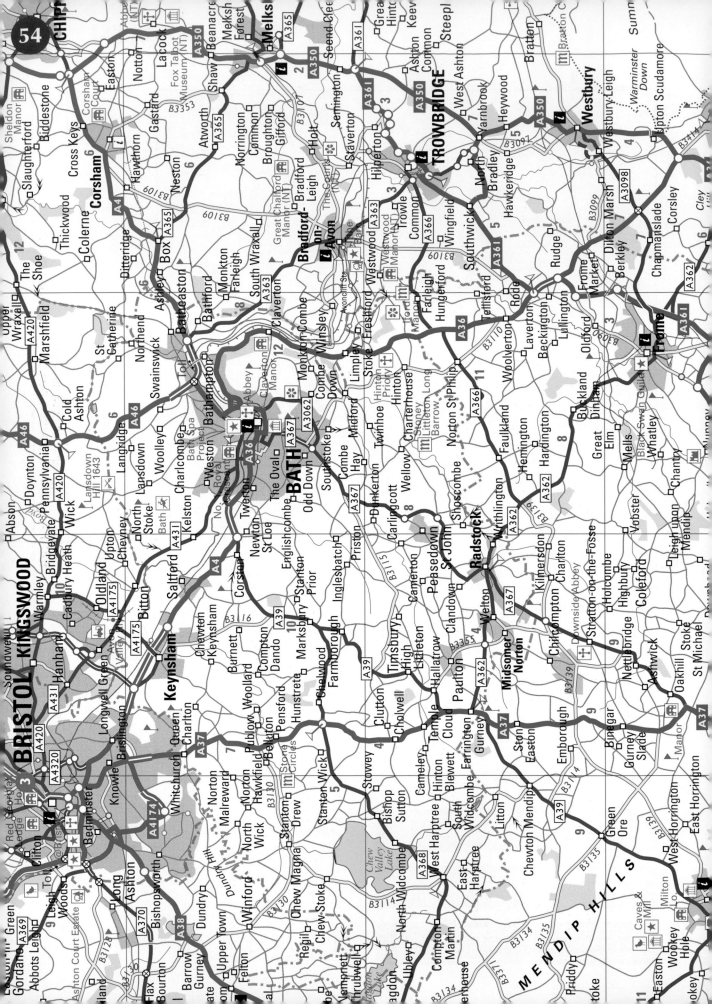

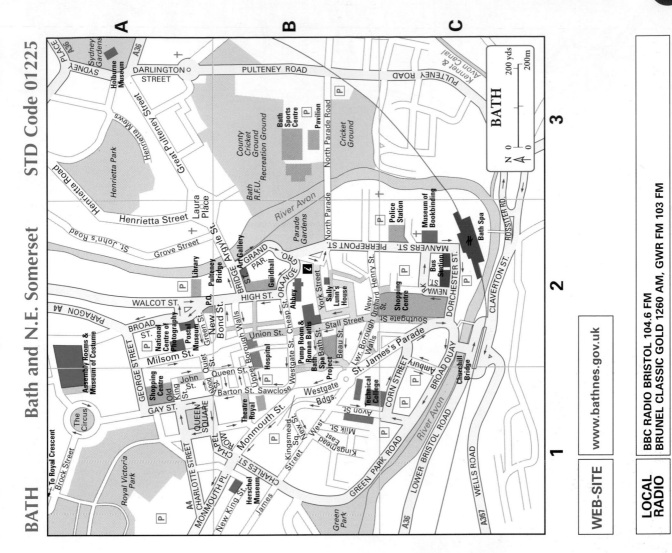

INDEX TO STREET NAMES

Ambury	C1	Grove Street	A2
Argyle Street	B2	Henrietta Mews	A3
Avon Street	B1	Henrietta Road	A2
Barton Street	B2	Henrietta Street	A2
Bath Street	B2	Henry Street	B2
Beau Street	B2	High Street	B2
Bridge Street	B2	James Street West	B1
Broad Quay	C1	John Street	A1
Broad Street	A2	Kingsmead East	B1
Brock Street	A1	Laura Place	A2
Chapel Row	B1	Lower Borough	B1
Charles Street	B1	Walls	
Charlotte Street	A1	Lower Bristol Road	C1
Cheap Street	B2	Manvers Street	C2
Claverton Street	C2	Milk Street	B1
Corn Street	C1	Milsom Street	A2
Darlington Street	A3	Monmouth Place	A1
Dorchester Street	C2	Monmouth Street	B1
Gay Street	A1	Newark Street	C2
George Street	A1	New Bond Street	B2
Grand Parade	B2	New King Street	B1
Great Pulteney	A3	New Orchard Street	B2
Street		New Street	B1
Green Park Road	B1	North Parade	B2
Green Street	A2	North Parade Road	B3

Old King Street	A1		
Orange Grove	B2		
Paragon	A2		
Pierrepont Street	B2		
Pulteney Road	B3		
Queen Street	B1		
Quiet Street	A1		
Rossiter Road	C2		
St. James's Parade	B1		
St. John's Road	A2		
Sawclose	B1		
Southgate Street	C2		
Stall Street	B2		
Sydney Place	A3		
The Circus	A1		
Union Street	B2		
Upper Borough	B1		
Walls			
Walcot Street	A2		
Wells Road	C1		
Westgate Buildings	B1		
Westgate Street	B2		
Wood Street	A1		
York Street	B2		

WEB-SITE www.bathnes.gov.uk

LOCAL RADIO
BBC RADIO BRISTOL 104.6 FM
BRUNEL CLASSIC GOLD 1260 AM, GWR FM 103 FM

TOURIST INFORMATION ☎ 01225 477107
AVVEY CAMBERS, ABBEY CHURCH YARD,
BATH, BA1 1LY

HOSPITAL A & E ☎ 01225 428331
ROYAL UNITED HOSPITAL, COMBE PARK,
BATH, BA1 3NG

COUNCIL OFFICE ☎ 01225 477000
THE GUILDHALL, HIGH STREET,
BATH, BA1 5AW

Bath *B. & N.E.Som.* Population: 85,202. City, spa on River Avon, 11m/18km SE of Bristol. Abbey church rebuilt 1501. Natural hot springs unique in Britain drew Romans to Bath, wh ch they named 'Aquae Sulis'. Roman baths and 18c Pump Room are open to visitors. n 18c, it was most fashionable resort in country. Many Georgian buildings and ele-gant crescents remain, including The Circus and Royal Crescent. Museum of Costume in restored Assembly Rooms. Holds annual sum-mer music festival. American Museum housed in Claverton Manor and University 3m/4km SE.

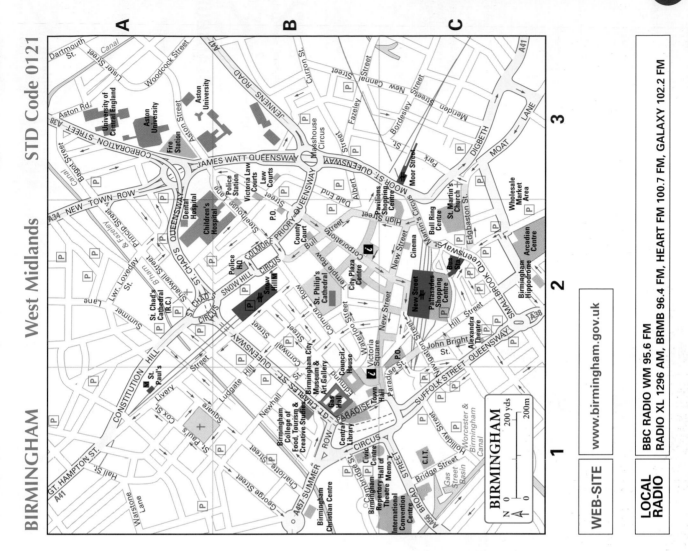

STD Code 0121   West Midlands   BIRMINGHAM

INDEX TO STREET NAMES

Albert Street	B3
Aston Road	A3
Aston Street	A3
Bagot Street	A3
Bordesley Street	C3
Bridge Street	C1
Broad Street	C1
Bull Street	B2
Cambridge Street	B1
Charlotte Street	B1
Colmore Circus	B2
Colmore Row	B2
Constitution Hill	A1
Cornwall Street	B2
Corporation Street	B2/A3
Cox Street	A1
Curzon Street	A3
Dale End	B2
Dartmouth Street	A3
Digbeth	C3
Edgbaston Street	C2
Edmund Street	B1
Fazeley Street	B3
George Street	B1

Great Charles Street	B1
Great Charles Street Queensway	A3
Great Hampton Street	A1
Hall Street	A1
High Street	C2
Hill Street	C1
Holliday Street	C1
James Watt Queensway	A3
Jennens Road	B3
John Bright Street	C2
Lister Street	A3
Lower Loveday Street	A1
Ludgate Hill	B2
Masshouse Circus	A3
Meriden Street	C3
Moat Lane	C3
Moor Street	C3
Navigation Street	C1
New Canal Street	C3
New Street	C2
New Town Row	B3
Newhall Street	B1

Paradise Circus	B1
Paradise Street	C1
Park Street	C3
Princip Street	A2
Priory Queensway	B2
Queensway	A2
St. Chad's Circus	A2
St. Chad's Queensway	A2
St. Martin's Circus	C2
St. Paul's Square	A1
Shadwell Street	A2
Smallbrook Queensway	C2
Snow Hill	B2
Steelhouse Lane	B2
Suffolk Street Queensway	C1
Summer Lane	A2
Summer Row	B1
Temple Row	B2
Victoria Square	B2
Warstone Lane	A1
Waterloo Street	B2
Woodcock Street	A3

TOURIST INFORMATION ☎ 0121 643 2514
2 CITY ARCADE, BIRMINGHAM,
WEST MIDLANDS, B2 4TX

HOSPITAL A & E ☎ 0121 554 3801
CITY HOSPITAL, DUDLEY ROAD,
BIRMINGHAM, B18 7QH

COUNCIL OFFICE ☎ 0121 303 9944
COUNCIL HOUSE, VICTORIA SQUARE,
BIRMINGHAM, B1 1BB

WEB-SITE   www.birmingham.gov.uk

LOCAL RADIO   BBC RADIO WM 95.6 FM
RADIO XL 1296 AM, BRMB 96.4 FM, HEART FM 100.7 FM, GALAXY 102.2 FM

Birmingham *W.Mid.* Population: 935,928. City, England's second city and manufacturing, commercial and communications centre, 100m/160km NW of London. Birmingham was home to many pioneers of industrial revolution. Current economic trend is towards post-industrial activities, concentrating on convention and exhibition trades and tourism. To S of city is planned village of Bournville, established by Quaker chocolate magnates George and Richard Cadbury in 1879, influenced by utopian ideas of William Morris. Universities. City has many galleries and museums, particularly around 19c Victoria and Chamberlain Squares. Anglican and Catholic cathedrals. Birmingham International Airport 7m/11km E of city centre.

BLACKPOOL

STD Code 01253

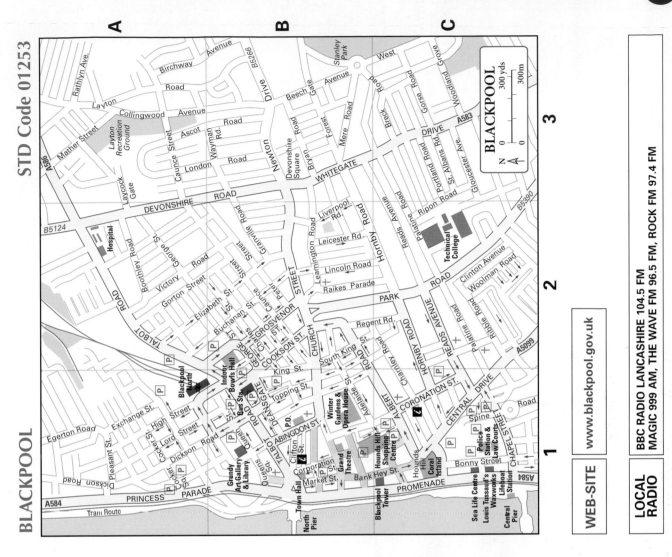

INDEX TO STREET NAMES

Abingdon Street	B1	Devonshire Road	A2	Mere Road	B3
Adelaide Street	B1	Devonshire Square	B3	Newton Drive	B3
Albert Road	C1	Dickson Road	A1	Palatine Road	C2
Ascot Road	A3	Egerton Road	A1	Park Road	C2
Bank Hey Street	B1	Elizabeth Street	A2	Peter Street	B2
Beech Avenue West	B3	Exchange Street	A1	Pleasant Street	A1
Birchway Avenue	A3	Forest Gate	33	Portland Road	C3
Bonny Street	C1	George Street	B2/A2	Princess Parade	A1
Boothley Road	A2	Gloucester Avenue	C3	Promenade	C1
Breck Road	C3	Gorse Road	C3	Queens Square	B1
Bryan Road	B3	Gorton Street	A2	Queen Street	B1
Buchanan Street	B2	Granville Road	C3	Rathlyn Avenue	A3
Caunce Street	B2/A3	Grosvenor Street	B2	Reads Avenue	C2
Central Drive	C1	High Street	A1	Regent Road	B2
Chapel Street	C1	Hornby Road	C1	Ribble Road	C2
Charles Street	B2	Hounds Hill	B1	Ripon Road	C2
Charnley Road	C1	King Street	B1	St. Albans Road	C3
Church Street	B2	Laycock Gate	A3	South King Street	B2
Clifton Street	B1	Layton Road	A3	Spine Road	C1
Clinton Avenue	C2	Leamington Road	B2	Talbot Road	B1/A2
Cocker Square	A1	Leicester Road	B2	Topping Street	B1
Cocker Street	A1	Lincoln Road	C2	Victory Road	A2
Collingwood Avenue	A3	Liverpool Road	B2	Wayman Road	B3
Cookson Street	B2	London Road	B2	Whitegate Drive	A3
Coronation Street	C1	Lord Street	A1	Woodland Grove	B3/C3
Corporation Street	B1	Market Street	B1	Woolman Road	C3
Deansgate	B1	Mather Street	B1		C2

TOURIST INFORMATION ☎ 01253 478222
1 CLIFTON STREET
BLACKPOOL, FY1 1LY

HOSPITAL A & E ☎ 01253 300000
VICTORIA HOSPITAL, WHINNEY HEYS ROAD,
BLACKPOOL, FY3 8NR

COUNCIL OFFICE ☎ 01253 477477
TOWN HALL, TALBOT SQUARE,
BLACKPOOL, FY1 1NB

Blackpool *B'pool* Population: 146,262. Town, large coastal resort and conference centre on Irish Sea, 15m/24km W of Preston. 19c fashionable resort, still very popular today. 7m/11km long 'Golden Mile' of tram route, beach, piers and amusement arcades. Blackpool Pleasure Beach funfair park, 518ft/158m high Tower entertainment complex, annual autumn Illuminations along 5m/8km of Promenade, Zoo, Sea Life Centre, The Sandcastle indoor pool complex and Winter Gardens. Airport 3m/5km S.

WEB-SITE www.blackpool.gov.uk

LOCAL RADIO BBC RADIO LANCASHIRE 104.5 FM
MAGIC 999 AM, THE WAVE FM 96.5 FM, ROCK FM 97.4 FM

BOURNEMOUTH

STD Code 01202

BOURNEMOUTH

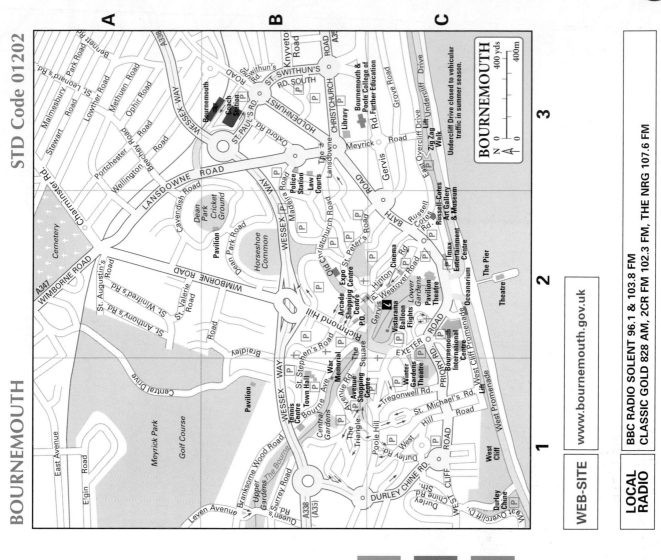

INDEX TO STREET NAMES

Avenue Road	B1	Hinton Road	C2	St. Pauls' Road	B3
Bath Road	C2	Holdenhurst Road	B3	St. Peter's Road	B2
Beechey Road	A3	Knyveton Road	B3	St. Stephen's Road	B1
Bennett Road	A3	Lansdowne Road	A2	St. Swithun's Road	B3
Bourne Avenue	B1	Leven Avenue	A1	St. Swithun's Road South	B3
Braidley Road	B2	Lowther Road	A3	St. Winifrec's Road	A2
Branksome Wood Road	B1	Madeira Road	B2	St. Valerie Road	A2
Cavendish Road	A2	Malmesbury Park Road	A3	Stewart Raod	A3
Central Drive	A1	Methuen Road	A3	Surrey Raod	B1
Charminster Road	A2	Meyrick Road	B3	The Landsdowne	B3
Christchurch Road	B3	Old Christchurch Road	B3	The Square	B2
Dean Park Road	B2	Ophir Road	A3	The Triangle	B1
Durley Chine Road	C1	Oxford Road	B3	Tregonwell Road	C1
Durley Chine Road South	C1	Poole Hill	C1	Undercliff Drive	C3
Durley Road	C1	Portchester Road	A3	Wellington Road	A2
East Avenue	A1	Priory Road	C1	Wessex Way	B1/A3
East Overcliff Drive	C3	Queen's Road	B1	West Cliff	C1
Elgin Road	A1	Richmond Hill	B2	Promenade	B1
Exeter Road	C2	Russell Cotes Road	C2	West Cliff Road	C1
Gervis Place	C2	St. Augustin's Road	A2	West Hill Road	C1
Gervis Road	C3	St. Anthony's Road	A2	West Overcliff Drive	C1
Grove Road	C3	St. Leonard's Road	A3	West Promenade	C2
		St. Michael's Road	C1	Westover Road	C2
				Wimborne Road	B2

TOURIST INFORMATION ☎ 09069 020 234
WESTOVER ROAD,
BOURNEMOUTH, BH1 2BU

HOSPITAL A & E ☎ 01202 303626
ROYAL BOURNEMOUTH HOSPITAL,
CASTLE LANE EAST, BOURNEMOUTH, BH7 7DW

COUNCIL OFFICE ☎ 01202 451451
TOWN HALL, BOURNE AVENUE,
BOURNEMOUTH, BH2 6EB

Bournemouth *Bourne.* Population: 155,488. Town, large seaside resort with mild climate, 24m/39km SW of Southampton. Town developed from a few cottages in 1810 to present conurbation. Sandy beach and pier. Extensive parks and gardens including Compton Acres, a display of international garden styles. Russell-Cotes Art Gallery and Museum houses Victorian and oriental collection. University. Conference, business and shopping centre. Bournemouth International Airport, 5m/8km NE of town centre.

WEB-SITE www.bournemouth.gov.uk

LOCAL RADIO BBC RADIO SOLENT 96.1 & 103.8 FM
CLASSIC GOLD 828 AM, 2CR FM 102.3 FM, THE NRG 107.6 FM

BRADFORD   **West Yorkshire**   **STD Code 01274**

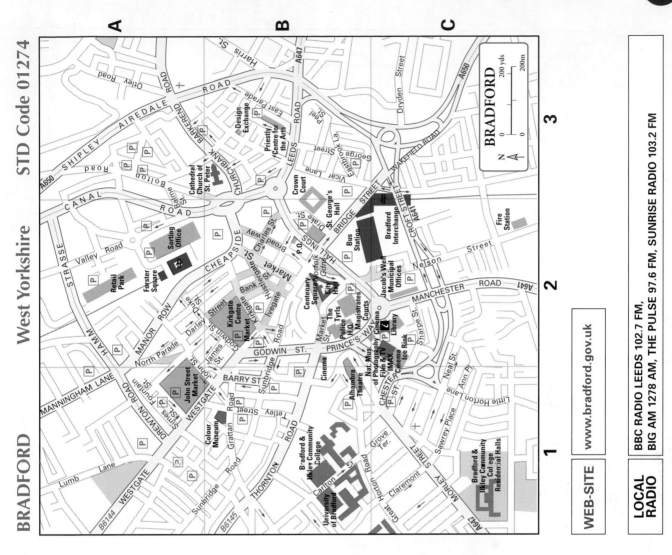

INDEX TO STREET NAMES

Ann Place	C1	Fountain Street	A1	Manor Row	A2
Balme Street	A2	George Street	B3	Market Street	B2
Bank Street	B2	Godwin Street	B2	Morley Street	C1
Barkerend Road	A3	Grattan Road	B1	Neal Street	C1
Barry Street	B1	Great Horton Road	C1	Nelson Street	C2
Bolton Road	A3			North Parade	A2
Bridge Street	B2	Grove Terrace	C1	Otley Road	A3
Broadway	B2	Hall Ings	B2	Peel Street	B3
Canal Road	A2	Hamm Strasse	A2	Prince's Way	B2
Carlton Street	B1	Harris Street	A3	Sawrey Place	C1
Charles Street	B2	Hustlergate	B2	Sharpe Street	C2
Cheapside	B2	Ivegate	B2	Shipley	A3
Chester Street	C1	James Street	B2	Airedale Road	A1
Churchbank	B3	John Street	B1	Simes Street	A1
Claremont	C1	Kirkgate	B2	Sunbridge Road	B3
Croft Street	C2	Leeds Road	A2	Tetley Street	B1
Darley Street	A2	Little Horton	C1	Thornton Road	B1
Drake Street	B2	Lane		Valley Road	A2
Drewton Road	A1	Lumb Lane	A1	Vicar Lane	B3
Dryden Street	C3	Manchester	C2	Wakefield Road	C3
Duke Street	A2	Road		Westgate	A1
East Parade	B3	Manningham			
Eastbrook Lane	B3	Lane	A1		

TOURIST INFORMATION ☎ 01274 753678
CENTRAL LIBRARY, PRINCES WAY,
BRADFORD, W.YORKS, BD1 1NN

HOSPITAL A & E ☎ 01274 542200
BRADFORD ROYAL INFIRMARY, DUCKWORTH LANE,
BRADFORD, BD9 6RJ

COUNCIL OFFICE ☎ 01274 752111
CITY HALL, CHANNING WAY,
BRADFORD, BD1 1HY

Bradford *W.Yorks.* Population: 283,376. City, industrial city, 8m/13km W of Leeds. Cathedral is former parish church. Previously known as wool capital of the world, Bradford is now less dependent upon the textile industry. Colour Museum documents history of dyeing and textile printing. University. Home to National Museum of Photography, Film and Television with IMAX cinema screen. Model industrial village of Saltaire 3m/5km N planned in 1852 for workers at Salt's Mill which now houses the David Hockney 1853 Gallery. Leeds Bradford International Airport at Yeadon, 6m/10km NE.

WEB-SITE | www.bradford.gov.uk

LOCAL RADIO | BBC RADIO LEEDS 102.7 FM, BIG AM 1278 AM, THE PULSE 97.6 FM, SUNRISE RADIO 103.2 FM

Brighton & Hove

STD Code 01273

INDEX TO STREET NAMES

Buckingham Road	B2	John Street	B3	Richmond Terrace	B3
Cheapside	B2	King's Road	B2	St. James's Street	C3
Church Street	B2	Lansdowne Road	B1	Southover Street	B3
Churchill Square	C2	Lewes Road	A3	Stanford Road	A2
Clifton Hill	B1	London Road	A2	The Lanes	C2
Davigdor Road	A1	Madeira Drive	C3	The Upper Drive	A1
Ditchling Rise	A2	Marine Parade	C3	Union Road	A3
Dyke Road	B2	Montefiore Road	A1	Upper Lewes	A3
Edward Street	C3	Montpelier Road	B1	Road	
Elm Grove	A3	North Street	B2	Upper North	B1
Florence Road	A2	Old Shoreham	A1	Street	
Freshfield Road	C3	Road		Viaduct Road	A2
Gloucester Road	B2	Old Steine	C3	West Street	C2
Grand Junction	C2	Preston Circus	A2	Western Road	B1
Road		Preston Road	A2	York Avenue	B1
Holland Road	B1	Queen's Park Road	B3	York Place	B3
Hollingdean Road	A3	Queen's Road	B2		
Islingword Road	A3	Richmond Place	B3		

TOURIST INFORMATION ☎ 01273 292599
10 BARTHOLOMEW SQUARE,
BRIGHTON, BN1 1JS

HOSPITAL A & E ☎ 01273 696955
ROYAL SUSSEX COUNTY HOSPITAL, EASTERN ROAD,
BRIGHTON, BN2 5BE

COUNCIL OFFICE ☎ 01273 290000
TOWN HALL, BARTHOLOMEWS,
BRIGHTON, BN1 1JA

Brighton *B. & H.* Population: 124,851. Town, seaside resort, sailing and conference centre, 48m/77km S of London. Previously a fishing village known as Brighthelmstone, centred on current Lanes area. Brighton became fashionable as a sea-bathing resort in the 18c. Patronized by the Prince Regent in 1780s who built the Royal Pavilion in Oriental style as a summer palace. Regency squares at Kemp Town. Amusement arcades on 1899 Palace Pier. Annual festivals. Language schools. Universities.

WEB-SITE www.brighton-hove.gov.uk

LOCAL RADIO
BBC SOUTHERN COUNTIES RADIO 95.3 FM
CAPITAL GOLD 945 & 1323 AM, SOUTHERN FM 103.5, SURF FM 107.2FM

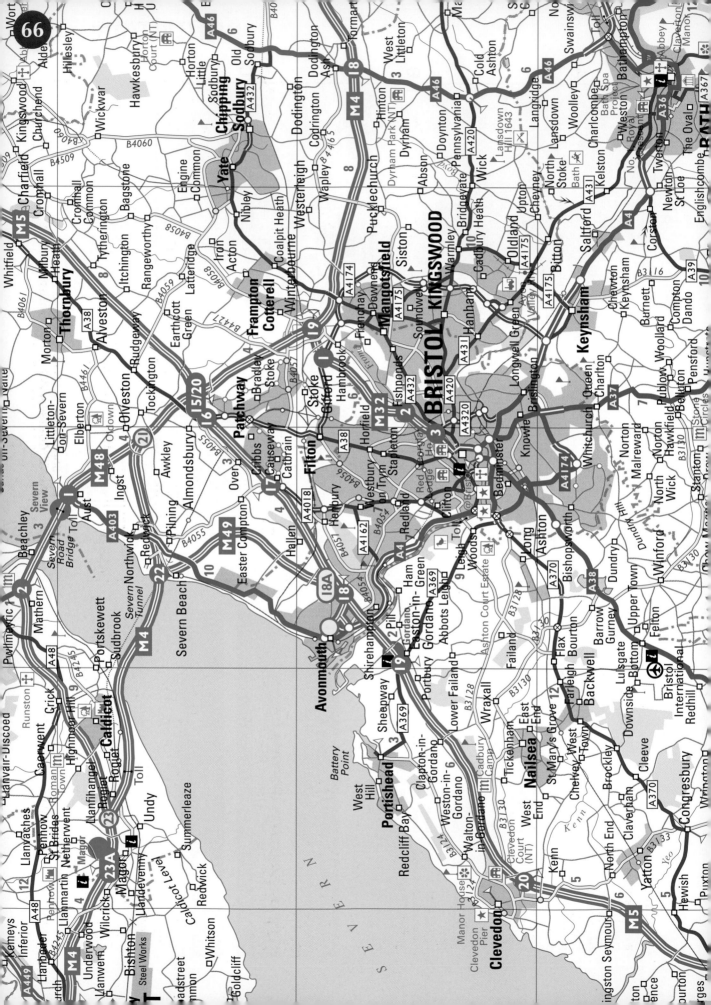

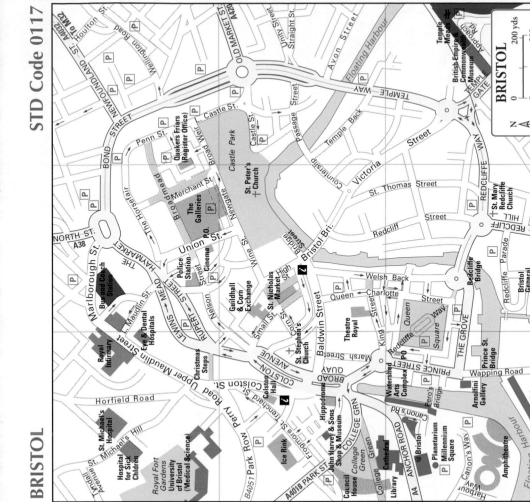

INDEX TO STREET NAMES

Anchor Road C1
Approach Road C3
Avon Street B3
Baldwin Street B1
Bond Street A2
Bridge Street B2
Bristol Bridge B2
Broadmead A2
Broad Quay B1
Broad Weir A3
Canon's Road C1
Canon's Way C1
Castle Street B3
Christmas Steps A1
College Green B1
Colston Avenue B1
Colston Street B1
Corn Street B1
Counterslip B2
Frogmore Street B1
Harbour Way C1
High Street B2
Horfield Road A1
Houlton Street A3
King Street B1

Lewins Mead C1
Lower Castle Street C3
Lower Maudlin B3
Street
Malborough Street A2
Marsh Street B1
Merchant Street B2
Nelson Street A2
Newfoundland A3
Street
Newgate B2
North Street A2
Old Market Street B3
Park Row B1
Park Street B1
Passage Street B3
Penn Street A3
Perry Road C1
Prince Street B2
Prince Street Bridge C1
Queen Charlotte B2
Street
Redcliffe Bridge C2
Redcliffe Parade C2

Redcliff Street B2
Redcliffe Way C1/C2
Rupert Street A1
St. Michael's Hill B2
St. Thomas Street B1
Small Street B3
Straight Street B3
Temple Back C3
Temple Gate C3
Temple Way A3
The Grove C1
The Haymarket A2
The Horsefair A2
Trenchard Street B1
Tyndall Avenue A1
Union Street A2
Unity Street B3
Upper Maudlin A1
Street
Victoria Street B2
Wapping Road C1
Wellington Road B2
Welsh Back C2
Wine Street B2

TOURIST INFORMATION ☎ 0117 926 0767
ST. NICHOLAS CHURCH, ST. NICHOLAS STREET,
BRISTOL, BS1 1UE

HOSPITAL A & E ☎ 0117 923 0000
BRISTOL ROYAL INFIRMARY,
MARLBOROUGH STREET, BRISTOL, BS2 8HW

COUNCIL OFFICE ☎ 0117 922 2000
THE COUNCIL HOUSE, COLLEGE GREEN,
BRISTOL, BS1 5TR

Bristol Population: 407,992. City, 106m/171km W of London. Port on River Avon dates from medieval times. Bristol grew from transatlantic trade in rum, tobacco and slaves. In Georgian times, Bristol's population was second only to London and many Georgian buildings still stand, including the Theatre Royal, the oldest working theatre in the country. Bristol is now a commercial and industrial centre. Cathedral dates from 12c and was originally an abbey. 15c Temple Church tower and walls (English Heritage). Restored iron ship SS Great Britain and Industrial Museum in city docks area. Universities. 245ft/75m high Clifton Suspension Bridge completed in 1864 across the Avon Gorge NW of the city. Bristol International Airport at Lulsgate 7m/11km SW.

WEB-SITE www.bristol-city.gov.uk

LOCAL RADIO BBC RADIO BRISTOL 95.5 FM
BRUNEL CLASSIC GOLD 1260 AM, GWR FM 96.3 FM, GALAXY 101 FM

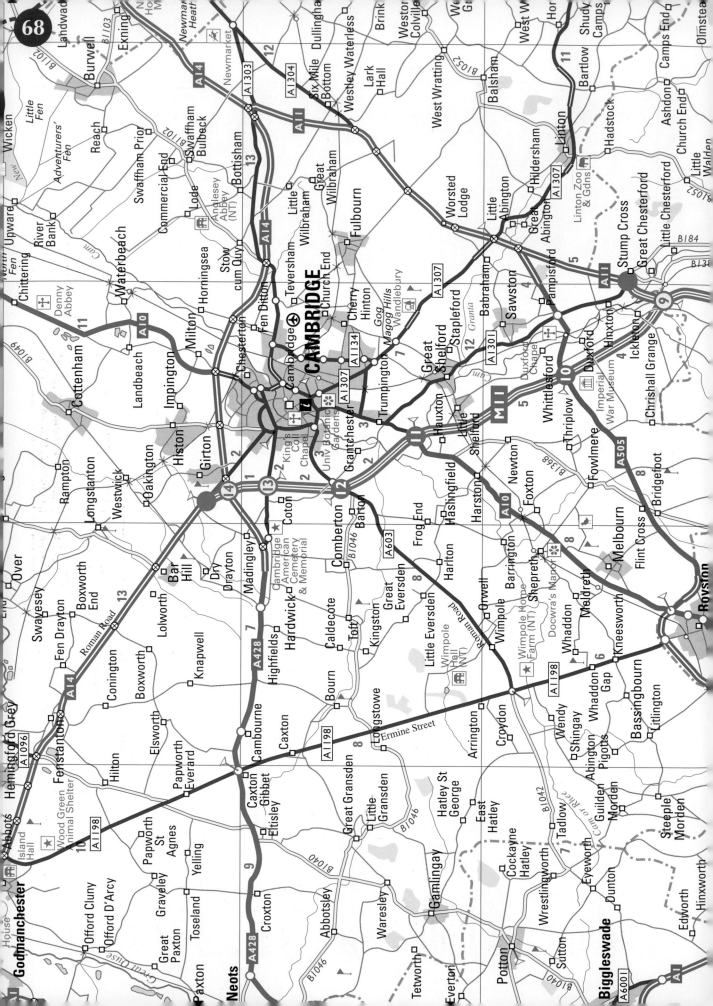

INDEX TO STREET NAMES

Street	Grid	Street	Grid	Street	Grid
Alpha Road	A2	Humberstone Road	A3	Regent Street	B2
Aylestone Road	A3	Huntingdon Road	A1	St. Andrew's Street	B2
Barton Road	C1	Jesus Lane	B2	St. John's Street	B2
Bateman Street	C2	King's Parade	B2	St. Paul's Road	C3
Carlyle Road	A2	King Street	B2	Searce Street	A1
Castle Street	A1	Lensfield Road	C2	Sidgwick Avenue	C1
Chesterton Lane	A2	Madingley Road	A1	Sidney Street	B2
Chesterton Road	A2	Magdalene Bridge Street	A2	Silver Street	C1
Clarendon Street	B3	Maids Causeway	B3	Storey's Way	A1
De Freville Avenue	A3	Market Street	B2	Tenison Road	C3
Downing Street	B2	Mawson Road	C3	Tennis Court Road	B2
East Road	B3	Mill Road	C3	Trinity Street	B2
Elizabeth Way	A3	Montague Road	A3	Trumpington Road	C2
Emmanuel Road	B2	Newmarket Road	B3	Trumpington Street	C2
Fen Causeway, The	C1	Newnham Road	C1	Union Road	C2
Glisson Road	C3	Norfolk Street	B3	Victoria Avenue	A2
Gonville Place	C3	Panton Street	C2	Victoria Road	A2
Grange Road	B1	Parker Street	B2	West Road	B1
Gresham Road	C3	Parkside	B3		
Hamilton Road	A3	Park Terrace	B2		
Harvey Road	C3	Pembroke Street	B2		
Hills Road	C3	Queen's Road	B1		

TOURIST INFORMATION ☎ 01223 322640
WHEELER STREET, CAMBRIDGE,
CAMBRIDGESHIRE, CB2 3QB

HOSPITAL A & E ☎ 01223 245151
ADDENBROOKE'S HOSPITAL, HILLS ROAD,
CAMBRIDGE, CB2 2QQ

COUNCIL OFFICE ☎ 01223 457000
THE GUILDHALL, MARKET SQUARE,
CAMBRIDGE, CB2 3QJ

Cambridge *Cambs.* Population: 95,682. City, university city on River Cam 49m/79km N of London. First college founded here in 1271. Historic tensions existed between students and townspeople since 14c, and came to a head during Peasants' Revolt of 1381 in which five townsfolk were hanged. Oliver Cromwell was a graduate of Sidney Sussex College and local MP at a time when the University was chiefly Royalist. 1870's saw foundation of first women's colleges, but women were not awarded degrees until after 1947. University's notable graduates include prime ministers, foreign heads of state, literary giants, philosophers and spies. Cambridge Footlights regularly provide a platform for future stars of stage, screen and television. Cambridge boasts many fine museums, art galleries and buildings of interest, including King's College Chapel and Fitzwilliam Museum. Airport at Teversham 3m/4km E.

WEB-SITE www.cambridge.gov.uk

LOCAL RADIO BBC RADIO CAMBRIDGESHIRE 96 FM
Q 103 FM, RED RADIO 107.9 FM

CAMBRIDGE

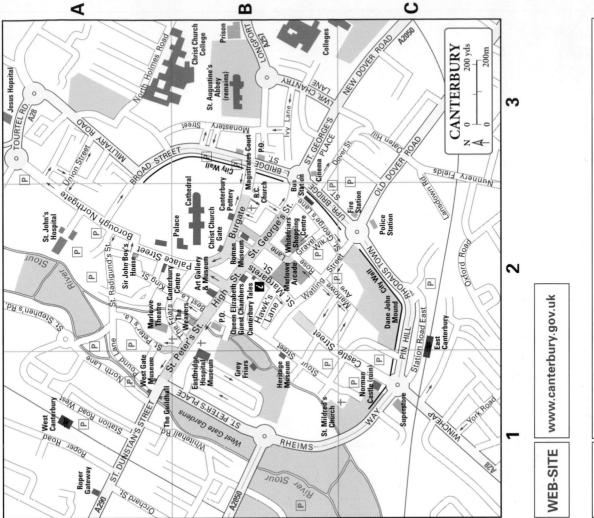

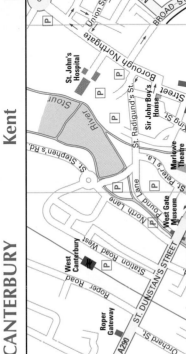

INDEX TO STREET NAMES

Best Lane	B2	North Holmes Road	A3
Borough	A2	North Lane	A1
Northgate		Nunnery Fields	C3
Broad Street	A3	Oaten Hill	C3
Burgate	B2	Old Dover Road	C2
Castle Street	C1	Orchard Street	A1
Dover Street	B3	Oxford Road	C2
Gravel Walk	B2	Palace Street	B2
Hawk's Lane	B2	Pin Hill	C1
High Street	B2	Pound Lane	A1
Ivy Lane	B3	Rheims Way	B1
King Street	A2	Rhodaus Town	C2
Lansdown Road	C2	Roper Road	A1
Longport	B3	Rose Lane	B2
Lower Bridge	B3	St. Dunstan's	A1
Street		Street	
Lower	B3	St. George's Lane	B2
Chantry Lane		St. George's	B3
Marlowe Avenue	C2	Place	
Military Road	A3	St. George's	B3
Monastery Street	B3	Street	
New Dover Road	C3		
St. Margarets	B2	Station Road East	C1
Street		Station Road	A1
St. Peter's Lane	A2	West	
St. Peter's Place	B1	Stour Street	B1
St. Peter's Street	A1	The Friar's	B2
St. Radigund's	A2	Tourtel Road	A3
Street		Union Street	A3
St. Stephen's	A2	Upper Bridge	C2
		Street	
		Watling Street	B2
		Whitehall Road	B1
		Wincheap	C1
		York Road	C1

TOURIST INFORMATION ☎ 01227 766567
34 ST. MARGARET'S STREET,
CANTERBURY, KENT, CT1 2TG

HOSPITAL A & E ☎ 01227 766877
KENT & CANTERBURY HOSPITAL, ETHELBERT ROAD,
CANTERBURY, CT1 3NG

COUNCIL OFFICE ☎ 01227 862000
COUNCIL OFFICES, MILITARY ROAD,
CANTERBURY, CT1 1YW

WEB-SITE www.canterbury.gov.uk

LOCAL RADIO BBC RADIO KENT 97.6 FM
INVICTA FM 103.1 FM, 106 CTFM 106 FM

Canterbury *Kent* Population: 36,464. City, premier cathedral city and seat of Primate of Church of England on Great Stour River 54m/88km E of London. Site of Roman settlement Durovernum. After Romans left, Saxons renamed town Cantwarabyrig. First cathedral in England built on site of current Christ Church Cathedral in AD 602. Thomas à Becket assassinated in Canterbury in 1170, turning Cathedral into great Christian shrine and destination of many pilgrimages, such as those detailed in Geoffrey Chaucer's Canterbury Tales. Becket's tomb destroyed on orders of Henry VIII. Cathedral was backdrop for premiere of T.S. Eliot's play 'Murder in the Cathedral' in 1935. City suffered extensive damage during World War II. Many museums and galleries explaining city's rich heritage. Roman and medieval remains, including city walls. Modern shopping centre; industrial development on outskirts. University of Kent on hill to N.

CARDIFF

STD Code 029

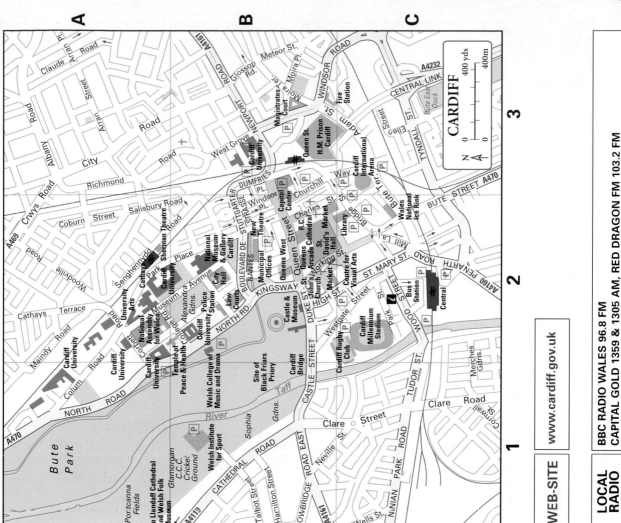

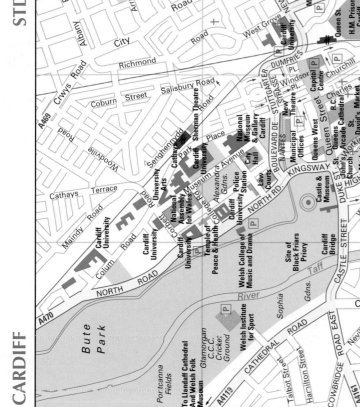

CARDIFF

N				
0	400 yds			
0	400m			

INDEX TO STREET NAMES

Adam Street	C3	Cornwall Street	C1	
Albany Road	A3	Cowbridge	B1	
Arran Place	A3	Road East	A2	
Arran Street	A3	Crwys Road	B2	
Boulevard	B2	Duke Street	B3	
de Nantes		Dumfries Place	C3	
Bridge Street	C2	Ellen Street	B3	
Bute Street	C2	Glossop Road	B1	
Bute Terrace	C2	Hamilton Street	B2	
Castle Street	B1	High Street	B2	
Cathays Terrace	A2	Kingsway	A1	
Cathedral Road	B1	Maindy Road	C1	
Central Link	C3	Merches Gardens	B3	
Charles Street	B2	Meteor Street	C2	
Churchill Way	B3	Mill Lane	B3	
City Road	A3	Moira Place	B3	
Clare Road	C1	Moira Terrace	B3	
Clare Street	B1	Museum Avenue	A2	
Claude Road	A3	Neville Street	B1	
Coburn Street	A2	Newport Road	B3	
College Road	B2	Ninian Park Road	C1	
Colum Road	A1	North Road	A1	
Corbett Road	A2	Park Place	A2	

Park Street	C2	
Penarth Road	C2	
Queen Street	B2	
Richmond Road	A3	
St. Mary Street	C2	
Salisbury Road	A2	
Senghennydd	A2	
Road		
Stuttgarter	B2	
Strasse		
Talbot Street	B1	
Tudor Street	C1	
Tyndall Street	C3	
Wells Street	C1	
West Grove	B3	
Westgate Street	B2	
Windsor Place	B3	
Windsor Road	B3	
Wood Street	C2	
Woodville Road	A2	
Working Street	B2	

TOURIST INFORMATION ☎ 029 2022 7281
CARDIFF VISITOR CENTRE, 16 WOOD STREET,
CARDIFF, CF10 1ES

HOSPITAL A & E ☎ 029 2074 7747
CARDIFF UNIVERSITY OF WALES HOSPITAL, HEATH PARK,
CARDIFF, CF14 4XW

COUNCIL OFFICE ☎ 029 2087 2000
COUNTY HALL, ATLANTIC WHARF,
CARDIFF, CF10 4UW

Cardiff (Caerdydd). Population: 272,129. City, capital of Wales since 1955. Romans founded military fort and small settlement on site of present day Cardiff. Uninhabited between departure of Romans and Norman conquest centuries later. Fishing village until development of coal mining in 19c. Population rose from 1000 in 1801 to 170,000 a century later, with city becoming one of busiest ports in the world. Dock trade collapsed in 1930's. Since establishment as Welsh capital, many governmental, administrative and media organisations have moved to city. Major refurbishment and development programme still under way. Cardiff Bay area now major tourist centre and includes Techniquest, a science discovery centre, and has been selected as the location of the new Welsh Assembly building. Millennium Stadium Cardiff Arms Park is the home of the Welsh Rugby Union and also hosts other sporting and entertainment events. Many museums including National Museum of Wales. Universities.

WEB-SITE www.cardiff.gov.uk

LOCAL RADIO BBC RADIO WALES 96.8 FM
CAPITAL GOLD 1359 & 1305 AM, RED DRAGON FM 103.2 FM

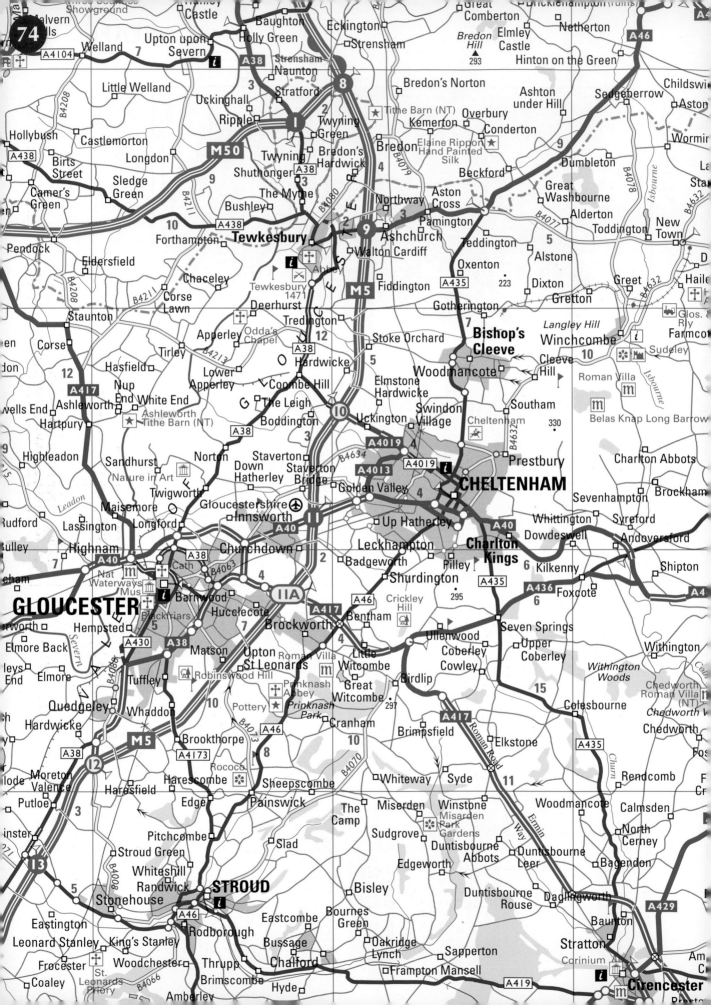

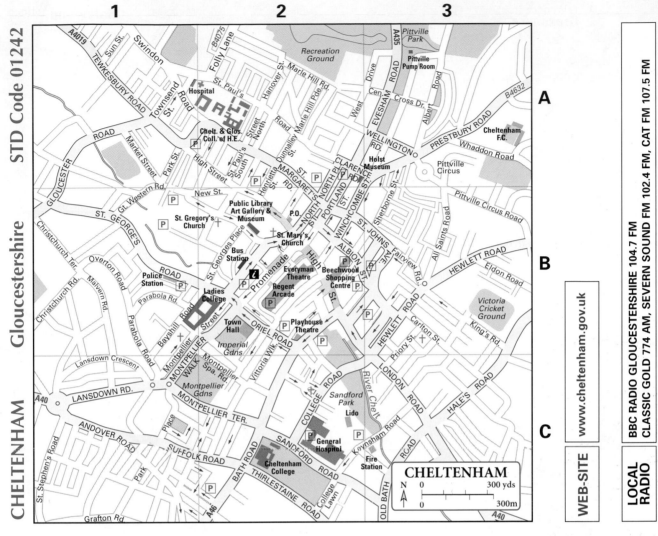

STD Code 01242

Gloucestershire

CHELTENHAM

WEB-SITE www.cheltenham.gov.uk

LOCAL RADIO BBC RADIO GLOUCESTERSHIRE 104.7 FM CLASSIC GOLD 774 AM, SEVERN SOUND FM 102.4 FM, CAT FM 107.5 FM

INDEX TO STREET NAMES

Albert Road	A3	Fairview Road	B3	Market Street	A1	Park Street	A1	St. Stephen's Road	C1
Albion Street	B2	Folly Lane	A2	Marle Hill Parade	A2	Pittville Circus	A3	Sandford Road	C2
All Saints Road	B3	Gloucester Road	B1	Marle Hill Road	A2	Pittville Circus Road	B3	Sherborne Street	B3
Andover Road	C1	Grafton Road	C1	Montpellier Spa		Portland Street	B2	Suffolk Road	C1
Bath Road	C2	Great Western Road	B1	Road	B2	Prestbury Road	A3	Sun Street	A1
Bayshill Road	B1	Hale's Road	C3	Montpellier Street	C1	Priory Street	C3	Swindon Road	A1
Carlton Street	B3	Hanover Street	A2	Montpellier Terrace	C1	Promenade	B2	Tewkesbury Road	A1
Central Cross Drive	A3	Henrietta Street	B2	Montpellier Walk	C1	St. George's Place	B2	Thirlestaine Road	C2
Christchurch Road	B1	Hewlett Road	B3	New Street	A2	St. George's Road	B1	Townsend Street	A1
Christchurch Terrace	B1	High Street	A2	North Place	B2	St. Johns Avenue	B2	Vittoria Walk	C2
Clarence Road	A2	Keynsham Road	C2	North Street	B2	St. Margaret's Road	A2	Wellington Road	A3
College Lawn	C2	King's Road	B3	Old Bath Road	C3	St. Paul's Road	A2	West Drive	A2
College Road	C2	Lansdown Crescent	C1	Oriel Road	B2	St. Paul's Street	A2	Whaddon Road	A3
Dunnally Street	A2	Lansdown Road	C1	Overton Road	B1	North		Winchcombe Street	B2
Eldon Road	B3	London Road	C3	Parabola Road	B1	St. Paul's Street	A2		
Evesham Road	A3	Malvern Road	B1	Park Place	C1	South			

TOURIST INFORMATION ☎ 01242 522878 77 THE PROMENADE, CHELTENHAM, GLOUCESTERSHIRE, GL50 1PP

HOSPITAL A & E ☎ 01242 222222 CHELTENHAM GENERAL HOSPITAL, SANDFORD ROAD, CHELTENHAM, GL53 7AN

COUNCIL OFFICE ☎ 01242 262626 MUNICIPAL OFFICES, THE PROMENADE, CHELTENHAM, GL50 1PP

Cheltenham *Glos.* Population: 91,301. Town, largest town in The Cotswolds, 8m/12km NE of Gloucester. Shopping and tourist centre, with some light industry. Mainly residential, with many Regency and Victorian buildings and public gardens. Formerly a spa town, Pittville Pump Room built between 1825 and 1830 overlooks Pittville Park and is now used for concerts. Art Gallery and Museum. Ladies' College founded 1853. Racecourse to the N hosts Cheltenham Gold Cup race meeting, Cheltenham International Music Festival and Festival of Literature, among other events. Birthplace of composer Gustav Holst.

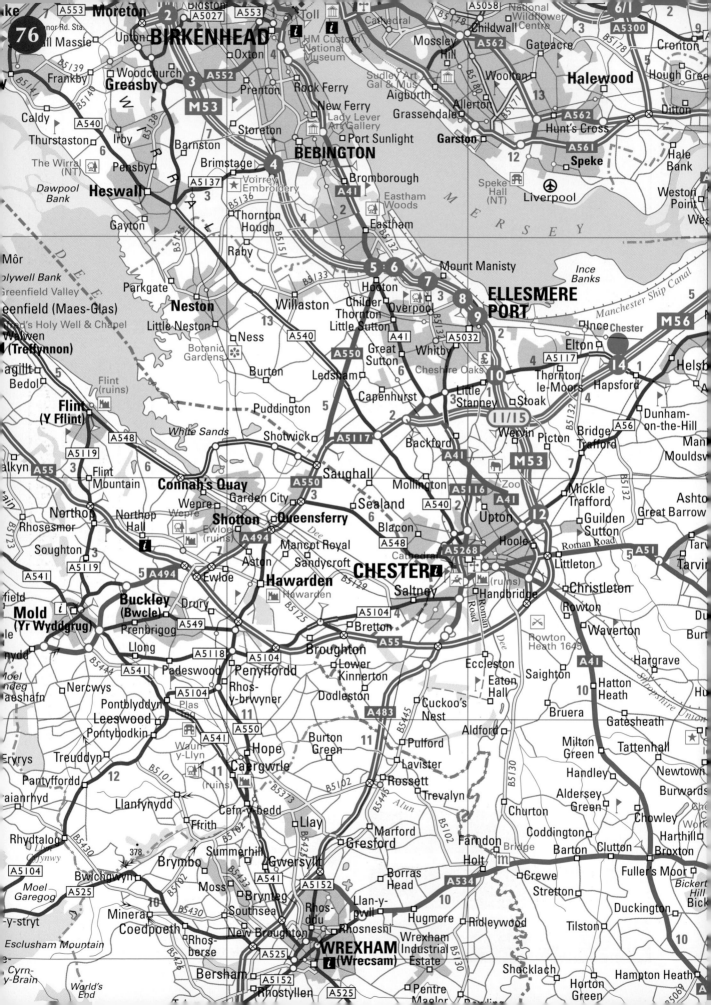

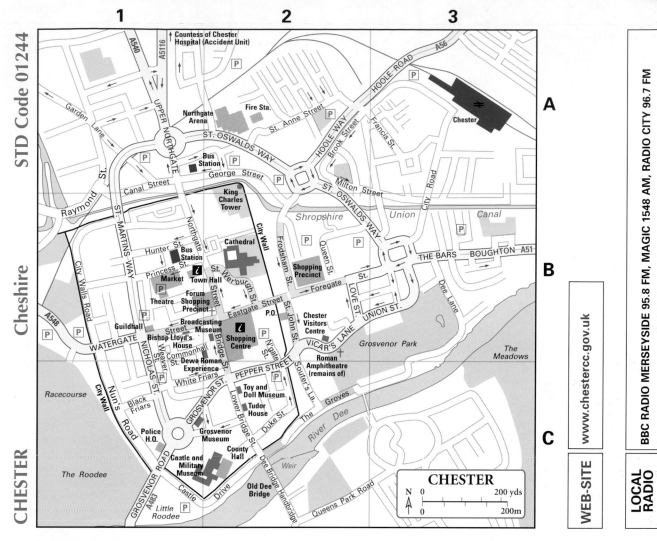

WEB-SITE www.chestercc.gov.uk

LOCAL RADIO BBC RADIO MERSEYSIDE 95.8 FM, MAGIC 1548 AM, RADIO CITY 96.7 FM

INDEX TO STREET NAMES

Black Friars	C1	Foregate Street	B2	Milton Street	A2	St. Martins Way	A1
Boughton	B3	Francis Street	A3	Newgate Street	B2	St. Oswalds Way	A2
Bridge Street	B2	Frodsham Street	B2	Nicholas Street	B1	St. Werburgh Street	B2
Brook Street	A2	Garden Lane	A1	Northgate Street	B1	Souter's Lane	C2
Canal Street	A1	George Street	A2	Nun's Road	C1	The Bars	B3
Castle Drive	C1	Grosvenor Road	C1	Old Dee Bridge	C2	The Groves	C2
City Road	B3	Grosvenor Street	C1	Pepper Street	C2	Union Street	B2
City Walls Road	B1	Handbridge	C2	Princess Street	B1	Upper Northgate	A1
Commonhall Street	B1	Hoole Road	A2	Queens Park Road	C2	Vicar's Lane	B2
Dee Bridge	C2	Hoole Way	A2	Queen Street	B2	Watergate Street	B1
Dee Lane	B3	Hunter Street	B1	Raymond Street	A1	Weaver Street	B1
Duke Street	C2	Love Street	B2	St. Anne Street	A2	White Friars	C1
Eastgate Street	B2	Lower Bridge Street	C2	St. John Street	B2		

TOURIST INFORMATION ☎ 01244 402111
TOWN HALL, NORTHGATE STREET,
CHESTER, CHESHIRE, CH1 2HJ

HOSPITAL A & E ☎ 01244 365000
COUNTESS OF CHESTER HOSPITAL, HEALTH PK,
LIVERPOOL ROAD, CHESTER, CH2 1UL

COUNCIL OFFICE ☎ 01244 324324
THE FORUM,
CHESTER, CH1 2HS

Chester *Ches.* Population: 80110. City, county town and cathedral city on River Dee, 34m/54km SW of Manchester and 15m/24km SE of Birkenhead. Commercial, financial and tourist centre built on Roman town of Deva. Includes biggest Roman amphitheatre in Britain (English Heritage) and well preserved medieval walls (English Heritage). Castle, now county hall, includes 12c Agricola Tower (English Heritage). Cathedral with remains of original Norman abbey. Famed for Tudor timber-framed buildings which include Chester Rows, two-tier galleried shops and Bishop Lloyd's House, with ornate 16c carved façade. Eastgate clock built to commemorate Queen Victoria's diamond jubilee in 1897. Racecourse 1m/2km SW of city centre; zoo 3m/4km N of city centre.

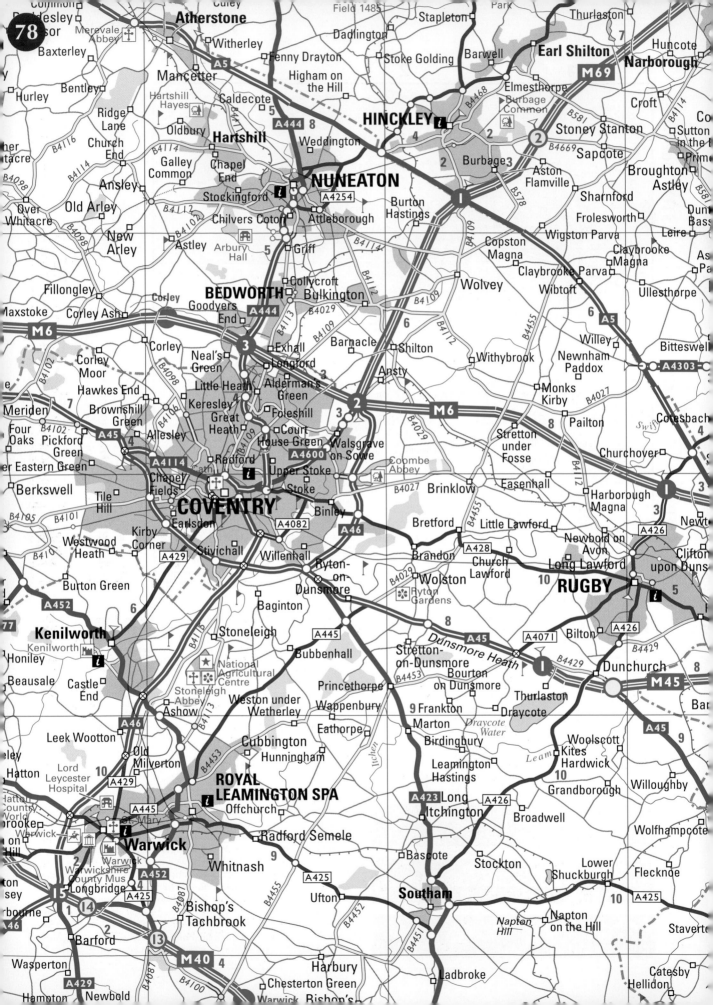

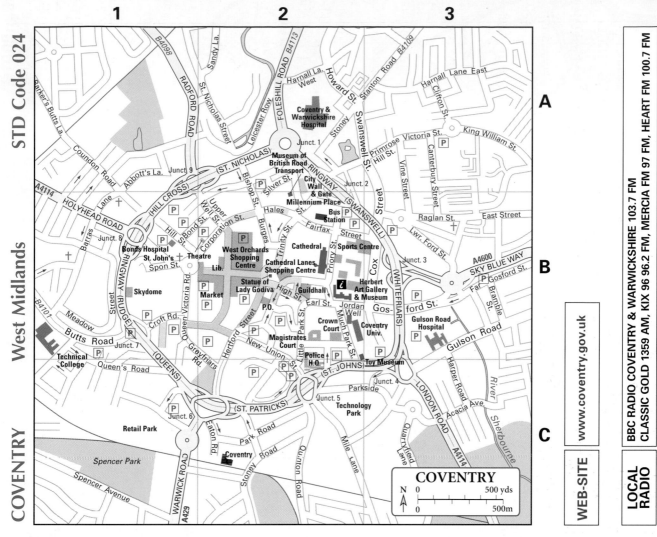

COVENTRY

N 0 500 yds

0 500m

STD Code 024

West Midlands

COVENTRY

WEB-SITE www.coventry.gov.uk

LOCAL RADIO

BBC RADIO COVENTRY & WARWICKSHIRE 103.7 FM
CLASSIC GOLD 1359 AM, KIX 96 96.2 FM, MERCIA FM 97 FM, HEART FM 100.7 FM

INDEX TO STREET NAMES

Abbott's Lane	A1	Eaton Road	C2	King William Street	A3	Quinton Road	C2

Abbott's Lane A1
Acacia Avenue C3
Barker's Butts Lane A1
Barras Lane B1
Bishop Street A2
Bond Street B1
Bramble Street B3
Burges B2
Butts Road B1
Canterbury Street A3
Clifton Street A3
Corporation Street B2
Coundon Road A1
Cox Street B3
Croft Road B1
Earl Street B2
East Street B3

Eaton Road C2
Fairfax Street B2
Far Gosford Street B3
Foleshill Road A2
Gosford Street B3
Greyfriars Road B1
Gulson Road B3
Hales Street B2
Harnall Lane East A3
Harnall Lane West A2
Harper Road C3
Hertford Street B2
High Street B2
Hill Street B1
Holyhead Road B1
Howard Street A2
Jordan Well B2

King William Street A3
Leicester Row A2
Little Park Street C2
London Road C3
Lower Ford Street B3
Meadow Street B1
Mile Lane C2
Much Park Street B2
New Union Street B2
Park Road C2
Parkside C2
Primrose Hill Street A3
Priory Street B2
Quarryfield Lane C3
Queen's Road C1
Queen Victoria B1
Road

Quinton Road C2
Radford Road A1
Raglan Street B3
Ringway Hill Cross B1
Ringway St. Johns C2
Ringway A2
St. Nicholas
Ringway C2
St. Patricks
Ringway Queens B1
Ringway Rudge B1
Ringway B2
Swanswell
Ringway B3
Whitefriars
St. Nicholas Street A2
Sandy Lane A2

Silver Street A2
Sky Blue Way B3
Spencer Avenue C1
Spon Street B1
Stoney Road C2
Stoney Stanton A2
Road
Swanswell Street A2
Trinity Street B2
Upper Well Street B2
Victoria Street A3
Vine Street A3
Warwick Road C1

TOURIST INFORMATION ☎ 024 7683 2303
BAYLEY LANE, COVENTRY,
WEST MIDLANDS, CV1 5RN

HOSPITAL A & E ☎ 024 7622 4055
COVENTRY & WARWICKSHIRE HOSPITAL,
STONEY STANTON ROAD, COVENTRY, CV1 4FH

COUNCIL OFFICE ☎ 024 7683 3333
COUNCIL HOUSE, EARL STREET,
COVENTRY, CV1 5RR

Coventry *W.Mid.* Population: 299,316. City, 17m/27km E of Birmingham. St. Michael's cathedral built 1954-62 beside ruins of medieval cathedral destroyed in air raid in 1940. The centre of the city was rebuilt in the 1950s and 1960s following WW II bombing, but some old buildings remain, including Bonds Hospital and the medieval Guildhall. A town rich from textile industry in middle ages, Coventry is now known for its motor car industry; other important industries are manufacturing and engineering. Museum of British Road Transport. Herbert Art Gallery and Museum. Universities. Civil airport at Baginton to S. Coventry Canal runs N to Trent and Mersey Canal at Fradley Junction near Lichfield.

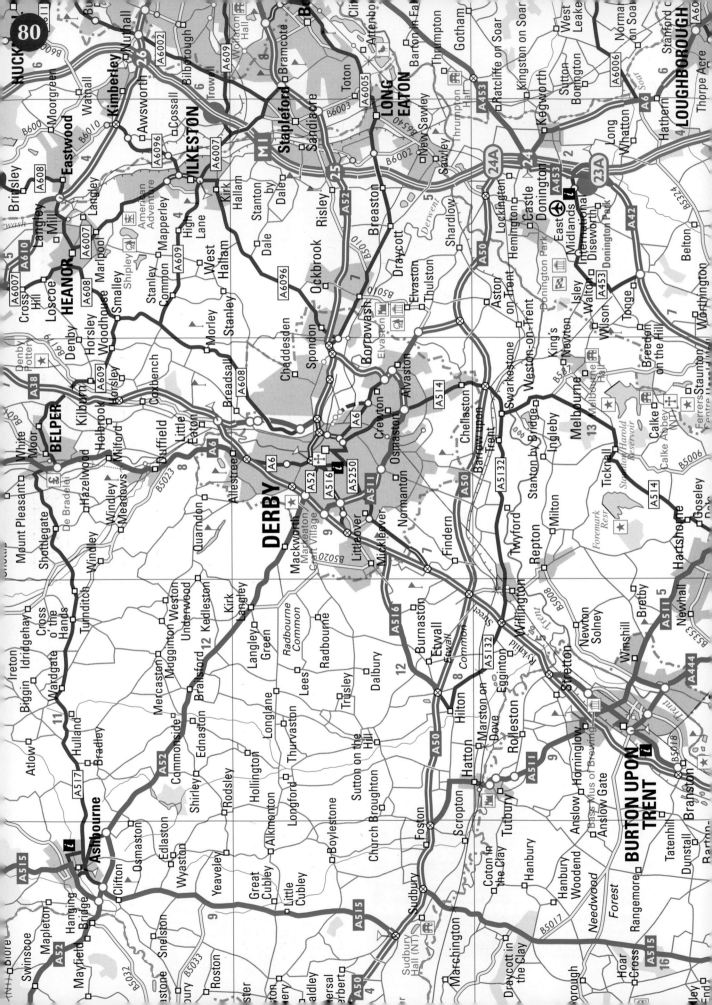

STD Code 01332

DERBY

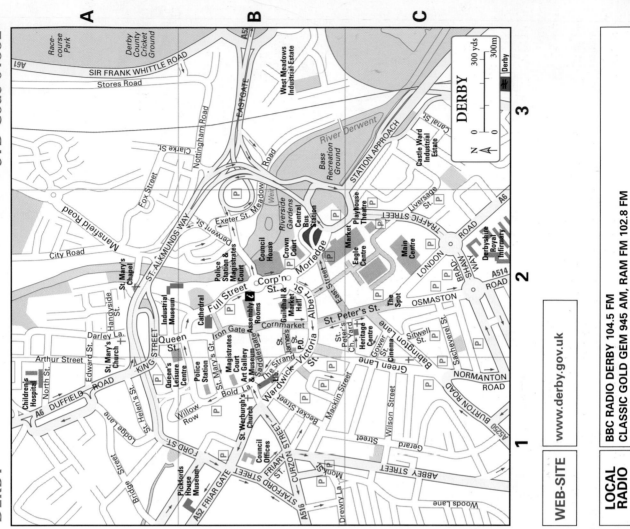

INDEX TO STREET NAMES

Abbey Street	C1	Fox Street	C1	Sacheverel Street	C1
Albert Street	B2	Friar Gate	B2	Saddlergate	B2
Arthur Street	A1	Friary Street	A1	St. Alkmunds Way	A2
Babington Lane	C1	Full Street	B1	St. Helen's Street	A1
Becket Street	B1	Gerard Street	C1	St. James Street	B2
Bold Lane	B1	Gower Street	C2	St. Mary's Gate	B1
Bradshaw Way	C2	Green Lane	C1	St. Peter's Church	C2
Bridge Street	A1	Handyside Street	A2	Yard	
Burton Road	C1	Iron Gate	B2	St. Peter's Street	B2
Canal Street	C3	King Street	A1	Sir Frank Whittle	A3
City Road	A2	Liversage Street	C2	Road	
Clarke Street	B3	Lodge Lane	A1	Sitwell Street	C2
Cornmarket	B2	London Road	C2	Stafford Street	B1
Corporation Street	B2	Macklin Street	B3	Station Approach	A3
Curzon Street	B1	Mansfield Road	A2	Stores Road	A2
Darley Lane	A2	Market Place	B2	The Strand	B1
Derwent Street	B2	Meadow Road	B1	Traffic Street	C2
Drewry Lane	B1	Monk Street	B2	Victoria Street	B1
Duffield Road	A1	Morledge	B2	Wardwick	B1
Eastgate	B3	Normanton Road	C1	Willow Row	A1
East Street	B2	North Street	A1	Wilson Street	C1
Edward Street	A1	Nottingham Road	B3	Woods Lane	C1
Exeter Street	B2	Osmaston Road	C2		
Ford Street	B1	Queen Street	A2		

**TOURIST INFORMATION ☎ 01332 255802
ASSEMBLY ROOMS, MARKET PLACE,
DERBY, DE1 3AH**

**HOSPITAL A & E ☎ 01332 347141
DERBYSHIRE ROYAL INFIRMARY,
LONDON ROAD, DERBY, DE1 2QY**

**COUNCIL OFFICE ☎ 01332 293111
THE COUNCIL HOUSE, CORPORATION STREET,
DERBY, DE1 2FS**

Derby Population: 223,836. City, industrial city and county town on River Derwent. 35m/56km NE of Birmingham. Shopping and entertainment centre. Cathedral mainly by James Gibbs, 1725. Both manufacturing and engineering are important to local economy. Derby Industrial Museum charts city's industrial history with emphasis on Rolls Royce aircraft engineering. Tours at Royal Crown Derby porcelain factory. University.

WEB-SITE www.derby.gov.uk

LOCAL RADIO
BBC RADIO DERBY 104.5 FM
CLASSIC GOLD GEM 945 AM, RAM FM 102.8 FM

STD Code 01304

Kent

DOVER

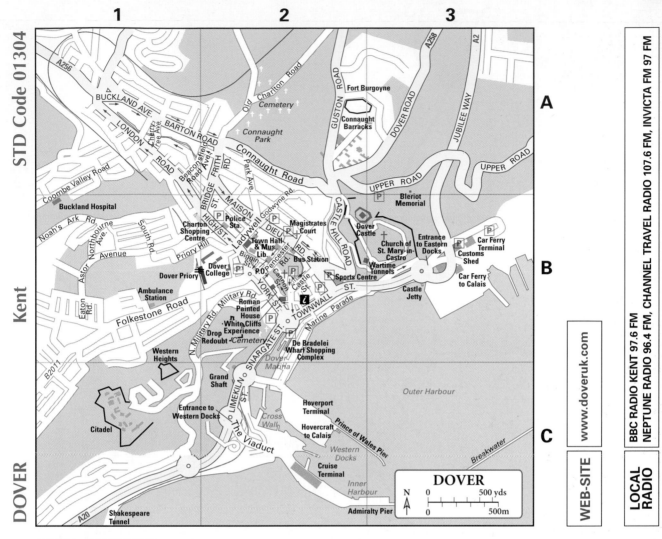

BBC RADIO KENT 97.6 FM
NEPTUNE RADIO 96.4 FM, CHANNEL TRAVEL RADIO 107.6 FM, INVICTA FM 97 FM

www.doveruk.com

WEB-SITE

LOCAL RADIO

INDEX TO STREET NAMES

Astor Avenue	B1	Cherry Tree Avenue	A1	Ladywell	B2	Pencester Road	B2
Barton Road	A1	Connaught Road	A2	Limekiln Street	C2	Priory Hill	B1
Beaconsfield Avenue	A1	Coombe Valley Road	B1	London Road	A1	Snargate Street	C2
Beaconsfield Road	A1	Dover Road	A3	Maison Dieu Road	B2	South Road	B1
Biggin Street	B2	Eaton Road	B1	Marine Parade	B2	The Viaduct	C2
Bridge Street	B2	Folkestone Road	B1	Military Road	B2	Townwall Street	B2
Buckland Avenue	A1	Frith Road	A2	Noah's Ark Road	B1	Upper Road	A3
Cannon Street	B2	Godwyne Road	B2	Northbourne Avenue	B1	York Street	B2
Canons Gate Road	B2	Guston Road	A2	North Military Road	B1		
Castle Hill Road	B2	High Street	B2	Old Charlton Road	A2		
Castle Street	B2	Jubilee Way	A3	Park Avenue	A2		

TOURIST INFORMATION ☎ 01304 205108
TOWNWALL STREET,
DOVER, KENT, CT16 1JR

HOSPITAL A & E ☎ 01227 766877
KENT & CANTERBURY HOSPITAL,
ETHELBERT ROAD, CANTERBURY, CT1 3NG

COUNCIL OFFICE ☎ 01304 821199
WHITE CLIFFS BUSINESS PARK, HONEYWOOD
ROAD, DOVER, CT16 3PJ

Dover *Kent* Population: 34,179. Town, cinque port, resort and Channel port on Strait of Dover, 15m/24km SE of Canterbury, with large modern docks for freight and passengers. Dominated by high white cliffs and medieval castle (English Heritage) enclosing the Pharos, 50AD remains of Roman lighthouse. Remains of 12c Knights Templar Church (English Heritage) across valley from castle. Sections of moat of 19c fort at Western Heights (English Heritage), above town on W side of harbour. White Cliffs Experience re-creates Roman and wartime Dover.

DUNDEE

STD Code 01382

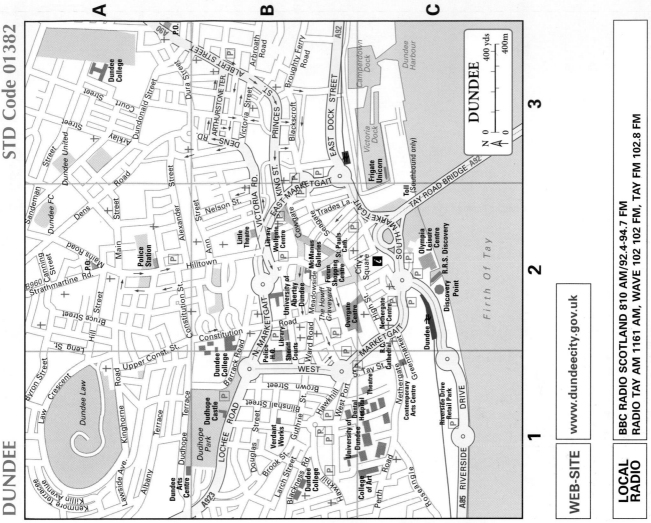

WEB-SITE www.dundeecity.gov.uk

LOCAL RADIO
BBC RADIO SCOTLAND 810 AM/92.4-94.7 FM
RADIO TAY AM 1161 AM, WAVE 102 102 FM, TAY FM 102.8 FM

INDEX TO STREET NAMES

Albany Terrace	A1	Douglas Street	B1
Albert Street	B3	Dudhope Street	A1
Alexander Street	A2	Dudhope Terrace	A3
Ann Street	B2	Dundonald Street	A3
Arbroath Road	B3	Dura Street	B3
Arklay Street	A3	East Dock Street	B3
Arthurstone	B3	East Marketgait	B2
Terrace		Greenmarket	C1
Barrack Road	B1	Guthrie Street	B1
Blackness Road	A1	Hawkhill	B1
Blackscroft	B3	High Street	B2
Blinshall Street	B1	Hill Street	C2
Brook Street	B1	Hilltown	C1
Broughty Ferry	B3	Kenmore Terrace	A2
Road		Killin Avenue	A1
Brown Street	B1	Kinghorne Road	A1
Bruce Street	A1	King Street	B2
Byron Street	A1	Larch Street	B1
Canning Street	A2	Law Crescent	A1
Constitution Road	B2	Lawside Avenue	A1
Constitution Street	A2	Leng Street	A2
Court Street	A3	Lochee Road	B1
Cowgate Street	B2	Mains Road	A2
Dens Road	A2	Main Street	A2

Meadowside	B2
Nelson Street	B2
Nethergate	C1
North Marketgait	B1
Perth Road	C1
Princes Street	B3
Roseangle	C1
Riverside Drive	C1
Seagate	B2
South Marketgait	C2
South Tay Street	C1
Strathmartine	A2
Road	
Tay Road Bridge	C2
Trades Lane	B2
Upper	A1
Constitution	
Street	
Victoria Road	B2
Victoria Street	B3
Ward Road	B1
West Marketgait	B1
West Port	B1

TOURIST INFORMATION ☎ 01382 527527
7-21 CASTLE STREET, DUNDEE, DD1 3BA

HOSPITAL A & E ☎ 01382 660111
NINEWELLS HOSPITAL, NINEWELLS ROAD, DUNDEE, DD1 9SY

COUNCIL OFFICE ☎ 01382 434000
CITY CHAMBERS, 21 CITY SQUARE, DUNDEE, DD1 3BY

Dundee Population: 158,981. City, Scotland's fourth largest city, commercial and industrial centre and port, 18m/29km E of Perth on N side of Firth of Tay, crossed here by a 1m/2km road bridge and a 2m/3km railway bridge. Robert the Bruce declared King of the Scots in Dundee in 1309. Sustained severe damage during Civil War and again prior to Jacobite uprising. City recovered in early 19c and became Britain's main processor of jute. One of largest employers in Dundee today is D.C. Thomson, publisher of The Beano and The Dandy. Many museums and art galleries. Cultural centre, occasional playing host to overflow from Edinburgh Festival. Episcopal cathedral on site of former castle. Universities. Ship 'Discovery' in which Captain Scott travelled to Antarctic has returned to Victoria dock, where she was built.

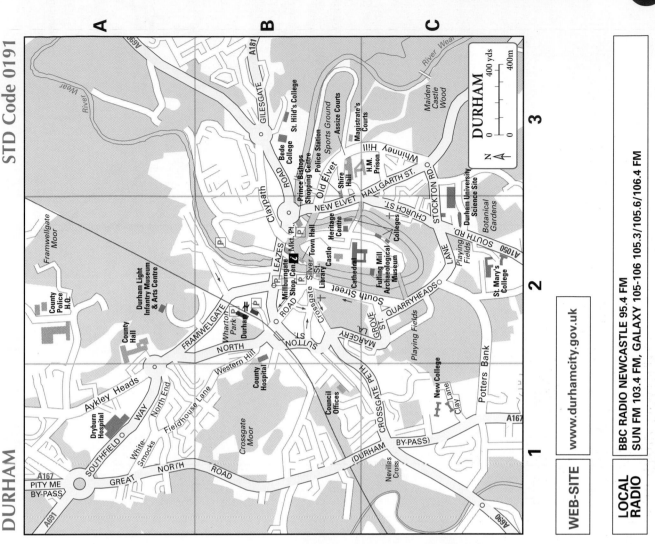

INDEX TO STREET NAMES

Aykley Heads	A1	New Elvet	B2
Church Street	C2	North End	A1
Clay Lane	C1	North Road	B2
Claypath	B2	Old Elvet	B3
Crossgate	B2	Pity Me By-Pass	A1
Crossgate Peth	C1	Potte's Bank	C1
Durham By-Pass		Quarryheads Lane	C2
Fieldhouse Lane	B1	Silver Street	B2
Framwelgate	A1	South Road	C2
Gilesgate	A2	South Street	C2
Great North Road	B3	Southfield Way	A1
Grove Street	A1	Stockton Road	C2
Hallgarth Street	C2	Sutton Street	B2
Leazes Road	C3	Western Hill	B1
Margery Lane	B2	Wh nney Hill	C3
Market Place	C2	Wh tesmocks	A1
Millburngate Bridge	B2		

TOURIST INFORMATION ☎ 0191 384 3720
MARKET PLACE, DURHAM,
COUNTY DURHAM, DH1 3NJ

HOSPITAL A & E ☎ 0191 333 2333
DRYBURN HOSPITAL, NORTH ROAD,
DURHAM, DH1 5TW

COUNCIL OFFICE ☎ 0191 386 4411
COUNTY HALL,
DURHAM, DH1 5UB

Durham *Dur.* Population: 36,937. Cathedral city on narrow bend in River Wear, 14m/22km S of Newcastle upon Tyne. Norman-Romanesque cathedral founded in 1093 on site of shrine of St. Cuthbert is World Heritage Site. England's third oldest University founded in 1832. Motte-and-bailey castle dating from 1072 now part of the University. Collection in Fulling Mill Museum of Archaelogy illustrates history of city. Museum of Oriental Art. Light Infantry Museum. Art Gallery. University Botanic Garden S of city.

WEB-SITE www.durhamcity.gov.uk

LOCAL RADIO
BBC RADIO NEWCASTLE 95.4 FM
SUN FM 103.4 FM, GALAXY 105-106 105.3/105.6/106.4 FM

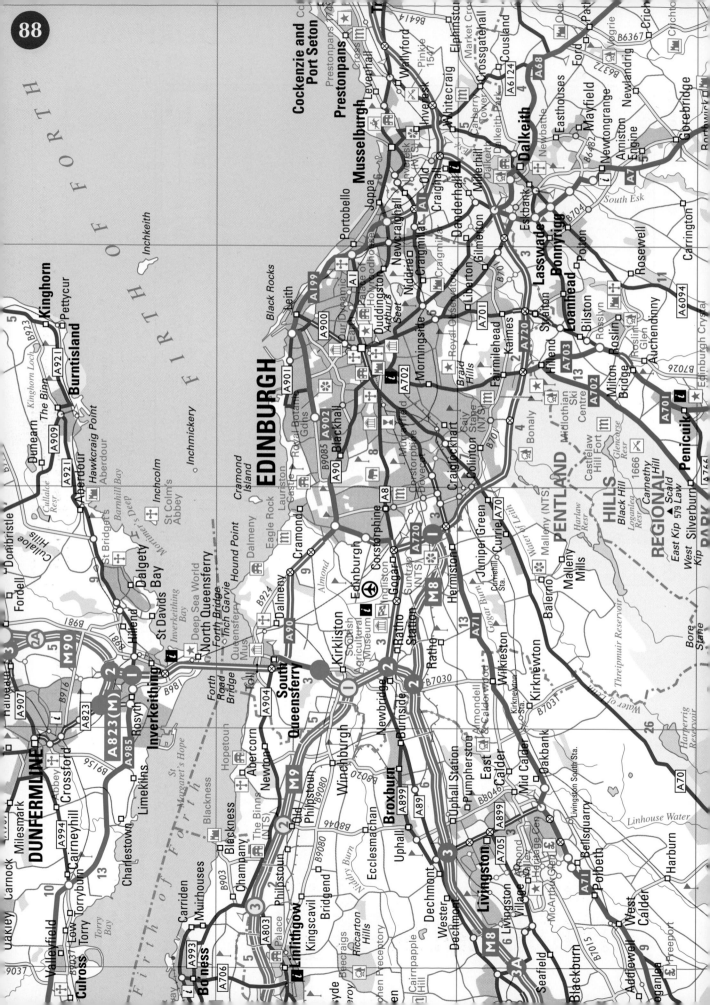

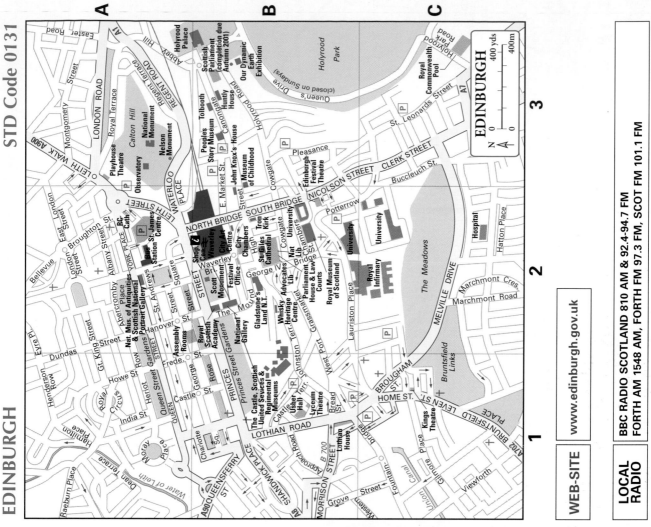

EDINBURGH

N 0 — 400 yds
0 — 400m

WEB-SITE   www.edinburgh.gov.uk

LOCAL RADIO   BBC RADIO SCOTLAND 810 AM & 92.4-94.7 FM
FORTH AM 1548 AM, FORTH FM 97.3 FM, SCOT FM 101.1 FM

INDEX TO STREET NAMES

Abbey Hill A3
Abercromby Place A2
Albany Street A2
Bellevue A2
Bread Street B1
Brougham Street C1
Broughton Street A2
Bruntsfield Place C1
Buccleuch Street C3
Canongate B3
Castle Street A1
Castle Terrace B1
Chambers Street B2
Charlotte Square B1
Clerk Street C3
Cowgate B2
Dean Terrace A1
Dundas Street A1
Easter Road A3
East London Street A2
East Market Street B2
Eyre Place A2
Fountainbridge C1
Frederick Street A1
George IV Bridge C2
George Street B1
Gilmore Place C1

Grassmarket B2
Great King Street A1
Grove Street B1
Hamilton Place A1
Hanover Street C1
Hatton Place C2
Henderson Row A2
Heriot Row C1
High Street B2
Holyrood Park Road C3
Holyrood Road A3
Home Street B1
Howe Street B1
India Street A1
Johnston Terrace A3
Lauriston Place B2
Leith Street A1
Leven Street C1
London Road A3
Lothian Road A2
Marchmont Road B1
Marchmont Crescent C2
Melville Drive C2
Montgomery Street B1
Moray Place C1

Morrison Street B1
Nicolson Street B2
North Bridge A2
Pleasance B3
Potterrow B2
Princes Street B1
Queen's Drive B3
Queensferry Street B1
Queen Street A1
Raeburn Place B2
Regent Road A3
Regent Terrace A3
Rose Street B1
Royal Circus A1
Royal Terrace A3
St. Andrew's Square A2
St. Leonards Street C3
Shandwick Place B1
South Bridge B2
The Mound C1
Viewforth C1
Waterloo Place A2
Waverley Bridge B2
Western Approach
Road C1

West Por. B1
York Place A2

TOURIST INFORMATION ☎ 0131 473 3800
INFORMATION CENTRE, 3 PRINCES STREET,
EDINBURGH, EH2 2QP

HOSPITAL A & E ☎ 0131 536 1000
ROYAL INFIRMARY OF EDINBURGH,
1 LAURISTON PLACE, EDINBURGH, EH3 9YW

COUNCIL OFFICE ☎ 0131 200 2000
CITY CHAMBERS, HIGH STREET,
EDINBURGH, EH1 1YJ

Edinburgh *Edin.* Population: 401,910. City, historic city and capital of Scotland, built on a range of rocky crags and extinct volcanoes, on S side of Firth of Forth, 41m/66km E of Glasgow. Administrative, financial and legal centre of Scotland. Medieval castle (Historic Scotland) on rocky eminence overlooks central area and was one of main seats of Royal court, while Arthur's Seat (largest of the volcanoes) guards eastern approaches. Three universities. Port at Leith, where Royal Yacht Britannia is now docked and open to public. Important industries include brewing, distilling, food and electronics. Palace of Holyroodhouse (Historic Scotland) is chief royal residence of Scotland. Old Town typified by Gladstone's Land (Historic Scotland), 17c six-storey tenement with arcaded front, outside stair and stepped gables. Numerous literary associations including Sir Arthur Conan Doyle who was born here. Many galleries and museums including National Gallery of Scotland. Annual arts festival attracts over a million visitors each year and is largest such event in the world.

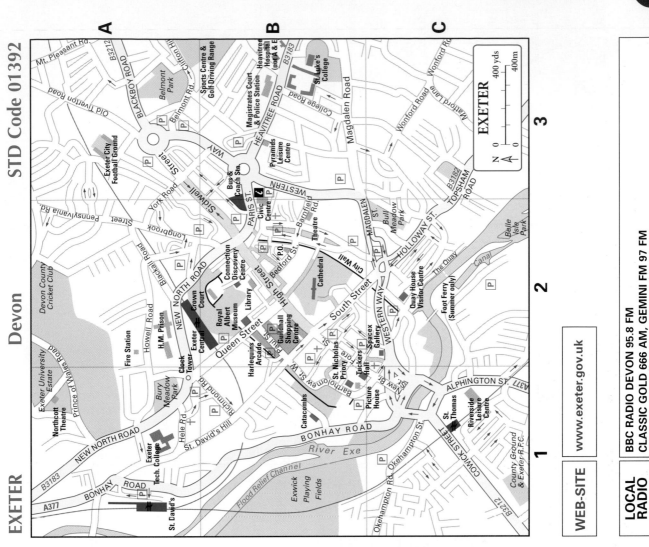

INDEX TO STREET NAMES

Alphington Street	C1
Barnfield Road	B2
Bartholomew Street West	B1
Bedford Street	B2
Belmont Road	A3
Blackboy Road	A3
Blackall Road	A2
Bonhay Road	B1
Clifton Hill	A3
College Road	B3
Cowick Street	C1
Fore Street	B2
Heavitree Road	B3
Hele Road	A1
High Street	B2
Holloway Street	C2
Howell Road	A2
Longbrook Street	A2
Magdalen Street	B3
Magdalen Street	C2
Matford Lane	C3
Mount Pleasant Road	A3
New Bridge Street	C1
New North Road	A1/A2
Okehampton Road	C1
Okehampton Street	C1
Old Tiverton Road	A3
Paris Street	B2
Paul Street	B2
Pennsylvania Road	A2
Prince of Wales Road	A1
Queen Street	B2
Richmond Road	B1
St. David's Hill	A1
Sidwell Street	B2
South Street	B2
The Quay	C2
Topsham Road	C2
Western Way	B2
Worford Road	B3
York Road	A2

TOURIST INFORMATION ☎ 01392 265700
CIVIC CENTRE, PARIS STREET, EXETER
DEVON, EX1 1RP

HOSPITAL A & E ☎ 01392 411611
ROYAL DEVON & EXETER HOSPITAL (WONFORD),
BARRACK ROAD, EXETER, EX2 5DW

COUNCIL OFFICE ☎ 01392 277888
CIVIC CENTRE, PARIS STREET,
EXETER, EX1 1JN

WEB-SITE www.exeter.gov.uk

LOCAL RADIO BBC RADIO DEVON 95.8 FM
CLASSIC GOLD 666 AM, GEMINI FM 97 FM

Exeter *Devon* Population: 94,717. City, county capital on River Exe, 64m/103km SW of Bristol. Major administrative, business and financial centre on site of Roman town Isca Dumnoniorum. Cathedral is Decorated, with Norman towers and façade with hundreds of stone statues. 15c guildhall. Modern buildings in centre built after extensive damage from World War II. Beneath the city lie remains of medieval water-supply system built in 14c to supply fresh water to city centre. Royal Albert Memorial Museum and Art Gallery. Early 16c mansion of Bowhill (English Heritage), with preserved Great Hall, 2m/3km SW. University 1m/2km N of city centre. Airport 5m,8km E at Clyst Honiton.

STD Code 01303 Kent FOLKESTONE

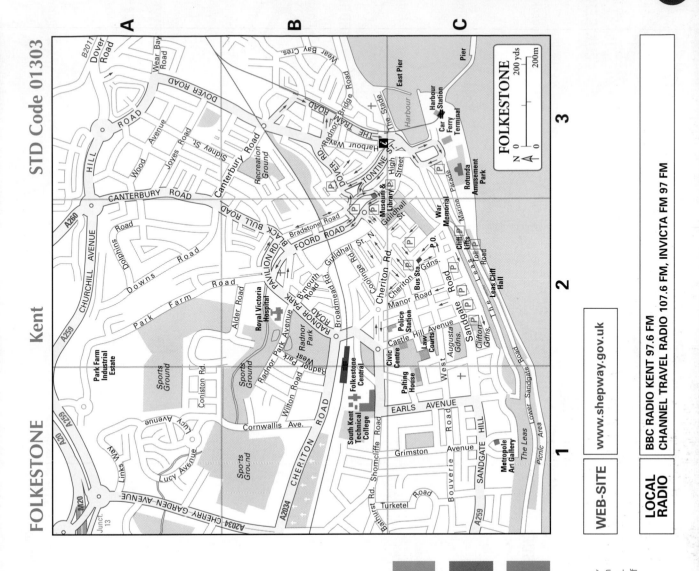

FOLKESTONE

N
200 yds
200m

INDEX TO STREET NAMES

Alder Road	B2
Bathurst Road	B1
Black Bull Road	B2
Bournemouth Road	B2
Bouverie Road West	C1
Bradstone Road	B2
Broadmead Road	B2
Canterbury Road	A3
Castle Hill Avenue	C2
Cheriton Gardens	C2
Cheriton Road	B1
Cherry Garden Avenue	A1
Churchill Avenue	A2
Coniston Road	A1
Coolinge Road	B2
Cornwallis Avenue	B1
Dolphins Road	A2
Dover Road	A3
Downs Road	A2
Earles Avenue	C1
Foord Road	B2
Grimston Avenue	C1
Guildhall Street	B2
Guildhall Street North	B2
Harbour Way	B3
High Street	C3

Hill Road	A3
Joyes Road	A3
Links Way	A1
Lower Sandgate Road	C1
Lucy Avenue	A1
Manor Road	C2
Marine Parade	C2
Park Farm Road	A2
Pavilon Road	B2
Radnor Bridge Road	B3
Radnor Park Avenue	B1
Radnor Park Road	B2
Radnor Park West	B1
Sandgate Hill	C1
Sandgate Road	C2
Shorncliffe Road	B1
Sidney Street	B3
The Leas	C2
The Stade	C3
The Tram Raod	B3
Tontine Street	B3
Turketel Road	C1
Wear Bay Crescent	B2
Wear Bay Road	B3
Wood Avenue	A3
Wilton Road	B1

TOURIST INFORMATION ☎ 01303 258594
HARBOUR STREET, FOLKESTONE,
KENT, CT20 1QN

HOSPITAL A & E ☎ 01233 633331
WILLIAM HARVEY HOSPITAL, KENNINGTON RD,
WILLESBOROUGH, ASHFORD, TN24 0LZ

COUNCIL OFFICE ☎ 01303 850388
CIVIC CENTRE, CASTLE HILL AVENUE,
FOLKESTONE, CT20 2QY

WEB-SITE www.shepway.gov.uk

LOCAL RADIO BBC RADIO KENT 97.6 FM
CHANNEL TRAVEL RADIO 107.6 FM, INVICTA FM 97 FM

Folkestone *Kent* Population: 45,537. *Town*, Channel port and resort, 14m/22km E of Ashford. Russian submarine docked in harbour is open to the public. The Lear marine promenade accessed by Victorian cliff lift. Ornate Victorian hotels. Martello tower on East Cliff. Kent Battle of Britain Museum at Hawkinge airfield 3m/5km N. Channel Tunnel : terminal on N side.

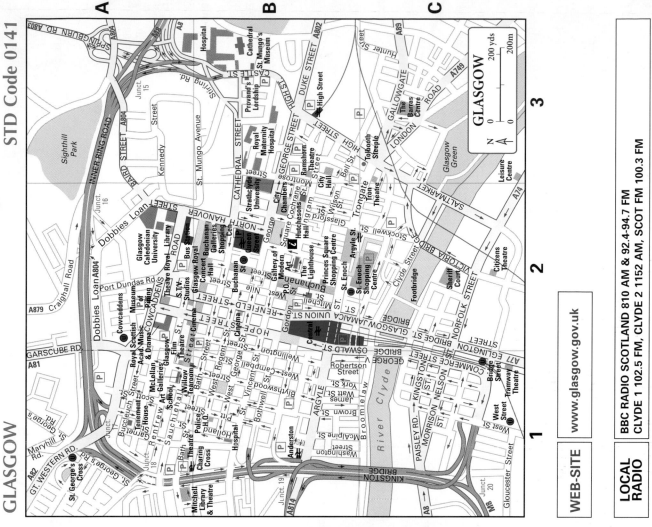

INDEX TO STREET NAMES

Argyle Street	B1
Baird Street	A3
Bath Street	A1/B1
Bell Street	B3
Blythswood Street	B1
Bothwell Street	B1
Bridge Street	C2
Broomielaw	C1
Brown Street	B1
Buccleuch Street	A1
Buchanan Street	B2
Castle Street	B3
Cathedral Street	B2
Clyde Street	C2
Cochrane Street	B2
Commerce Street	C1
Cowcaddens Road	A2
Craighall Road	A2
Dobbie's Loan	A2
Duke Street	B3
Eglington Street	C1
Gallowgate	C3
Garnet Street	A1
Garscube Road	A2
George Square	B2
George Street	B3
George V Bridge	C1
Glasgow Bridge	C2

Glassford Street	B2
Gloucester Street	C1
Gordon Street	B2
Great Western Road	A1
High Street	B3
Holland Street	B1
Hope Street	B2
Hunter Street	B3
Ingram Street	B2
Inner Ring Road	A3
Jamaica Street	C2
James Watt Street	C1
Kennedy Street	A3
Kingston Bridge	C1
Kingston Street	C1
London Road	C3
Maryhill Road	A1
McAlpine Street	A2
Mitchell Street	B2
Montrose Street	B3
Morrison Street	C1
Nelson Street	C1
Norfolk Street	C2
North Hanover Street	B2

Pitt Street	B1
Port Dundas Road	A2
Renfield Street	B2
Renfrew Street	A1
Robertson Street	C1
Saltmarket	C2
Sauchiehall Street	A1
Scott Street	A1
Springburn Road	A3
St. George's Road	A1
St. Mungo Avenue	B3
St. Vincent Street	B1
Stirling Road	B3
Stockwell Street	C2
Trongate	B2
Union Street	B2
Victoria Bridge	C2
Washington Street	C1
Wellington Street	B1
West Campbell Street	B1
West George Street	B1
West Nile Street	B2
West Regent Street	B1
West Street	C1
Wilson Street	B2
York Street	B1

TOURIST INFORMATION ☎ 0141 204 4400
11 GEORGE SQUARE,
GLASGOW, G2 1DY

HOSPITAL A & E ☎ 0141 211 2000
WESTERN INFIRMARY, DUMBARTON ROAD,
GLASGOW, G11 6NT

COUNCIL OFFICE ☎ 0141 287 2000
CITY CHAMBERS, GEORGE SQUARE,
GLASGOW, G2 1DU

Glasgow *Glas.* Population: 662,954. City, largest city in Scotland. Port and commercial, industrial, cultural and entertainment centre on River Clyde, 41m/66km W of Edinburgh and 346m/557km NW of London. Major industrial port and important trading point with America until War of Independence. During industrial revolution, nearby coal seams boosted Glasgow's importance and its population increased ten-fold between 1800 and 1900. By beginning of 20c shipbuilding dominated the city, although industry went into decline in 1930's. Glasgow is now seen to be a city of culture and progress. It has a strong performing arts tradition and many museums and galleries including Burrell Collection (set in Pollok Country Park). Cathedral is rare example of an almost complete 13c church. Early 19c Hutcheson's Hall (National Trust for Scotland) in Ingram Street is one of city's most elegant buildings; Tenement House (National Trust for Scotland) is late Victorian tenement flat retaining many original features. Three universities. Airport 7m/11km W.

WEB-SITE | www.glasgow.gov.uk

LOCAL RADIO | BBC RADIO SCOTLAND 810 AM & 92.4-94.7 FM
CLYDE 1 102.5 FM, CLYDE 2 1152 AM, SCOT FM 100.3 FM

GLOUCESTER   Gloucestershire   STD Code 01452

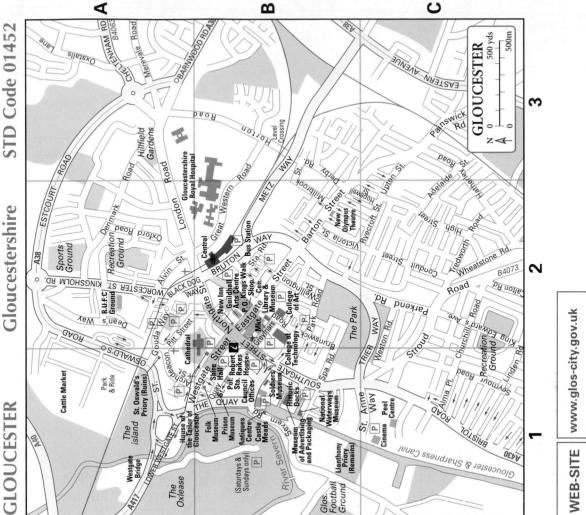

INDEX TO STREET NAMES

Adelaide Street	C2	Great Western	
Alma Place	C1	Road	C2
Alvin Street	A2	Greyfriars	B2
Archdeacon	A1	Hatherley Road	C2
Street		High Street	C2
Barnwood Road	A3	Hopewell Street	C2
Barton Street	B2	Horton Road	B3
Black Dog Way	A2	King Edward's	C2
Bristol Road	C1	Avenue	
Brunswick Road	B2	Kingsholm Road	B2
Bruton Way	B2	Linden Road	B2
Calton Road	C2	London Road	C2
Cheltenham Road	A3	Lower Westgate	A1
Churchill Street	C1	Street	
Conduit Street	C2	Merevale Road	A3
Dean's Way	A2	Metz Way	B2
Denmark Road	A2	Millbrook Street	B2
Derby Road	B2	Northgate Street	B2
Estcourt Road	A2	Oxford Road	A2
Eastern Avenue	C3	Oxstalls Lane	C3
Eastgate Street	B2	Painswick Road	C2
Gouda Way	A1	Park Road	A2

Parkend Road	C2
Pitt Street	A2
Quay Street	B1
Ryecroft Street	C2
St. Ann Way	C1
St. Oswald's Road	A1
Severn Road	B1
Seymour Road	C1
Southgate Street	B1
Spa Road	B2
Station Road	C1
Stroud Road	C1
The Quay	B1
Tredworth Road	C2
Trier Way	C1
Upton Street	C2
Victoria Street	B2
Wellington Street	B2
Westgate Street	A1
Weston Road	C1
Wheatstone Road	C2
Worcester Street	A2

TOURIST INFORMATION ☎ 01452 421188
28 SOUTHGATE STREET, GLOUCESTER,
GLOUCESTERSHIRE, GL1 2DP

HOSPITAL A & E ☎ 01452 528555
GLOUCESTER ROYAL HOSPITAL
GREAT WESTERN RD, GLOUCESTER, GL1 3NN

COUNCIL OFFICE ☎ 01452 522232
COUNCIL OFFICES, NORTH WAREHOUSE,
THE DOCKS, GLOUCESTER, GL1 2EP

Gloucester *Glos.* Population: 114,003. City, industrial city on River Severn, on site of Roman town of Glevum, 32m/52km NE of Bristol. Norman era saw Gloucester grow in political importance, from here William the Conqueror ordered survey of his Kingdom which resulted in Domesday Book of 1086. City became a religious centre during middle ages. Cathedral built in mixture of Norman and Perpendicular styles, has cloisters and England's largest stained glass window, dating from 14c. Remains of 15c-16c Franciscan friary, Greyfriars, (English Heritage). Historic docks, now largely redeveloped, on Gloucester and Sharpness Canal. Three Choirs Festival held every third year.

WEB-SITE www.glos-city.gov.uk

LOCAL RADIO BBC RADIO GLOUCESTERSHIRE 104.7 FM
CLASSIC GOLD 774 AM, SEVERN SOUND FM 102.4 FM

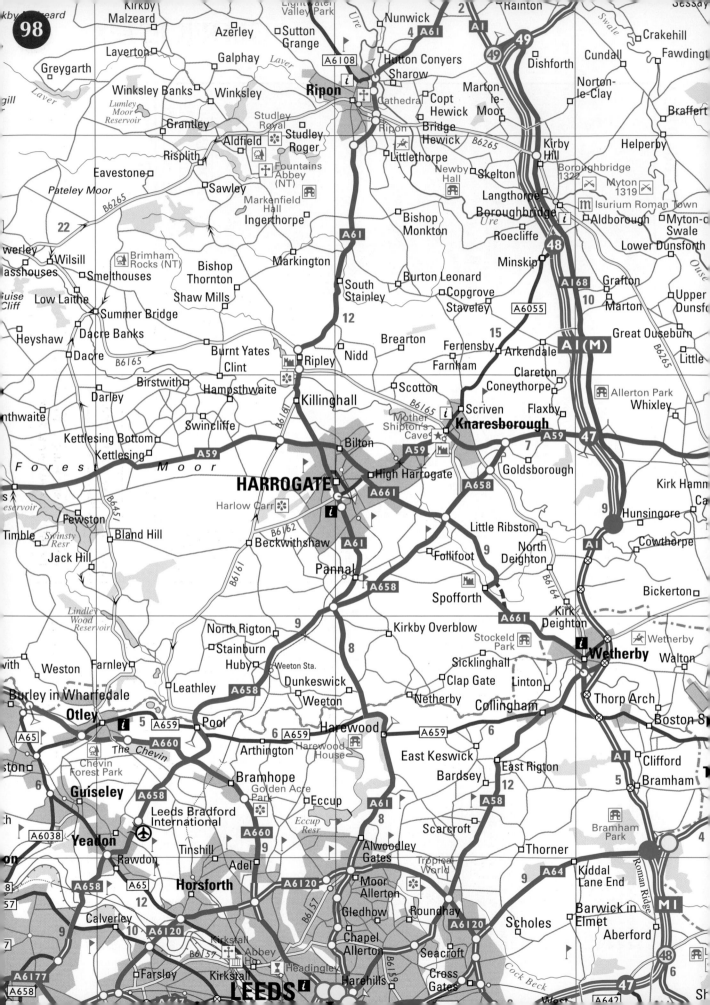

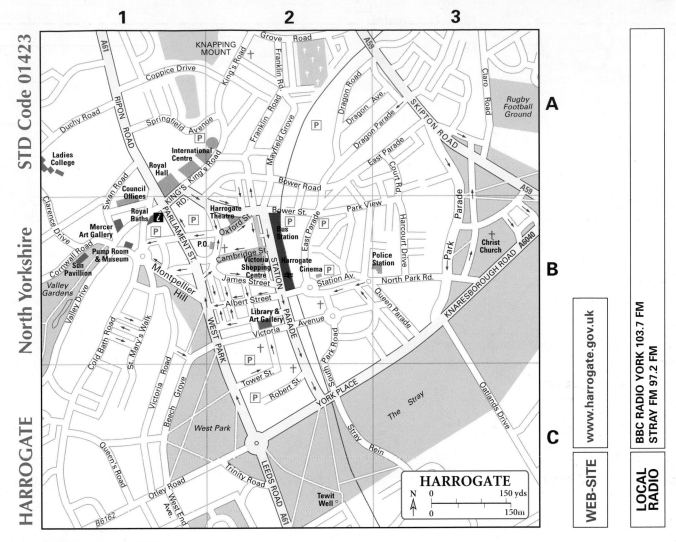

STD Code 01423

North Yorkshire

HARROGATE

WEB-SITE www.harrogate.gov.uk

LOCAL RADIO BBC RADIO YORK 103.7 FM STRAY FM 97.2 FM

HARROGATE
N 0 — 150 yds
0 — 150m

INDEX TO STREET NAMES

Street	Grid	Street	Grid	Street	Grid	Street	Grid
Albert Street	B2	Dragon Road	A2	Oatlands Drive	C3	Springfield Avenue	A1
Beech Grove	C1	Duchy Road	A1	Otley Road	C1	Station Avenue	B2
Bower Road	A2	East Parade	B2	Oxford Street	B2	Station Parade	B2
Bower Street	B2	Franklin Road	A2	Park Parade	B3	Stray Rein	C2
Cambridge Street	B2	Grove Road	A2	Park View	B2	Swan Road	B1
Clarence Drive	B1	Harcourt Drive	B3	Parliament Street	B1	Tower Street	C2
Claro Road	A3	James Street	B2	Queen Parade	B3	Trinity Road	C2
Cold Bath Road	C1	King's Road	B1	Queen's Road	C1	Valley Drive	B1
Coppice Drive	A1	Knaresborough Road	B3	Ripon Road	A1	Victoria Avenue	B2
Cornwall Road	B1	Leeds Road	C2	Robert Street	C2	Victoria Road	C1
Court Road	A3	Mayfield Grove	A2	St. Mary's Walk	C1	West End Avenue	C1
Dragon Avenue	A2	Montpellier Hill	B1	Skipton Road	A3	West Park	B2
Dragon Parade	A2	North Park Road	B3	South Park Road	C2	York Place	C2

TOURIST INFORMATION ☎ 01423 537300
ROYAL BATHS ASSEMBLY ROOMS, CRES. ROAD,
HARROGATE, NORTH YORKSHIRE, HG1 2RR

HOSPITAL A & E ☎ 01423 885959
HARROGATE DISTRICT HOSPITAL,
LANCASTER PARK ROAD, HARROGATE, HG2 7SX

COUNCIL OFFICE ☎ 01423 568954
COUNCIL OFFICES, CRESCENT GARDENS
HARROGATE, HG1 2SG

Harrogate *N. Yorks.* Population: 66,178. Town, spa town and conference centre, 12m/21km N of Leeds. Fashionable spa town of 19c with many distinguished Victorian buildings, extensive gardens and pleasant tree-lined streets. Royal Baths Assembly Rooms (1897) open for Turkish baths. Royal Pump Room (1842) now a museum. The Stray park and gardens are S of town centre. The Valley Gardens to the SW are the venue for band concerts and flower shows. Harlow Carr Botanical Gardens and Museum of Gardening 2m/3km SW. Mother Shipton's cave, reputed home to the 16c prophetess, near Knaresborough, 4m/6km NW.

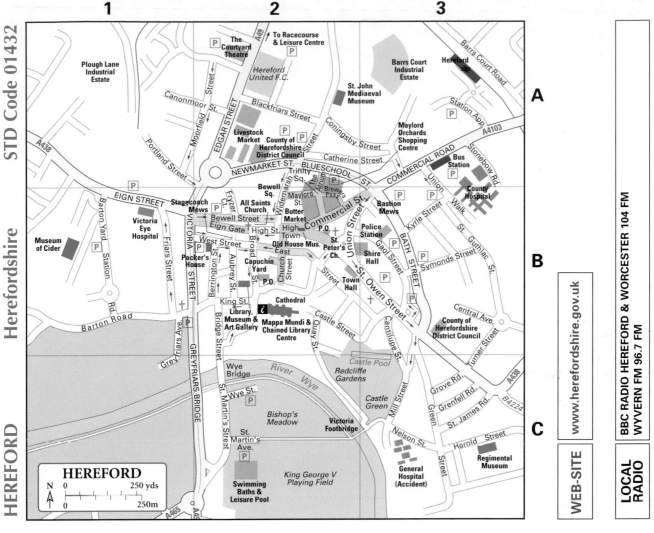

STD Code 01432

Herefordshire

HEREFORD

WEB-SITE www.herefordshire.gov.uk

LOCAL RADIO — BBC RADIO HEREFORD & WORCESTER 104 FM WYVERN FM 96.7 FM

INDEX TO STREET NAMES

Aubrey Street	B2	Cantilupe Street	B3	Fryzer Court	B2	Mill Street	C3	Stonebow Road	A3
Barrs Court Road	A3	Castle Street	B2	Gaol Street	B3	Moorfield Street	A1	Symonds Street	B3
Barton Road	B1	Catherine Street	A2	Green Street	C3	Nelson Street	C3	The Atrium	A2
Barton Yard	B1	Central Avenue	B3	Grenfell Road	C3	Newmarket Street	A2	Turner Street	C3
Bath Street	B3	Church Street	B2	Greyfriars Avenue	C1	Portland Street	A1	Union Street	B2
Berrington Street	B2	Commercial Road	A3	Greyfriars Bridge	B2	Quay Street	B2	Union Walk	A3
Bewell Street	B2	Commercial Street	B2	Grove Road	C3	St. Guthiac Street	B3	Victoria Street	B1
Blackfriars Street	A2	Coningsby Street	A2	Harold Street	C3	St. James Road	C3	West Street	B2
Blueschool Street	A2	East Street	B2	High Street	B2	St. Martin's Avenue	C2	Widemarsh Street	B2
Brewers Passage	B2	Edgar Street	A2	High Town	B2	St. Martin's Street	C2	Wye Street	C2
Bridge Street	B2	Eign Gate	B2	King Street	B2	St. Owen Street	B3		
Broad Street	B2	Eign Street	B1	Kyrle Street	B3	Station Approach	A3		
Canonmoor Street	A1	Friars Street	B1	Maylord Street	B2	Station Road	B1		

TOURIST INFORMATION ☎ 01432 268430
1 KING STREET,
HEREFORD, HR4 9BW

HOSPITAL A & E ☎ 01432 355444
HEREFORD GENERAL HOSPITAL,
NELSON STREET, HEREFORD, HR1 2PA

COUNCIL OFFICE ☎ 01432 260000
COUNCIL OFFICES, ST. OWEN STREET,
HEREFORD, HR1 2PJ

Hereford *Here.* Population: 54,326. City, county town and cathedral city on River Wye, 45m/72km SW of Birmingham. Many old buildings and museums, including Waterworks museum and City Museum and Art Gallery. 1621 Old House is a museum of local history. Medieval Wye Bridge. Cathedral includes richly ornamented Early English style Lady chapel. New building houses Chained Library of 1500 volumes and 1289 Mappa Mundi Map of the world. Three Choirs Festival every third year. Cider Museum and King Offa Distillery W of city centre depicts history of cider making.

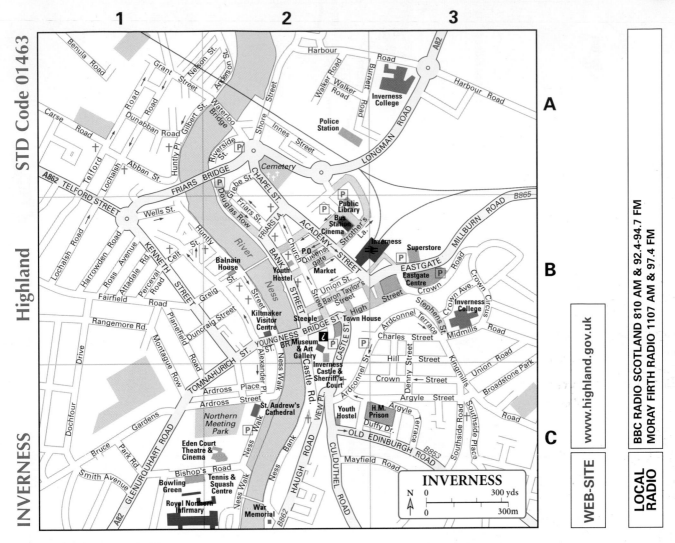

STD Code 01463

Highland

INVERNESS

INDEX TO STREET NAMES

Street	Ref	Street	Ref	Street	Ref	Street	Ref	Street	Ref
Abban Street	A1	Burnett Road	A3	Eastgate	B3	Kenneth Street	B1	Riverside Street	A2
Academy Street	B2	Carse Road	A1	Fairfield Road	B1	Kingsmills Road	B3	Ross Avenue	B1
Alexander Place	B2	Castle Road	B2	Friars Bridge	A1	Lochalsh Road	A1	Shore Street	A2
Anderson Street	A2	Castle Street	B2	Friars Lane	B2	Longman Road	A2	Smith Avenue	C1
Ardconnel Street	C2	Celt Street	B1	Friars Street	B2	Mayfield Road	C2	Southside Place	C3
Ardconnel Terrace	B3	Chapel Street	A2	Gilbert Street	A1	Midmills Road	B3	Southside Road	C3
Ardross Place	D2	Charles Street	B3	Glebe Street	A2	Millburn Road	B3	Stephens Street	B3
Ardross Street	C1	Church Street	B2	Glen Urquhart Road	C1	Montague Row	B1	Strother's Lane	B2
Argyle Street	C3	Crown Avenue	B3	Grant Street	A1	Nelson Street	A1	Telford Road	A1
Argyle Terrace	C3	Crown Circus	B3	Greig Street	B1	Ness Bank	C2	Telford Street	A1
Attadale Road	B1	Crown Road	B3	Harbour Road	A2	Ness Bridge	B2	Tomnahurich Street	C1
Bank Street	B2	Crown Street	C3	Harrowden Road	A1	Ness Walk	C2	Union Road	C3
Baron Taylor's Street	B2	Culduthel Road	C2	Haugh Road	C2	Old Edinburgh Road	C2	Union Street	B2
Benula Road	A1	Denny Street	C3	High Street	B2	Park Road	C1	View Place	C2
Bishop's Road	C1	Dochfour Drive	C1	Hill Street	B3	Perceval Road	B1	Walker Road	A2
Bridge Street	B2	Douglas Row	A2	Hontly Place	A1	Planefield Road	B1	Waterloo Bridge	A2
Broadstone Park	C3	Duffy Drive	C2	Huntly Street	B1	Queensgate	B2	Wells Street	B1
Bruce Gardens	C1	Duncraig Street	B1	Innes Street	A2	Rancemore Road	B1	Young Street	B2

TOURIST INFORMATION ☎ 01463 234353
CASTLE WYND,
INVERNESS, HIGHLAND, IV2 3BJ

HOSPITAL A & E ☎ 01463 704000
RAIGMORE HOSPITAL, OLD PERTH ROAD,
INVERNESS, IV2 3UJ

COUNCIL OFFICE ☎ 01463 702000
COUNCIL OFFICES, GLENURQUHART ROAD,
INVERNESS, IV3 5NX

Inverness *High.* Population: 41,234. Town, at mouth of River Ness at entrance to Beauly Firth, 105m/169km NW of Aberdeen and 113m/181km NW of Edinburgh. Administrative, commercial and tourist centre. Caledonian Canal passes to W of town. Victorian castle in town centre used as law courts. Inverness Museum and Art Gallery depicts history of Highlands. Balnain House is a museum of Highland music and musical instruments. University of the Highlands and Islands. 1746 Culloden battle site 5m/8km E. Airport at locality of Dalcross, 7m/11km NE of town.

WEB-SITE www.highland.gov.uk

LOCAL RADIO BBC RADIO SCOTLAND 810 AM & 92.4-94.7 FM · MORAY FIRTH RADIO 1107 AM & 97.4 FM

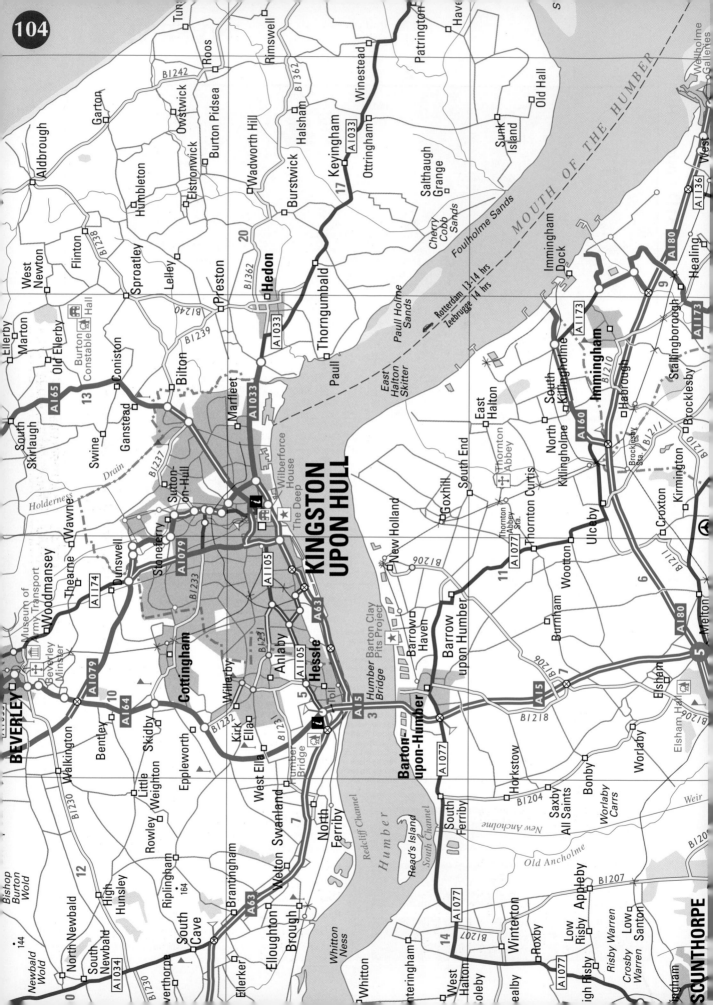

KINGSTON UPON HULL   Hull   STD Code 01482

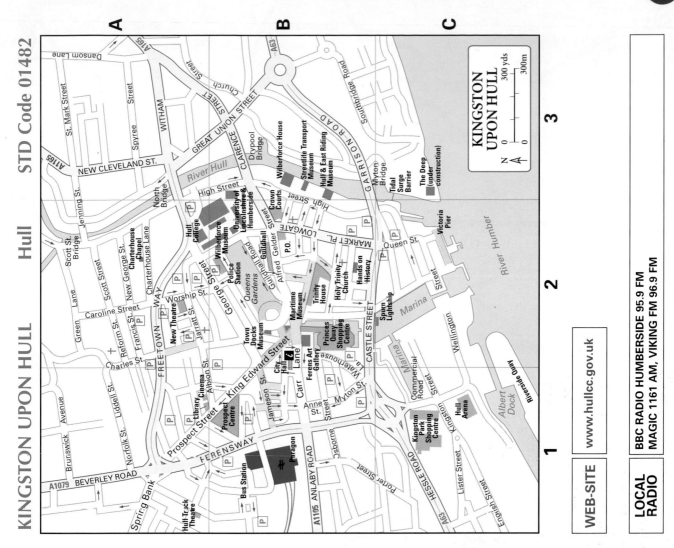

KINGSTON UPON HULL

N
0   300 yds
0   300m

INDEX TO STREET NAMES

Street	Grid
Albion Street	B1
Alfred Gelder Street	B2
Anlaby Road	B1
Anne Street	B1
Beverley Road	A1
Brunswick Avenue	A1
Caroline Street	A2
Carr Lane	B1
Castle Street	B2
Charles Street	A2
Charterhouse Lane	A2
Church Street	C1
Clarence Street	B3
Cleveland Street	A3
Dansom Lane	A3
English Street	C1
Ferensway	A1
Francis Street	A2
Freetown Way	A1
Garrison Road	B1
George Street	B2
Great Union Street	A3
Green Lane	A2
Guildhall Road	B2
Hessle Road	C1
High Street	A1
Jameson Street	B1
Jarratt Street	A2
Jenning Street	A2
King Edward Street	B1
Kingston Street	C1
Liddell Street	A1
Lister Street	C1
Lowgate	B2
Market Place	C1
Myton Street	B2
New Cleveland Street	A1
New George Street	A2
Norfolk Street	A1
North Bridge	A2
Osborne Street	B1
Porter Street	C1
Prospect Street	A1
Queen Street	C2
Reform Street	B1
St. Mark Street	A3
Scott Street	A2
Scott Street Bridge	A2
Southbridge Road	B3
Spring Bank	A1
Spyree Street	A3
Waterhouse Lane	B1
Wellington Street	C2
Witham	A3
Worship Street	A2

TOURIST INFORMATION ☎ 01482 223559
1 PARAGON STREET,
KINGSTON UPON HULL, HU1 3NA

HOSPITAL A & E ☎ 01482 328541
HULL ROYAL INFIRMARY, ANLABY ROAD,
KINGSTON UPON HULL, HU3 2JZ

COUNCIL OFFICE ☎ 01482 610610
GUILDHALL, ALFRED GELDER STREET,
KINGSTON UPON HULL, HU1 2AA

Kingston upon Hull (Commonly known as Hull.) *Hull* Population: 310,636. City, port at confluence of Rivers Humber and Hull, 50m/80km E of Leeds. Much of town destroyed during bombing of World War II; town centre has been rebuilt. Formerly had a thriving fishing industry. Major industry nowadays is frozen food processing. Restored docks, cobble streeted Old Town and modern marina. Universities. Birthplace of William Wilberforce, slavery abolitionist, 1759. Wilberforce Museum covers history of slavery. Streetlife Transport Museum. Town Docks Museum explores city's maritime history. Famous for associations with poets Andrew Marvell, Stevie Smith and Philip Larkin.

WEB-SITE
www.hullcc.gov.uk

LOCAL RADIO
BBC RADIO HUMBERSIDE 95.9 FM
MAGIC 1161 AM, VIKING FM 96.9 FM

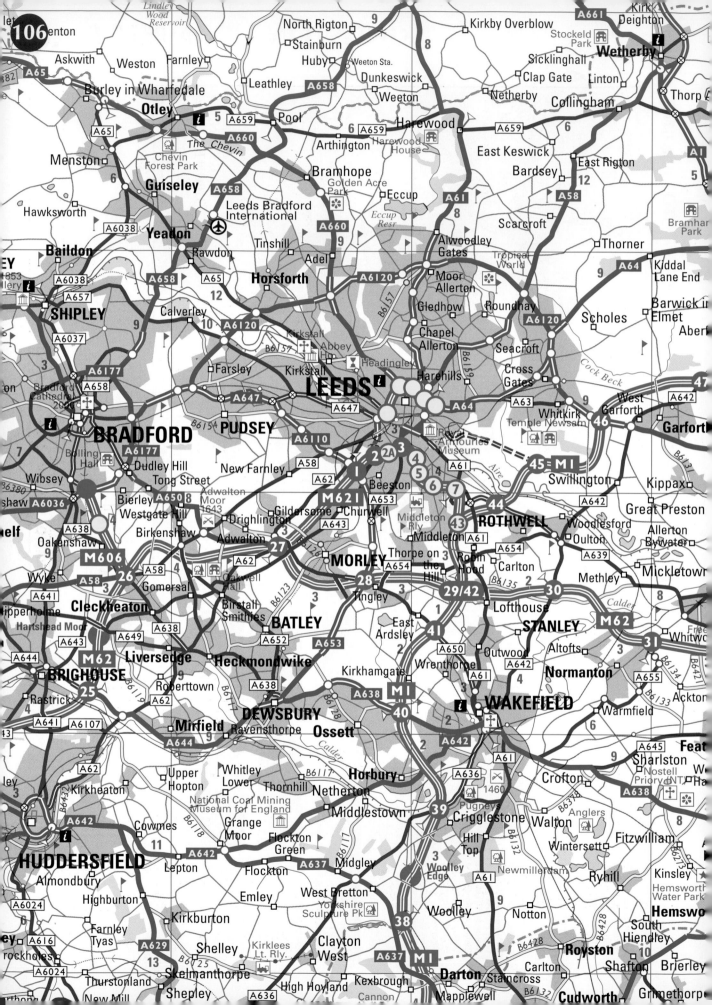

STD Code 0113

West Yorkshire

LEEDS

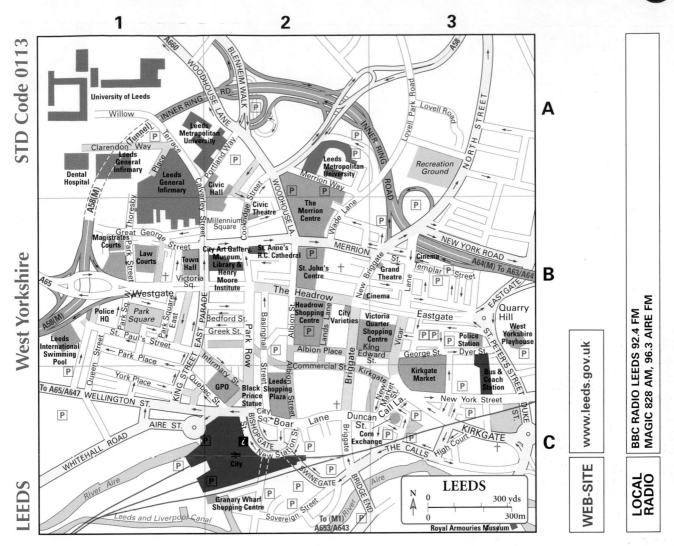

WEB-SITE www.leeds.gov.uk

LOCAL RADIO BBC RADIO LEEDS 92.4 FM · MAGIC 828 AM, 96.3 AIRE FM

INDEX TO STREET NAMES

Aire Street	C1	Cookridge Street	B2	King Street	C1	Park Place	B1	Thoresby Place	B1
Albion Place	B2	Duke Street	C3	Kirkgate	C2/C3	Park Row	B2	Vicar Lane	B3
Albion Street	B2	Duncan Street	C2	Lands Lane	B2	Park Square East	B1	Victoria Square	B1
Basinghall Street	B2	Dyer Street	B3	Lovell Park Road	A3	Park Square West	B1	Wade Lane	B2
Bedford Street	B2	East Parade	B1	Lovell Road	A3	Park Street	B1	Wellington Street	C1
Bishopgate Street	C2	Eastgate	B3	Morrion Street	B2	Portland Way	A2	Westgate	B1
Blenheim Walk	A2	George Street	B3	Merrion Way	A2	Quebec Street	C1	Whitehall Road	C1
Boar Lane	C2	Great George		Merrion Street	B2	Queen Street	C1	Willow Terrace	A1
Bridge End	C2	Street	B1	New Briggate	B2	Sovereign Street	C2	Woodhouse	A1/A2
Briggate	C2	Greek Street	B2	New Market	C3	St. Paul's Street	B1	Lane	
Call Lane	C3	High Court	C3	Street		St. Peter's Street	B3	York Place	C1
Calverley Street	A1	Infirmary Street	B1	New Station	C2	Swinegate	C2		
City Square	C2	Inner Ring Road	A1/A2	Street		Templar Street	B3		
Clarendon Way	A1	King Edward		New York Road	B3	The Calls	C3		
Commercial Street	B2	Street		New York Street	C3	The Headrow	B2		
				North Street	A3				

TOURIST INFORMATION ☎ 0113 242 5242 GATEWAY YORKSHIRE, THE ARCADE, CITY STATION, LEEDS, W. YORKSHIRE, LS1 1PL

HOSPITAL A & E ☎ 0113 243 2799 LEEDS GENERAL INFIRMARY, GREAT GEORGE STREET, LEEDS, LS1 3EX

COUNCIL OFFICE ☎ 0113 247 4023 CIVIC HALL, CALVERLEY STREET, LEEDS, LS1 1UR

Leeds *W. Yorks.* Population: 424,194. City, commercial and industrial city on River Aire and on Leeds and Liverpool Canal, 36m/58km NE of Manchester and 170m/274km NW of London. Previously important for textile industry. Prospered during Victorian period, the architecture of a series of ornate arcades containing some magnificent clocks reflecting the affluence of this time. City Art Gallery has a fine collection of 20c British Art. Edwardian Kirkgate Market is the largest in north of England. Royal Armouries Museum houses arms and armour collection from the Tower of London. Universities. Leeds Bradford International Airport at Yeadon, 7m/11km NW.

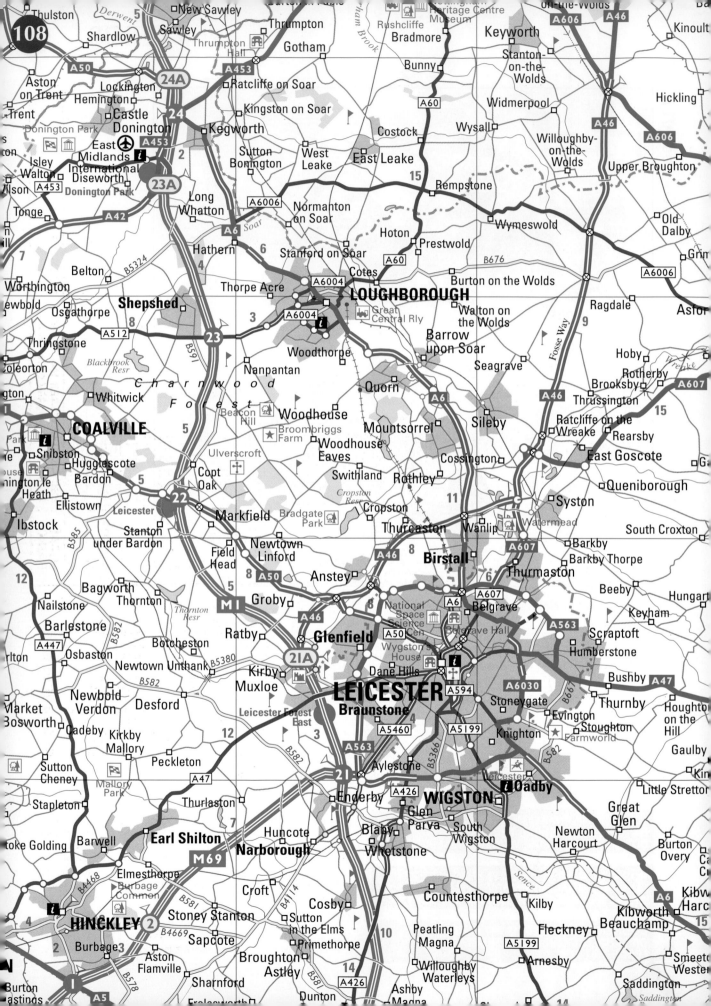

STD Code 0116

LEICESTER

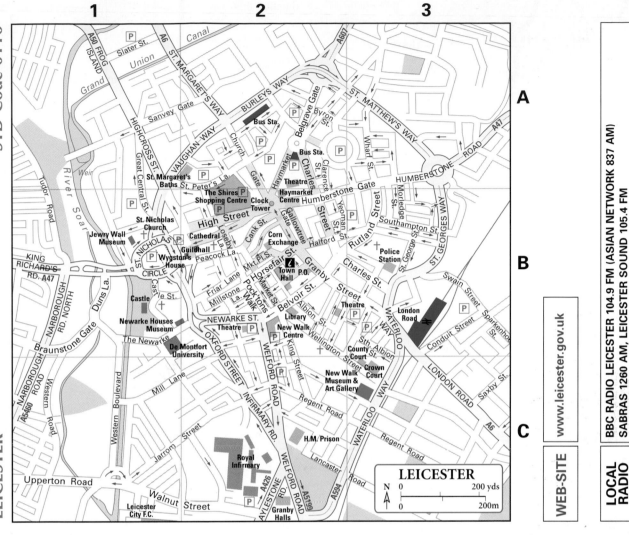

LEICESTER

N 0 .... 200 yds
0 .... 200m

WEB-SITE — www.leicester.gov.uk

LOCAL RADIO — BBC RADIO LEICESTER 104.9 FM (ASIAN NETWORK 837 AM) SABRAS 1260 AM, LEICESTER SOUND 105.4 FM

INDEX TO STREET NAMES

Albion Street	B2	Frog Island	A1	Lancaster Road	C2
Aylestone Road	C2	Gallowtree Gate	B2	London Road	C3
Belgrave Gate	A2	Granby Street	B2	Loseby Lane	B2
Belvoir Street	B2	Great Central Street	A1	Market Place South	B2
Braunstone Gate	B1	Halford Street	B2	Market Street	B2
Burleys Way	A2	Haymarket	A2	Mill Lane	C1
Byron Street	A2	High Street	B2	Millstone Lane	B2
Cank Street	B2	Highcross Street	A1	Morledge Street	B3
Castle Street	B1	Horsfair Street	B2	Narborough Road	C1
Charles Street	B3	Humberstone Gate	B2	Narborough Road North	B1
Church Gate	A2	Humberstone Road	A3	Newarke Street	B2
Clarence Street	A2	Infirmary Road	C2	Oxford Street	B2
Conduit Street	B3	Jarrom Street	C1	Peacock Lane	B2
Duns Lane	B1	King Richard's Road	B1	Pocklingtons Walk	B2
Friar Lane	B2	King Street	B2		

Regent Road	C2	Swain Street	B3
Rutland Street	B3	The Newarke	B1
St. George Street	B3	Tudor Road	A1
St. George's Way	B3	Upperton Road	C1
St. Margaret's Way	A1	Vaughan Way	A1
St. Matthew's Way	A3	Walnut Street	C1
St. Nicholas Circle	B1	Waterloo Way	C3
St. Peter's Lane	A2	Welford Road	B2
Sanvey Gare	A1	Wellington Street	B2
Saxby Street	C3	Western Boulevard	C1
Slater Street	A1	Western Road	C1
South Albion Street	B3	Wharf Street	A3
Southampton Street	B3	Yeoman Street	B2
Sparkenhoe Street	B3		

TOURIST INFORMATION ☎ 0116 299 8888
7 - 9 EVERY STREET, TOWN HALL SQUARE,
LEICESTER, LE1 6AG

HOSPITAL A & E ☎ 0116 254 1414
LEICESTER ROYAL INFIRMARY,
INFIRMARY SQUARE, LEICESTER, LE1 5WW

COUNCIL OFFICE ☎ 0116 252 6480
COUNCIL OFFICES, NEW WALK CENTRE,
WELFORD PLACE, LEICESTER, LE1 6ZG

Leicester *Leic.* Population: 318,518. City, county town and commercial and industrial centre on River Soar, on site of Roman town of Ratae Coritanorum, 89m/143km NW of London. Industries include hosiery and footwear, alongside more modern industries. Universities. Many historic remains including Jewry Wall (English Heritage), one of largest surviving sections of Roman wall in the country, Roman baths and a medieval guildhall. Saxon Church of St. Nicholas. 11c St. Martin's Cathedral. Victorian clock tower. Newarke Houses Museum explores the city's social history. Home to England's second biggest street festival after Notting Hill Carnival. Joseph Merrick, the 'Elephant Man' born and lived here.

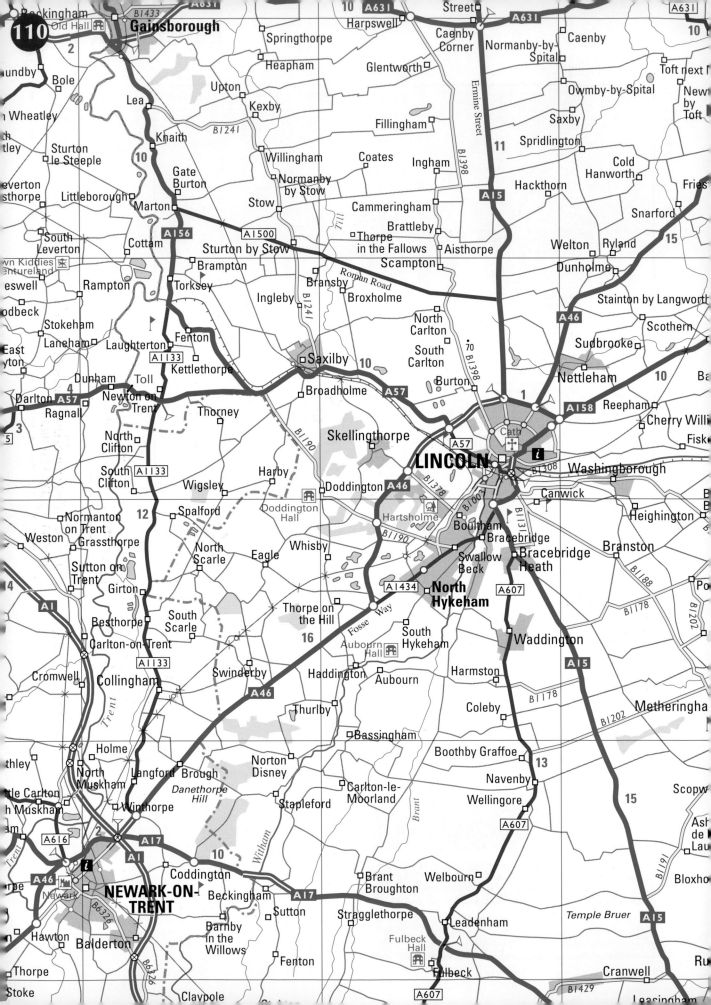

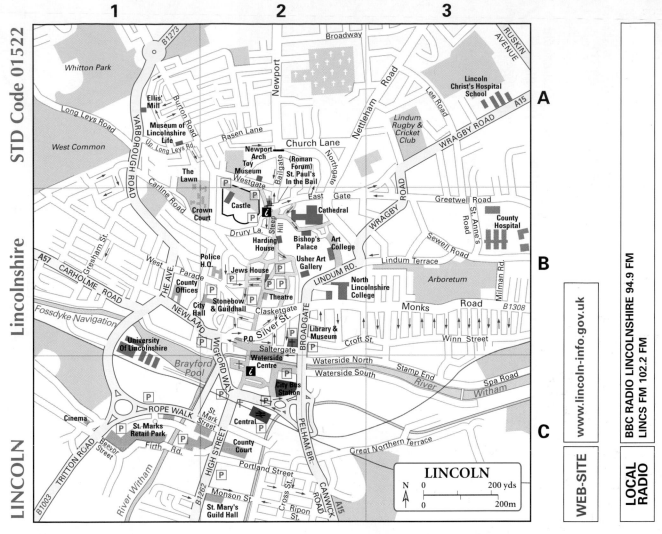

STD Code 01522

Lincolnshire

LINCOLN

WEB-SITE www.lincoln-info.gov.uk

LOCAL RADIO — BBC RADIO LINCOLNSHIRE 94.9 FM LINCS FM 102.2 FM

LINCOLN

N

0		200 yds
0		200m

INDEX TO STREET NAMES

Bailgate	A2	Firth Road	C1	Newport	A2	Stamp End	C3
Beevor Street	C1	Great Northern Terrace	C2	Northgate	A2	Steep Hill	B2
Broadgate	B2	Greetwell Road	B3	Pelham Bridge	C2	The Avenue	B1
Broadway	A2	Gresham Street	B1	Portland Street	C2	Tritton Road	C1
Burton Road	A1	High Street	C2	Rasen Lane	A2	Upper Long Leys Road	A1
Canwick Road	C2	Lee Road	A3	Ripon Street	C2	Waterside North	C2
Carholme Road	B1	Lindum Road	B2	Rope Walk	C1	Waterside South	C2
Carline Road	A1	Lindum Terrace	B3	Ruskin Avenue	A3	West Parade	B1
Church Lane	A2	Long Leys Road	A1	St. Anne's Road	B3	Westgate	A2
Clasketgate	B2	Milman Road	B3	St. Mark Street	C2	Wigford Way	B2
Croft Street	B2	Monks Road	B3	Saltergate	B2	Winn Street	B3
Cross Street	C2	Monson Street	C2	Sewell Road	B3	Wragby Road	B3
Drury Lane	B2	Nettleham Road	A2	Silver Street	B2	Yarborough Road	A1
East Gate	B2	Newland	B1	Spa Road	C3		

TOURIST INFORMATION ☎ 01522 873700
9 CASTLE HILL, LINCOLN,
LINCOLNSHIRE, LN1 3AA

HOSPITAL A & E ☎ 01522 512512
LINCOLN COUNTY HOSPITAL,
GREETWELL ROAD, LINCOLN, LN2 5QY

COUNCIL OFFICE ☎ 01522 552222
CITY HALL, BEAUMONT FEE,
LINCOLN, LN1 1DD

Lincoln *Lincs.* Population: 80,281. City, county town and cathedral city on River Witham, on site of Roman town of Lindum, 120m/193km N of London. City grew as a result of strategic importance in the wool trade. Many ancient monuments and archaeological features. Castle built by William I. 13c cathedral, is the third largest in Britain with its three towers on hilltop dominating the skyline. Carvings in the Angel Choir include the stone figure of the Lincoln Imp which is the city's emblem. Lincoln Bishop's Old Palace (English Heritage) is medieval building on S side of cathedral. 12c Jew's House. Museum of Lincolnshire Life. Universities.

LIVERPOOL

Merseyside   STD Code 0151

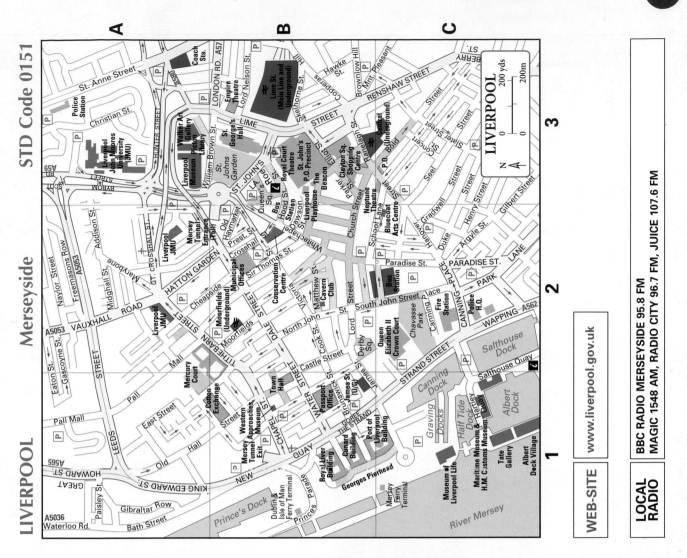

INDEX TO STREET NAMES

Addison Street	A2	Goree	B1	Pall Mall	A2
Argyle Street	C2	Gradwell Street	C2	Paradise Street	C2
Bath Street	A1	Great Crosshall Street	A2	Park Lane	B3
Berry Street	C3	Great Howard Street	A1	Parker Street	C2
Bold Street	C3	Hanover Street	C2	Preston Street	B2
Brownlow Hill	B3	Hartley Quay	B3	Princes Parade	A1
Brunswick Street	B1	Hatton Garden	B2	Queens Square	B2
Byrom Street	A3	Hawke Street	C2	Ranelagh Street	B3
Canning Place	C2	Henry Street	C3	Renshaw Street	B3
Castle Street	B2	Hood Street	B2	Roe Street	B2
Chapel Street	B1	Hunter Street	A3	Salthouse Quay	C1
Cheapside	A2	James Street	B1	School Lane	B2
Christian Street	A3	King Edward Street	A1	Scotland Road	A3
Church Street	C2	Leeds Street	A1	Seel Street	C3
Concert Street	C3	Lime Street	B3	Sir Thomas Street	B2
Cook Street	B2	London Road	B3	Skelhorne Street	B3
Copperas Hill	B3	Lord Nelson Street	B3	Slater Street	C3
Crosshall Street	B2	Lord Street	B2	South John Street	B2
Dale Street	B2	Marybone	A2	St. Anne Street	A3
Dawson Street	B2	Matthews Street	B2	St. John's Lane	B3
Derby Square	B2	Midghall Street	A2	The Strand	B1
Duke Street	C3	Moorfields	B2	Tithebarn Street	B2
East Street	A1	Mount Pleasant	B3	Vauxhall Road	A2
Eaton Street	A1	Naylor Street	A2	Victoria Street	B2
Elliot Street	B3	New Quay	B1	Wapping	C2
Freemasons Row	A2	North John Street	B2	Water Street	B1
Gascoyne Street	A1	Old Hall Street	A1	Waterloo Road	A1
Gibraltar Row	A1	Old Haymarket	B2	Whitechapel	B2
Gilbert Street	C2	Paisley Street	A1	William Brown Street	A3

TOURIST INFORMATION ☎ 09066 806886
MERSEYSIDE WELCOME CENTRE, CLAYTON SQ.
SHOPPING CEN, LIVERPOOL, MERSEYSIDE, L1 1QR

HOSPITAL A & E ☎ 0151 525 5980
UNIVERSITY HOSPITAL OF AINTREE, LOWER LANE,
FAZAKERLEY, LIVERPOOL, L9 7AL

COUNCIL OFFICE ☎ 0151 227 3911
MUNICIPAL BUILDINGS, DALE STREET,
LIVERPOOL, L69 2DH

Liverpool *Mersey.* Population: 481,786. City, major port and industrial city on River Mersey estuary, 178m/286km NW of London. Originally a fishing village it experienced rapid expansion during early 18c due to transatlantic trade in sugar, spice and tobacco and was involved in slave trade. Docks declined during 20c, now Albert Dock is home to shops, museums and Tate Liverpool. In 19c a multicultural city developed as Liverpool docks were point of departure for Europeans emigrating to America and Australia. Also became home to refugees from Irish potato famine of 1845. Present day Liverpool is home to variety of industries and many museums and art galleries. Also home of the Beatles, who performed at Liverpool's Cavern Club. Universities. Modern Anglican and Roman Catholic cathedrals. On Pier Head the famous Royal Liver Building is situated, topped by Liver Birds. Railway tunnel and two road tunnels under River Mersey to Wirral peninsula. Airport at Speke, 6m/10km.

WEB-SITE www.liverpool.gov.uk

LOCAL RADIO BBC RADIO MERSEYSIDE 95.8 FM, MAGIC 1548 AM, RADIO CITY 96.7 FM, JUICE 107.6 FM

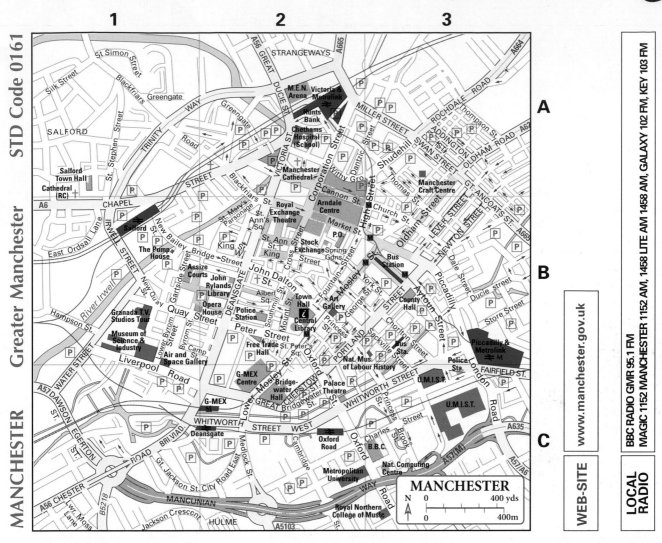

STD Code 0161

Greater Manchester

MANCHESTER

MANCHESTER

N 0 ——— 400 yds
   0 ——— 400m

WEB-SITE
www.manchester.gov.uk

LOCAL RADIO
BBC RADIO GMR 95.1 FM
MAGIC 1152 MANCHESTER 1152 AM, 1458 LITE AM 1458 AM, GALAXY 102 FM, KEY 103 FM

INDEX TO STREET NAMES

Addington Street	A3	Corporation Street	A2	High Street	B2	New Quay Street	B1	Shudehill	A3
Albert Square	B2	Cross Street	B2	Irwell Street	B1	Newton Street	B3	Silk Street	A1
Aytoun Street	B3	Dale Street	B3	Jackson Crescent	C1	Oldham Road	A3	Southmill Street	B2
Blackfriars Road	A1	Dantzic Street	A2	John Dalton Street	B2	Oldham Street	B3	Spring Gardens	B2
Blackfriars Street	A2	Dawson Street	C1	King Street	B2	Oxford Road	C2	Store Street	B3
Bridge Street	B1	Deansgate	B2	King Street West	B2	Oxford Street	B2	Swan Street	A3
Bridge Viaduct	C1	Ducie Street	B3	Lever Street	B3	Peter Street	B2	Thomas Street	A3
Brook Street	C3	East Ordsall Lane	B1	Liverpool Road	B1	Piccadilly	B3	Thompson Street	A3
Byrom Street	B1	Egerton Street	C1	London Road	B3	Portland Street	B2	Trinity Way	A1
Cambridge Street	C2	Fairfield Street	C3	Lower Byrom Street	B1	Princess Street	B2/C3	Victoria Street	A2
Camp Street	B1	Fountain Street	B2	Lower Mosley Street	C2	Quay Street	B1	Water Street	C1
Cannon Street	A2	Gartside Street	B1	Lower Moss Lane	C1	Rochdale Road	A3	Whitworth Street	C2
Chapel Street	B1	George Street	B2	Mancunian Way	C1	Sackville Street	B3	Whitworth Street West	C1
Charles Street	C3	Great Jackson Street	C1	Market Street	B2	St. Ann's Square	B2	Withy Grove	A2
Chepstow Street	C2	Greengate	A1/A2	Medlock Street	C2	St. Ann Street	B2	York Street	B3
Chester Road	C1	Gt. Ancoats Street	A3	Miller Street	A2	St. Mary's Parsonage	B2		
Chorlton Street	B3	Gt. Bridgewater Street	C2	Mosley Street	B2	St. Peter's Square	B2		
Church Street	B3	Gt. Ducie Street	A2	Mount Street	B2	St. Simon Street	A1		
City Road East	C2	Hampson Street	B1	New Bailey Street	B1	St. Stephen Street	A1		

TOURIST INFORMATION ☎ 0161 234 3157/8
MANCHESTER VISITOR CENTRE, TOWN HALL
EXTENSION, LLOYD ST, MANCHESTER, M60 2LA

HOSPITAL A & E ☎ 0161 276 1234
MANCHESTER ROYAL INFIRMARY,
OXFORD ROAD, MANCHESTER, M13 9WL

COUNCIL OFFICE ☎ 0161 234 5000
TOWN HALL, ALBERT SQUARE,
MANCHESTER, M60 2LA

Manchester *Gt.Man.* Population: 402,889. City, important industrial, business, cultural and commercial centre and port, 164m/264km NW of London. Access for ships by River Mersey and Manchester Ship Canal, opened in 1894. 15c cathedral, formerly parish church, has widest nave in England. Experienced rapid growth during industrial revolution. In 1750, Manchester was essentially still a village. During Victorian era, city was global cotton milling capital. Present day city is home to wide range of industries and is unofficial capital of nation's 'youth culture'. Major shopping centres include Arndale and Trafford Centres. Universities. International airport 9m/14km S of city centre.

MIDDLESBROUGH

STD Code 01642

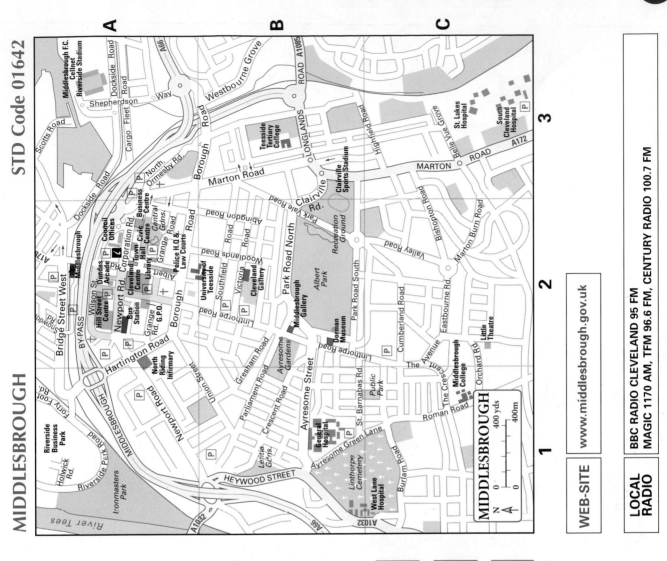

INDEX TO STREET NAMES

Abingdon Road	B2
Albert Road	A2
Ayresome Green Lane	B1
Ayresome Street	B1
Belle Vue Grove	C3
Bishopton Road	C2
Borough Road	A2/C3
Bridge Street West	A2
Burlam Road	C1
Cargo Fleet Road	A3
Clairville Road	B2
Corporation Road	A2
Crescent Road	B1
Cumberland Road	C2
Dockside Road	A2/A3
Eastbourne Road	C2
Forty Foot Road	A1
Grange Road	A2
Gresham Road	B1
Hartington Road	A1
Heywood Street	B1
Highfield Road	C3
Holwick Road	A1
Linthorpe Road	C2
Longlands Road	B3

Marton Burn Road	C2
Marton Road	B3/C3
Newport Road	A1/A2
North Ormesby Road	A3
Orchard Road	C1
Park Road North	B2
Park Road South	B2
Park Vale Road	B2
Parliament Road	B1
Riverside Park Road	A1
Roman Road	C1
St. Barnabas Road	B1
Scotts Road	A3
Sheperdson Way	A3
Snowdon Road	A2
Southfield Road	B2
The Avenue	C2
The Crescent	C1
Union Street	B1
Valley Road	C2
Victoria Road	B2
Westbourne Grove	B3
Wilson Street	A2
Woodlands Road	B2

TOURIST INFORMATION ☎ 01642 264330/243425
51 CORPORATION ROAD,
MIDDLESBROUGH, TS1 1LT

HOSPITAL A & E ☎ 01642 617617
NORTH TEES GENERAL HOSPITAL, HARDWICK ROAD,
STOCKTON-ON-TEES, TS19 8PE

COUNCIL OFFICE ☎ 01642 245432
MUNICIPAL BUILDINGS, PO BOX 99A,
RUSSELL STREET, MIDDLESBROUGH, TS1 2QQ

WEB-SITE www.middlesbrough.gov.uk

LOCAL RADIO BBC RADIO CLEVELAND 95 FM
MAGIC 1170 AM, TFM 96.6 FM, CENTURY RADIO 100.7 FM

Middlesbrough *Middbro.* Population: 147,430. Town, port, with extensive dock area, on S bank of River Tees, forming part of Teesside urban complex. A former iron and steel town, its chief industries now involve oil and petrochemicals. Unusual *1911 transporter bridge over River Tees. University of Teesside. Captian Cook Birthplace Museum in Stewart Park at Marton.

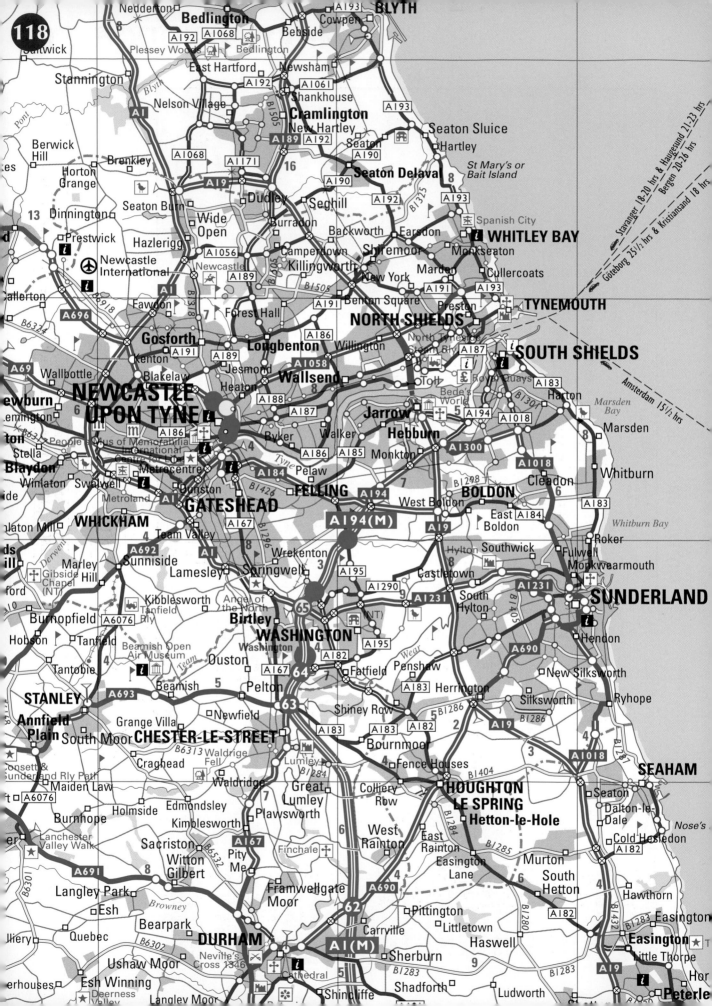

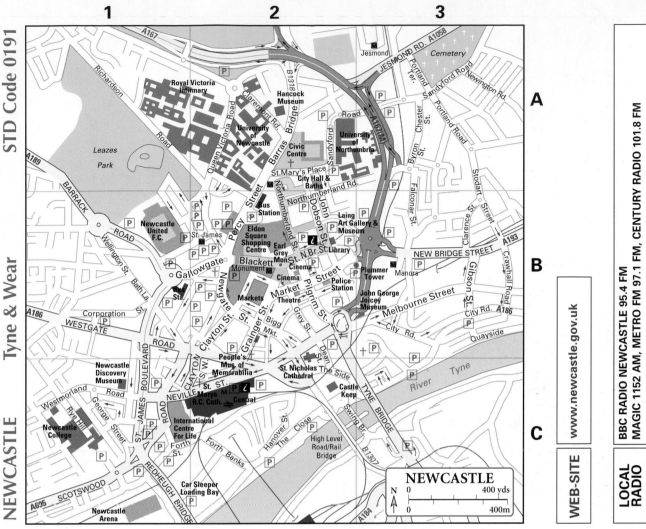

STD Code 0191   **Tyne & Wear**   **NEWCASTLE**

WEB-SITE www.newcastle.gov.uk

LOCAL RADIO BBC RADIO NEWCASTLE 95.4 FM MAGIC 1152 AM, METRO FM 97.1 FM, CENTURY RADIO 101.8 FM

INDEX TO STREET NAMES

Barrack Road	A1	Dean Street	B2	Neville Street	C1	Rye Hill	C1
Barras Bridge	A2	Falconar Street	A3	New Bridge Street	B3	St. James Boulevard	C1
Bath Lane	B1	Forth Banks	C2	Newgate Street	B2	St. Mary's Place	A2
Bigg Market	B2	Forth Street	C1	Newington Road	A3	Sandyford Road	A2/A3
Blackett Street	B2	Gallowgate	B1	Northumberland Road	B2	Scotswood Road	C1
Byron Street	A3	George Street	C1	Northumberland Street	A2	Stodart Street	A3
Chester Street	A3	Gibson Street	B3	Percy Street	B2	Swing Bridge	C2
City Road	B3	Grainger Street	B2	Pilgrim Street	B2	The Close	C2
Claremont Road	A2	Grey Street	B2	Portland Road	A3	The Side	B2
Clarence Street	B3	Hanover Street	C2	Portland Terrace	A3	Tyne Bridge	C3
Clayton Street	B2	Jesmond Road	A3	Quayside	B3	Wellington Street	B1
Clayton Street West	C1	John Dobson Street	B2	Queen Victoria Road	A2	Westgate Road	B1
Corporation Street	B1	Market Street	B2	Redheugh Bridge	C1	Westmorland Road	C1
Crawhall Road	B3	Melbourne Street	B3	Richardson Road	A1		

TOURIST INFORMATION ☎ 0191 261 0610
CENTRAL LIBRARY, PRINCESS SQ, NEWCASTLE
UPON TYNE, TYNE & WEAR, NE99 1DX

HOSPITAL A & E ☎ 0191 273 8811
NEWCASTLE GENERAL HOSPITAL, WESTGATE
ROAD, NEWCASTLE UPON TYNE, NE64 6BE

COUNCIL OFFICE ☎ 0191 232 8520
CIVIC CENTRE, BARRAS BRIDGE,
NEWCASTLE UPON TYNE, NE99 2BN

Newcastle upon Tyne *T. & W.* Population: 189,150. City, port on River Tyne about 11m/17km upstream from river mouth and 80m/129km N of Leeds. The 'new castle' of city's name started in 1080 by Robert Curthose, eldest son of William the Conqueror. 13c castle gatehouse known as 'Black Gate'. Commercial and industrial centre, previously dependent upon coalmining and shipbuilding. In its heyday, 25 percent of world's shipping built here. Cathedral dates from 14 to 15c. Bessie Surtees House (English Heritage) comprises 16c and 17c merchants' houses. Tyne Bridge, opened in 1928 and longest of its type at the time. Venerable Bede (AD 672-735) born near Jarrow. Catherine Cookson, writer, also born in Jarrow. Universities. Newcastle International Airport 5m/8km NW.

STD Code 01603

NORWICH Norfolk

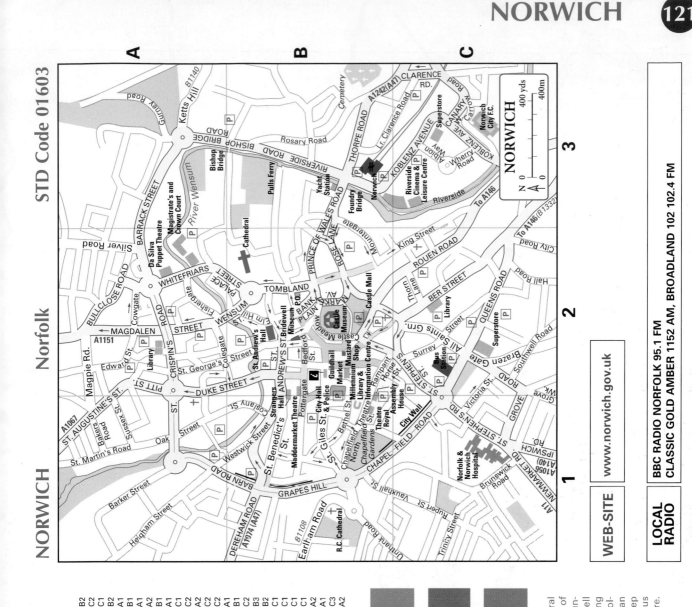

INDEX TO STREET NAMES

Albion Way	C3	Elm Hill	C2
All Saints Green	C2	Fishergate	A2
Bakers Road	A1	Grapes Hill	B1
Bank Plain	B2	Grove Road	C1
Barker Street	A1	Grove Walk	C1
Barn Road	B1	Gurney Road	A3
Barrack Street	A2	Hall Road	C2
Bedford Street	B2	Heigham Street	A1
Ber Street	C2	Ipswich Road	C1
Bethel Street	B1	Ketts Hill	A3
Bishopbridge Road	B3	King Street	C2
Brazen Gate	C2	Koblenz Avenue	C3
Brunswick Road	C1	Lower Clarence Road	B3
Bullclose Road	A2	Magdalen Street	A2
Canary Way	C3	Magpie Road	A2
Carrow Road	C3	Market Avenue	B2
Castle Meadow	B2	Mountergate	B2
Chapel Field Road	B1	Newmarket Road	C1
Chapelfield North	B1	Oak Street	A1
City Road	C2	Palace Street	B2
Clarence Road	C3	Pitt Street	A2
Colegate	A2	Pottergate	B1
Coslany Street	A2	Prince of Wales Road	B2
Cowgate	A2	Queens Road	C2
Dereham Road	B1	Rampant Horse Street	B2
Duke Street	B1	Riverside	C3
Earlham Road	B1	Rosary Road	B3
Edward Street	A2	Rose Lane	B2
		Rouen Road	C2
		Rupert Street	C1
		St. Andrew's Street	B2
		St. Augustine's Street	A1
		St. Benedict's Street	B1
		St. Crispin's Road	A1
		St. George's Street	A2
		St. Giles Street	B1
		St. Martin's Road	A1
		St. Stephen's Road	C1
		St. Stephen's Street	C2
		Silver Road	A2
		Southwell Road	C2
		Surrey Street	C2
		Sussex Street	A1
		Theatre Street	B1
		Thorn Lane	C2
		Thorpe Road	B3
		Tombland	B2
		Trinity Street	C1
		Unthank Road	C1
		Vauxhall Street	C1
		Victoria Street	C1
		Wensum Street	A2
		Westwick Street	A1
		Wherry Road	C3
		Whitefriars	A2

TOURIST INFORMATION ☎ 01603 666071
THE GUILDHALL, GAOL HILL, NORWICH,
NORFOLK, NR2 1NF

HOSPITAL A & E ☎ 01603 286286
NORFOLK & NORWICH HOSPITAL,
BRUNSWICK ROAD, NORWICH, NR1 3SR

COUNCIL OFFICE ☎ 01603 622233
CITY HALL, ST. PETER'S STREET,
NORWICH, NR2 1NH

WEB-SITE www.norwich.gov.uk

LOCAL RADIO BBC RADIO NORFOLK 95.1 FM
CLASSIC GOLD AMBER 1152 AM, BROADLAND 102 102.4 FM

Norwich *Norf.* Population: 171,304. City, county town and cathedral city at confluence of River Wensum and River Yare, 98m/158km NE of London. Middle ages saw Norwich become second richest city in country through exporting textiles. Medieval streets and buildings are well preserved. Sections of 14c flint city wall defences still exist, including Cow Tower (English Heritage). Current chief industries are high technology and computer based. Notable buildings include partly Norman cathedral with second highest spire in Britain, Norman castle with keep (now museum and art gallery), 15c guildhall, modern city hall, numerous medieval churches. University of East Anglia 2m/4km W of city centre. Airport 3m/5km N.

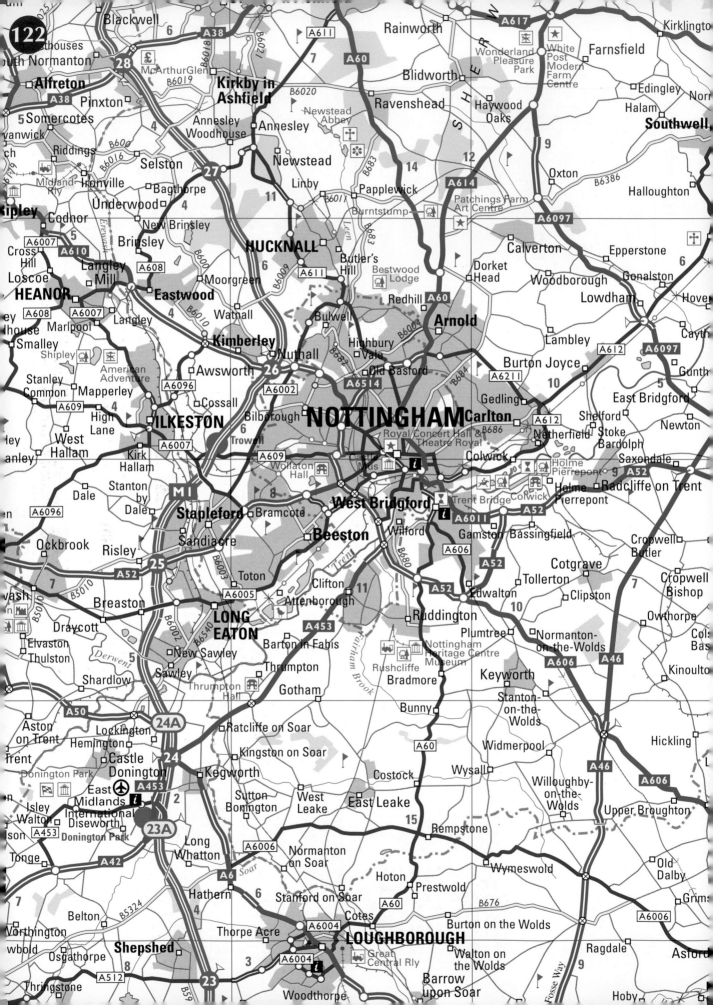

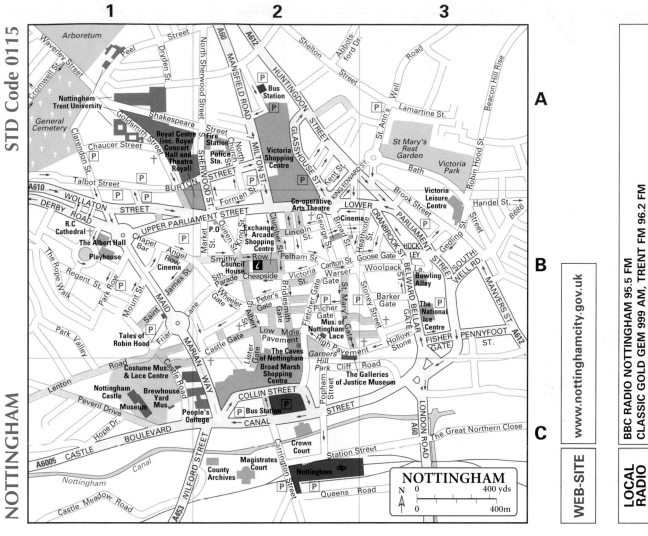

STD Code 0115

NOTTINGHAM

WEB-SITE   www.nottinghamcity.gov.uk

LOCAL RADIO   BBC RADIO NOTTINGHAM 95.5 FM   CLASSIC GOLD GEM 999 AM, TRENT FM 96.2 FM

INDEX TO STREET NAMES

Abbotsford Drive	A2	Chapel Bar	B1	Goose Gate	B3	Maid Marian Way	B1
Albert Street	B2	Chaucer Street	A1	Handel Street	B3	Mansfield Road	A2
Angel Row	B1	Cheapside	B2	Heathcote Street	B2	Manvers Street	B3
Barker Gate	B3	Clarendon Street	A1	High Pavement	B2	Market Street	B2
Bath Street	A3	Cliff Road	C2	Hockley	B3	Middle Pavement	B2
Beacon Hill Rise	A3	Clumber Street	B2	Hollowstone	B3	Milton Street	A2
Bellar Gate	B3	Collin Street	C2	Hope Drive	C1	Mount Street	B1
Belward Street	B3	Cranbrook Street	B3	Huntingdon Street	A2	North Church Street	A2
Bridlesmith Gate	B2	Cromwell Street	A1	Kent Street	A2	North Sherwood Street	A2
Broad Street	B2	Derby Road	B1	King Edward Street	B2	Park Row	B1
Brook Street	A3	Dryden Street	A1	King Street	B2	Park Valley	B1
Burton Street	A1	Fisher Gate	B3	Lamartine Street	A3	Peel Street	A1
Canal Street	C2	Fletcher Gate	B2	Lenton Road	C1	Pelham Street	B2
Carlton Street	B2	Forman Street	B2	Lincoln Street	B2	Pennyfoot Street	B3
Carrington Street	C2	Friar Lane	B1	Lister Gate	C2	Peveril Drive	C1
Castle Boulevard	C1	Gedling Street	B3	London Road	C3	Pilcher Gate	B2
Castle Gate	B2	George Street	B2	Low Pavement	B2	Popham Street	C2
Castle Meadow Road	C1	Glasshouse Street	A2	Lower Parliament Street	B2	Queens Road	C2
Castle Road	C1	Goldsmith Street	A1			Queen Street	B2
						Regent Street	B1
						Robin Hood Street	A3
						St. Ann's Well Road	A3
						St. James Street	B1
						St. Mary's Gate	B2
St. Peter's Gate	B2
Shakespeare Street	A1
Shelton Street	A2
Smithy Row	B2
South Parade	B2
South Sherwood Street	A2
Southwell Road	B3
Station Street	C2
Stoney Street	B3
Talbot Street	A1
The Great Northern Close	C3
The Rope Walk	B1
Upper Parliament Street	B1
Victoria Street	B2
Warser Gate	B2
Waverley Street	A1
Wheeler Gate	B2
Wilford Street	C1
Wollaton Street	B1
Woolpack Lane	B3

TOURIST INFORMATION ☎ 0115 915 5330
1-4 SMITHY ROW,
NOTTINGHAM, NG1 2BY

HOSPITAL A & E ☎ 0115 924 9924
QUEENS MEDICAL CENTRE, UNIVERSITY HOSP,
DERBY ROAD, NOTTINGHAM, NG7 2UH

COUNCIL OFFICE ☎ 0115 915 5555
THE GUILDHALL, BURTON STREET,
NOTTINGHAM, NG1 4BT

Nottingham *Nott.* Population: 270,222. City, on River Trent, 45m/72km NE of Birmingham. Originally Saxon town built on one of a pair of hills. In 1068, Normans built castle on other hill and both communities traded in valley between. Important commercial, industrial, entertainment and sports centre. Key industries include manufacture of lace, mechanical products, tobacco and pharmaceuticals. 17c castle, restored 19c, houses museum and art gallery. Two universities. Repertory theatre.

STD Code 01738

Perth & Kinross

PERTH

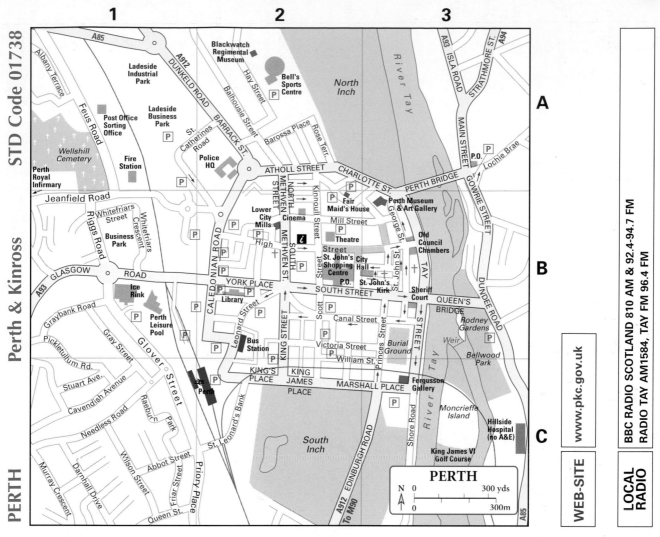

PERTH

N 0   300 yds

0   300m

WEB-SITE

www.pkc.gov.uk

LOCAL RADIO

BBC RADIO SCOTLAND 810 AM & 92.4-94.7 FM
RADIO TAY AM1584, TAY FM 96.4 FM

INDEX TO STREET NAMES

Abbot Street	C1	Feus Road	A1	King Street	B2	Priory Place	C2
Albany Terrace	A1	Friar Street	C1	Kinnoull Street	A2	Queen Street	C1
Atholl Street	A2	George Street	B3	Leonard Street	B2	Queens Bridge	B3
Balhousie Street	A2	Glasgow Road	B1	Lochie Brae	A3	Raeburn Park	C1
Barossa Place	A2	Glover Street	B1	Main Street	A3	Riggs Road	B1
Barrack Street	A2	Gowrie Street	A3	Marshall Place	C2	Rose Terrace	A2
Caledonian Road	B2	Gray Street	B1	Mill Street	B2	St. Catherines	
Canal Street	B2	Graybank Road	B1	Murray Crescent	C1	Road	A1
Cavendish Avenue	C1	Hay Street	A2	Needless Road	C1	St. John Street	B3
Charlotte Street	A2	High Street	B2	North Methven	A2	St. Leonard's Bank	C2
Darnhall Drive	C1	Isla Road	A3	Street		Scott Street	B2
Dundee Road	B3	Jeanfield Road	B1	Porth Bridge	A3	Shore Road	C3
Dunkeld Road	A1	King's Place	C2	Pickletullum Road	B1	South Methven	B2
Edinburgh Road	C2	King James Place	C2	Princes Street	C3	Street	

South Street	B2
Strathmore Street	A3
Stuart Avenue	C1
Tay Street	B3
Victoria Street	B2
Whitefriars	
Crescent	B1
Whitefriars Street	B1
William Street	B2
Wilson Street	C1
York Place	B2

TOURIST INFORMATION ☎ 01738 638353
45 HIGH STREET,
PERTH, PH1 5TJ

HOSPITAL A & E ☎ 01738 623311
PERTH ROYAL INFIRMARY,
TAYMOUNT TERRACE, PERTH, PH1 1NX

COUNCIL OFFICE ☎ 01738 475000
PERTH & KINROSS COUNCIL, PO BOX 77,
2 HIGH STREET, PERTH, PH1 5PH

Perth *P. & K.* Population: 41,453. City, ancient cathedral city (Royal Charter granted 1210) on River Tay, 31m/50km N of Edinburgh. Once capital of Medieval Scotland. Centre of livestock trade. Previously cotton manufacturing centre; now important industries include whisky distilling. St. John's Kirk founded 1126. 15c Balhousie Castle houses regimental headquarters and Museum of the Black Watch. Art Gallery and Museum. 16c Fair Maid's House. Gothic mansion Scone Palace 2m/3km N contains collections of furniture, needlework and porcelain with site of Coronation Stone of Destiny in its grounds. Airfield (Scone) to NE.

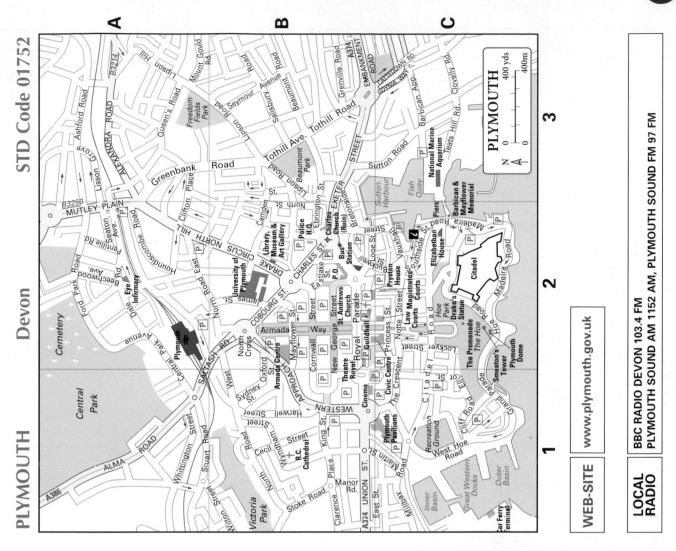

PLYMOUTH

N

0   400 yds
0   400m

WEB-SITE   www.plymouth.gov.uk

LOCAL RADIO   BBC RADIO DEVON 103.4 FM
PLYMOUTH SOUND AM 1152 AM, PLYMOUTH SOUND FM 97 FM

INDEX TO STREET NAMES

Alexandra Road	A3	Exeter Street	B2
Alma Road	A1	Ford Park Road	A2
Armada Way	B2	Gdynia Way	C3
Ashford Road	A3	Grand Parade	C1
Barbican Approach	C3	Greenbank Road	A3
Beaumont Road	B3	Grenville Road	B3
Beechwood Avenue	A2	Harwell Street	B1
		Hoe Road	C2
Bretonside	B2	Houndiscombe	A2
Buckwell Street	C2	Road	
Camden Street	B2	James Street	B2
Cattledown Road	C3	King Street	B1
Cecil Street	B1	Lipson Hill	A3
Central Park	A1	Lipson Road	B3
Avenue		Lisson Grove	A3
Charles Street	B2	Lockyer Street	C2
Citadel Road	C1	Looe Street	B2
Clarence Place	B1	Madeira Road	C2
Cliff Road	C1	Manor Road	B1
Clifton Place	A2	Martin Street	C1
Clovelly Road	C3	Mayflower Street	B2
Cobourg Street	B2	Millbay Road	C1
Cornwall Street	B2	Mount Gould	A3
Dale Road	A2	Road	
Drake Circus	B2	Mutley Plain	A2
East Street	C1	New George	B1
Eastlake Street	B2	Street	
Ebrington Street	B2	North Cross	B2
Elliot Street	C1	North Hill	B2
Embankment Road	B3	North Road East	B3

North Road West	B1		
North Street	B2		
Notte Street	C2		
Oxford Street	B1		
Pentillie Road	A2		
Princess Street	C2		
Queen's Road	A3		
Royal Parade	B2		
Salisbury Road	B3		
Saltash Road	A1		
Seaton Avenue	A2		
Seymour Avenue	B3		
Southside Street	C2		
Stoke Road	B1		
Stuart Road	A1		
Sutton Road	B3		
Sydney Street	B1		
Teats Hill Road	C3		
The Crescent	C1		
Tothill Avenue	B3		
Tothill Road	B3		
Union Street	B1		
Vauxhall Street	C2		
West Hoe Road	C1		
Western Approach	B1		
Whittington Street	A1		
Wilton Street	B1		
Wyndham Street	B1		

TOURIST INFORMATION ☎ 01752 264849
ISLAND HOUSE, 9 THE BARBICAN,
PLYMOUTH, DEVON, PL1 2LS

HOSPITAL A & E ☎ 01752 777111
DERRIFORD HOSPITAL, DERRIFORD ROAD,
CROWNHILL, PLYMOUTH, PL6 8DH

COUNCIL OFFICE ☎ 01752 668000
CIVIC CENTRE, ARMADA WAY,
PLYMOUTH, PL1 2EW

Plymouth *Plym.* Population: 245,295. City, largest city in SW England, 100m/160km SW of Bristol. Port and naval base. Regional shopping centre. City centre rebuilt after bombing in World War II. Has strong commercial and naval tradition. In 1588 Sir Francis Drake sailed from Plymouth to defeat Spanish Armada. Captain Cook's voyages to Australia, South Seas and Antarctica all departed from here. University. Plymouth City Airport to N of city.

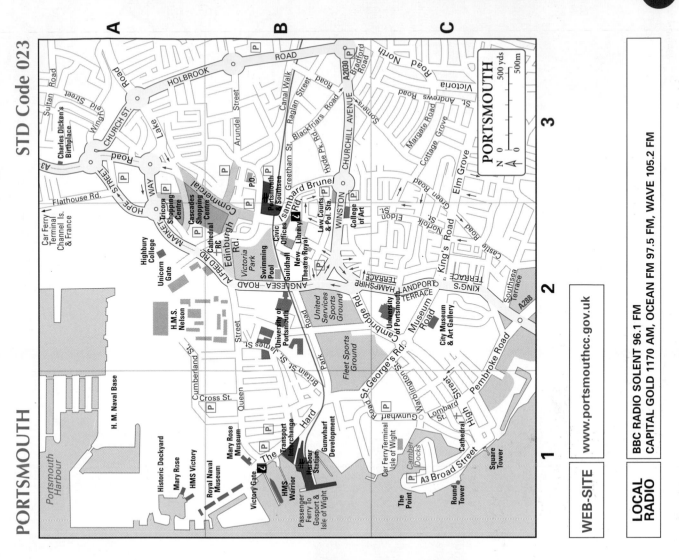

PORTSMOUTH

N 0   500 yds
  0   500m

BBC RADIO SOLENT 96.1 FM
CAPITAL GOLD 1170 AM, OCEAN FM 97.5 FM, WAVE 105.2 FM

WEB-SITE www.portsmouthcc.gov.uk

LOCAL RADIO

INDEX TO STREET NAMES

Alfred Road	B2	Flathouse Road	A3
Anglesea Road	B2	Green Road	C2
Arundel Street	B3	Greetham Street	B3
Blackfriars Road	B3	Gunwharf Road	C1
Bradford Road	B3	Hampshire Terrace	C2
Britain Street	B1	High Street	C1
Broad Street	C1	Holbrook Road	A3
Cambridge Road	C2	Hope Street	A2
Canal Walk	B3	Hyde Park Road	B3
Castle Road	C2	Isambard Brunel	B2
Church Street	A3	Road	
Commercial Road	B2	King's Road	C2
Cottage Grove	C3	King's Terrace	C2
Cross Street	A1	Lake Road	A3
Cumberland	A1	Landport Terrace	C2
Street		Lombard Street	C1
Edinburgh Road	B2	Margate Road	C3
Eldon Street	C2	Market Way	A2
Elm Grove	C3	Museum Road	C2

Norfolk Street	C2
Park Road	B2
Pembroke Road	C1
Queen Street	B1
Raglan Street	B3
St. Andrews Road	C3
St. George's Road	B1
St. James Street	B2
Somers Road	C3
Southsea Terrace	C2
Sultan Road	A3
The Hard	B1
Victoria Road	C3
North	
Warblington	C1
Street	
Wingfield Street	A3
Winston Churchill	A2
Avenue	C2

TOURIST INFORMATION ☎ 023 9282 6722
THE HARD,
PORTSMOUTH, PO1 3QJ

HOSPITAL A & E ☎ 023 9228 6000
QUEEN ALEXANDRA HOSPITAL, SOUTHWICK
HILL ROAD, COSHAM, PORTSMOUTH, PO6 3LY

COUNCIL OFFICE ☎ 023 9282 2251
CIVIC OFFICES, GUILDHALL SQUARE,
PORTSMOUTH, PO1 2AL

Portsmouth *Ports.* Population: 174,690. City, port and naval base (Portsmouth Harbour, on W side of city) 65m/105km SW of London, extending from S end of Portsea Island to S slopes of Ports Down. Various industries, including tourism, financial services and manufacturing. Partly bombed in World War II and now rebuilt; however, some 18c buildings remain. Boat and hovercraft ferries to Isle of Wight. University. Two cathedrals. Nelson's ship, HMS Victory, in harbour, alongside which are remains of Henry VIII's flagship, Mary Rose, which sank in 1545. King James's Gate and Landport Gate were part of 17c defences, and Fort Cumberland is 18c coastal defence at Eastney (all English Heritage). Royal Garrison Church (English Heritage) was 16c chapel prior to Dissolution. Museums, many with nautical theme. City airport at N end of Portsea Island.

STD Code 0118

READING

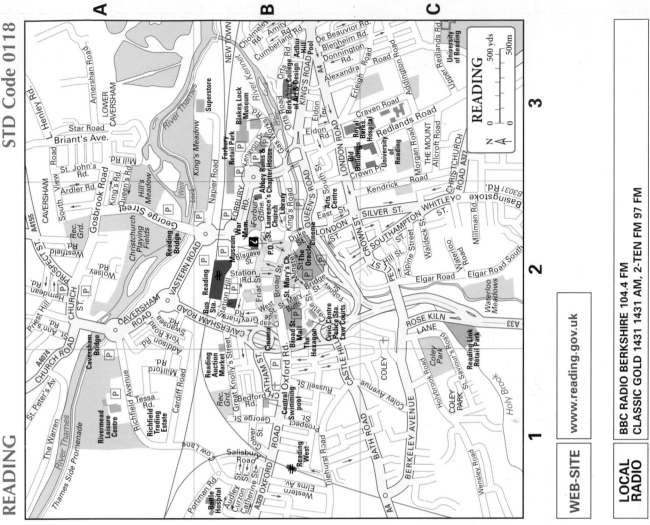

INDEX TO STREET NAMES

Addington Road	C3	Eldon Road	C3
Addison Road	A1	Eldon Terrace	C3
Alexandra Road	C3	Elgar Road	C2
Allcroft Road	C3	Elgar Road South	C2
Alpine Street	C2	Erleigh Road	C2
Amersham Road	A3	Fobney Street	B1
Amity Road	B1	Forbury Road	A2
Ardler Road	A2	Friar Street	B1
Audley Street	B1	Gas Work Road	B1
Basingstoke Road	C2	George Street	C2
Bath Road	C1	George Street:	
Bedford Road	B1	Caversham	B1
Berkeley Avenue	C1	George Stree:	
Blagave Street	B2	Reading	C1
Blenheim Road	B3	Gosbrook Road	A2
Briant's Avenue	A3	Gower Street	B1
Bridge Street	B2	Great Knollys Street	B1
Broad Street	B2	Greyfriars Road	B1
Cardiff Road	A2	Hemdean Road	A2
Castle Hill	C2	Hill Street	B2
Castle Street	B1	Holybrook Rcad	B1
Catherine Street	B2	Kenavon Drive	B2
Caversham Road	A2	Kendrick Roa1	B1
Chatham Street	B1	King's Road:	
Cheapside	B2	Caversham	B1
Cholmeley Road	A3	King's Road Reading	B2
Christchurch Roac	A1	London Road	B3
Church Road	C2	London Street	B2
Church Street	A2	Lower Henley	A3
Coley Avenue	C1	Road	
Cow Lane	A1	Mill Road	A3
Craven Road	B3	Millroc Roac	A1
Crown Place	B3	Millman Road	C2
Crown Street	C2	Minster Street	B1
Cumberland Road	B3	Morgan Roac	C2
Curzon Street	A1	Napier Road	A2
De Beauvoir Road	C3	Orts Road	B2
Donnington Road	B3	Oxford Road	B1
Duke Street	B2	Pell Street	C2
East Street	B2	Priest Hill	A2

Prospect Street	A2		
Caversham			
Prospect Street	B1		
Reading			
Queen's Road	A2		
Caversham			
Queen's Road	B2		
Reading			
Redlands Avenue	C3		
Richfield Avenue	A1		
Rose Kiln Lane	C2		
Russell Street	B1		
St. Ann's Road	A2		
St. John's Road	A3		
St. Mary's Road	B2		
St. Peters Avenue	A1		
St. Saviours Road	C1		
Silver Street	C2		
South Street	B2		
Southampton Street	C2		
South View Road	A3		
Star Roac	B2		
Station Hill	B2		
Station Road	A2		
Swansea Road	A1		
Tessa Roed	B2		
The Warren	A3		
Tilehurst Road	C1		
Upper Redlands Road	C3		
Vastern Road	A2		
Waldelk Street	C2		
Waterloo Road	C2		
Wensley Road	C1		
Western Elms Avenue	B1		
Westfield Road	A2		
West Street	B1		
Whitley Street	C2		
Wolsey R>ad	A2		
York Road	A2		

TOURIST INFORMATION ☎ **0118 956 6226**
TOWN HALL, BLAGRAVE STREET,
READING, RG1 1QH

HOSPITAL A & E ☎ **0118 987 5111**
ROYAL BERKSHIRE HOSPITAL, LONDON ROAD,
READING, RG1 5AN

COUNCIL OFFICE ☎ **0118 939 0900**
CIVIC CENTRE, CIVIC OFFICES, (OFF CASTLE ST.)
READING, RG1 7TD

Reading *Read* Population: 213,474. Town, county and industrial town and railway centre on River Thames, 36m/58km W of London. During Victorian times Reading was an important manufacturing town, particularly for biscuit-making and brewing. University. Remains of Norman abbey, founded by Henry I who lies buried there.

WEB-SITE www.reading.gov.uk

LOCAL RADIO BBC RADIO BERKSHIRE 104.4 FM
CLASSIC GOLD 1431 1431 AM, 2-TEN FM 97 FM

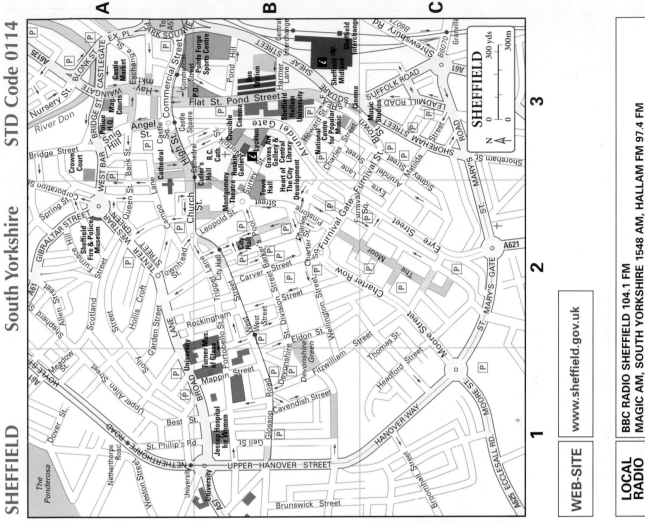

INDEX TO STREET NAMES

Allen Street	A2	Eyre Street	A2	Portobello Street	C2
Angel Street	A3	Fitzwilliam Street	A3	Queen Street	B1
Arundel Gate	B3	Flat Street	B3	Rockingham Street	A3
Arundel Street	C2	Furnace Hill	A2	St. Mary's Gate	A2
Bank Street	A3	Furnival Gate	B2	St. Mary's Road	B2
Barker's Pool	B2	Furnival Square	B2	St. Philip's Road	A1
Best Street	A1	Furnival Street	B2	Scotland Street	A2
Blonk Street	A3	Garden Street	A2	Sheaf Gate	B3
Bridge Street	A3	Gell Street	A1	Sheaf Square	B3
Broad Lane	A2	Gibraltar Street	A2	Shepherd Street	A2
Broomhall Street	C1	Glossop Road	B1	Shoreham Street	C3
Brown Street	C3	Hanover Way	C1	Shrewsbury Road	C3
Brunswick Street	B1	Harmer Lane	B3	Sidney Street	C2
Campo Lane	A2	Haymarket	A3	Snig Hill	A3
Carver Street	B2	Headford Street	C1	Solly Street	A1
Castle Square	A3	High Street	A3	Spring Street	A2
Castlegate	A3	Hollis Croft	A2	Suffolk Road	C3
Cavendish Street	B1	Howard Street	B3	Surrey Street	B2
Charles Street	B2/B3	Hoyle Street	A1	Tenter Street	A2
Charter Row	C2	Leadmill Road	C3	The Moor	C2
Charter Square	B2	Leopold Street	B2	Thomas Street	C1
Church Street	A2	Mappin Street	B1	Townhead Street	A2
Commercial Street	A3	Matilda Street	C3	Trippet Lane	B2
Corporation Street	A2	Meadow Street	A2	Upper Allan Street	A1
Devonshire Street	B1	Moore Street	C1	Upper Hanover Street	B1
Division Street	B2	Netherthorpe Road	B2	Waingate	A3
Dover Street	A1	Norfolk Street	B3	Wellington Street	B2
Ecclesall Road	C1	Nursery Street	A3	West Bar	A2
Eldon Street	B2	Pinstone Street	B2	West Street	B2
Exchange Street	A3	Pond Hill	B3	Westbar Green	A2
Eyre Lane	C2	Pond Street	B3	Weston Street	A1

TOURIST INFORMATION ☎ 0114 221 1900
PEACE GARDENS, SHEFFIELD,
SOUTH YORKSHIRE, S1 2HH

HOSPITAL A & E ☎ 0114 243 4343
NORTHERN GENERAL HOSPITAL, HERRIES ROAD,
SHEFFIELD, S5 7AU

COUNCIL OFFICE ☎ 0114 272 6444
TOWN HALL, PINSTONE STREET,
SHEFFIELD, S1 2HH

Sheffield S.Yorks. Population: 431,607. City, on River Don, 144m/232km NW of London. Former centre of heavy steel industry, now largely precision steel and cutlery industries. University of Sheffield and Sheffield Hallam University. Various museums dedicated to Sheffield's industrial past. National Centre for Popular Music in city centre. Meadowhall shopping centre and Sheffield City Airport, 3m/5km NE of city centre.

WEB-SITE www.sheffield.gov.uk

LOCAL RADIO
BBC RADIO SHEFFIELD 104.1 FM
MAGIC AM, SOUTH YORKSHIRE 1548 AM, HALLAM FM 97.4 FM

SOUTHAMPTON

STD Code 023

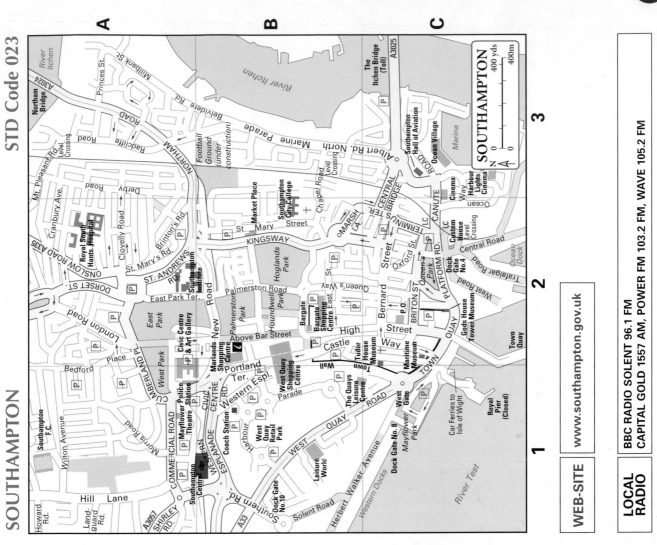

SOUTHAMPTON

400 yds

400m

BBC RADIO SOLENT 96.1 FM
CAPITAL GOLD 1557 AM, POWER FM 103.2 FM, WAVE 105.2 FM

WEB-SITE www.southampton.gov.uk

LOCAL RADIO

INDEX TO STREET NAMES

Above Bar Street	B2
Albert Road North	C3
Bedford Place	A1
Belvidere Road	B3
Bernard Street	C2
Brintons Road	A2
Briton Street	C2
Canute Road	C2
Castle Way	B2
Central Bridge	C2
Central Road	C2
Chapel Road	B2
Civic Centre Road	B1
Clovelly Road	A2
Commercial Road	A1
Cranbury Avenue	A2
Cumberland Place	A1
Derby Road	A3
Dorset Street	A2
East Park Terrace	A2
East Street	B2

Harbour Parade	B2
Herbert Walker	B1
Avenue	A1
High Street	B2
Hill Lane	A1
Howard Road	A1
Kingsway	B2
Landguard Road	A1
London Road	A2
Marine Parade	B3
Marsh Lane	C2
Millbank Street	B2
Morris Road	A1
Mount Pleasant	A3
Road	
New Road	B2
Northam Road	A3
Ocean Way	C2
Onslow Road	A2
Oxford Street	C2
Palmerston Road	B2

Platform Road	C2
Portland Terrace	B1
Princes Street	A3
Queen's Way	C2
Radcliffe Road	A3
St. Andrews Road	A2
St. Mary's Road	A2
St. Mary Street	B2
Shirley Road	A1
Solent Road	B1
Southern Road	B1
Terminus Terrace	C2
Town Quay	C1
Trafalgar Road	C2
West Quay Road	B1
West Road	C2
Western	B1
Esplanade	
Wilton Avenue	A1

TOURIST INFORMATION ☎ 023 8022 1106
9 CIVIC CENTRE ROAD,
SOUTHAMPTON, SO14 7JP

HOSPITAL A & E ☎ 023 8077 7222
SOUTHAMPTON GENERAL HOSP, TREMONA RD,
SHIRLEY, SOUTHAMPTON, SO16 6YD

COUNCIL OFFICE ☎ 023 8022 3855
CIVIC CENTRE, CIVIC CENTRE ROAD,
SOUTHAMPTON, SO14 7LY

Southampton *S'ham.* Population: 210,138. City, at confluence of Rivers Itchen and Test at head of Southampton Water, 70m/113km SW of London. Southern centre for business, culture and recreation. Container and transatlantic passenger port, dealing with 7 percent of UK's seaborne trade. Site of many famous departures: Henry V's army bound for Agincourt; the Pilgrim Fathers sailed to America on the Mayflower in 1620; maiden voyage of Queen Mary and only voyage of Titanic. Remains of medieval town walls. Medieval Merchant's House (English Heritage) has authentically recreated furnishings. Boat and helicopter ferries to Isle of Wight. Host to many international boating events including Southampton International Boat Show, Whitbread Round the World, and BT Global Challenge. University. Southampton International Airport 1m/2km S of Eastleigh.

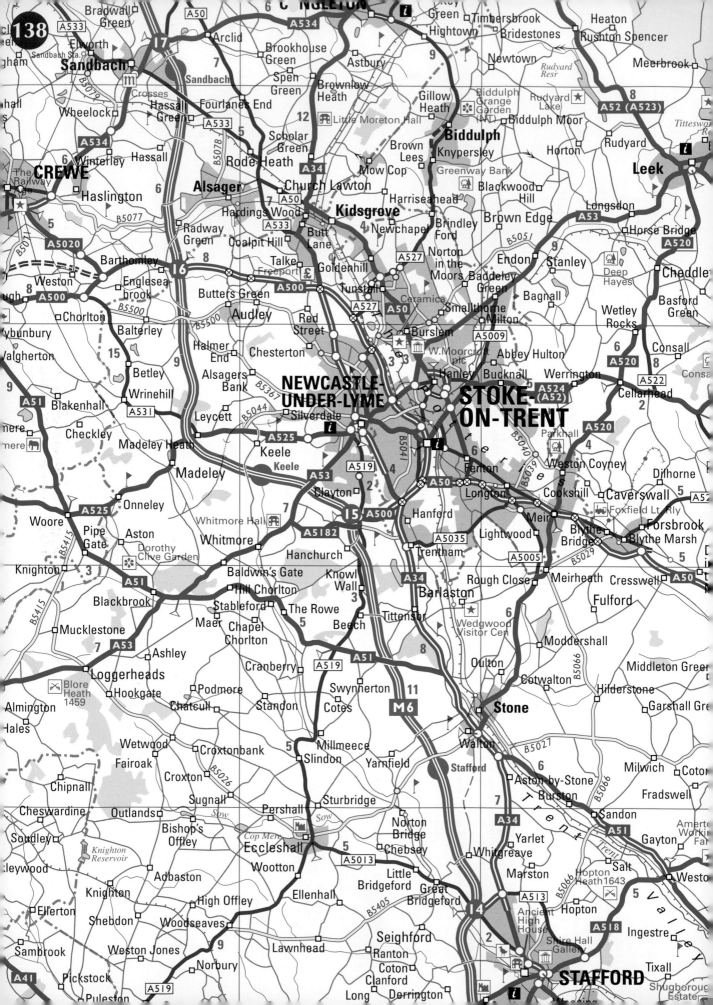

STD Code 01782

STOKE-ON-TRENT

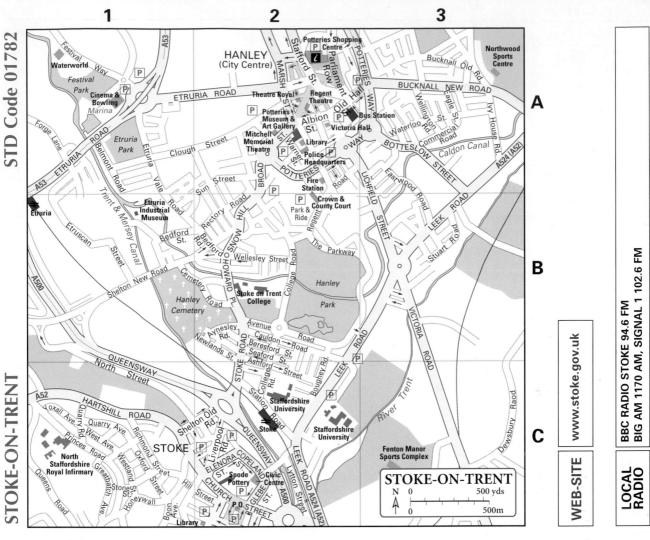

www.stoke.gov.uk

WEB-SITE

BBC RADIO STOKE 94.6 FM
BIG AM 1170 AM, SIGNAL 1 102.6 FM

LOCAL RADIO

INDEX TO STREET NAMES

Albion Street	A2	Church Street	C2	Hanley	A2	Potteries Way	A2	Stoke	C2
Ashford Street	B2	Clough Street	A1	Hartshill Road	C1	Potters Way	A3	Stoke Road	C2
Avenue Road	B2	College Road	B2	Hill Street	C1	Prince's Road	C1	Stone Street	C1
Aynsley Road	B2	Commercial Road	A3	Honeywall	C1	Quarry Avenue	C1	Stuart Road	B3
Bedford Road	B2	Copeland Street	C2	Howard Place	B2	Quarry Road	C1	Sun Street	A2
Bedford Street	B1	Dewsbury Road	C3	Ivy House Road	A3	Queen's Road	C1	The Parkway	B2
Belmont Road	A1	Eagle Street	A3	Leek Road	C2	Queensway	B1	Victoria Road	B3
Beresford Street	B2	Eastwood Road	A3	Lichfield Street	A3	Rectory Road	B2	Warner Street	A2
Botteslow Street	A3	Elenora Street	C2	Liverpool Road	C2	Regent Road	B2	Waterloo Street	A3
Boon Avenue	C1	Etruria Road	A1	Lytton Street	C2	Richmond Street	C1	Wellesley Street	B2
Boughey Road	C2	Etruria Vale Road	A1	Marsh Street	A2	Seaford Street	B2	Wellington Road	A3
Broad Street	A2	Etruscan Street	B1	Newlands Street	B2	Shelton New Road	B1	West Avenue	C1
Bucknall New Road	A3	Festival Way	A1	North Street	B1	Shelton Old Road	C1	Westland Street	C1
Bucknall Old Road	A3	Forge Lane	A1	Old Hall Street	A2	Snow Hill	B2	Yoxall Avenue	C1
Cauldon Road	B2	Glebe Street	C2	Oxford Street	C1	Stafford Street	A2		
Cemetery Road	B1	Greatbatch Avenue	C1	Parliament Row	A2	Station Road	C2		

TOURIST INFORMATION ☎ 01782 236000
POTTERIES SHOPPING CENTRE, QUADRANT RD,
STOKE-ON-TRENT, ST1 1RZ

HOSPITAL A & E ☎ 01782 715444
NORTH STAFFORDSHIRE ROYAL INFIRMARY,
PRINCE'S ROAD, STOKE-ON-TRENT, ST4 7LN

COUNCIL OFFICE ☎ 01782 234567
TOWN HALL, CIVIC CENTRE, GLEBE STREET,
STOKE-ON-TRENT, ST4 1HH

Stoke-on-Trent *Stoke* Population: 266,543. City, on River Trent, 135m/217km NW of London. Centre for employment, shopping and leisure. Created by an amalgamation of former Stoke-upon-Trent and the towns of Burslem, Fenton, Hanley, Longton and Tunstall in 1910. Capital of The Potteries (largest claywear producer in the world), now largely a finishing centre for imported pottery. Many pottery factories open to public including Wedgewood, Royal Doulton and Spode. Potteries Museum in Hanley charts history of the potteries. Gladstone Pottery Museum in Longton is centred around large bottle-kiln and demonstrates traditional skills of pottery production. Staffordshire University.

STRATFORD-UPON-AVON Warwickshire STD Code 01789

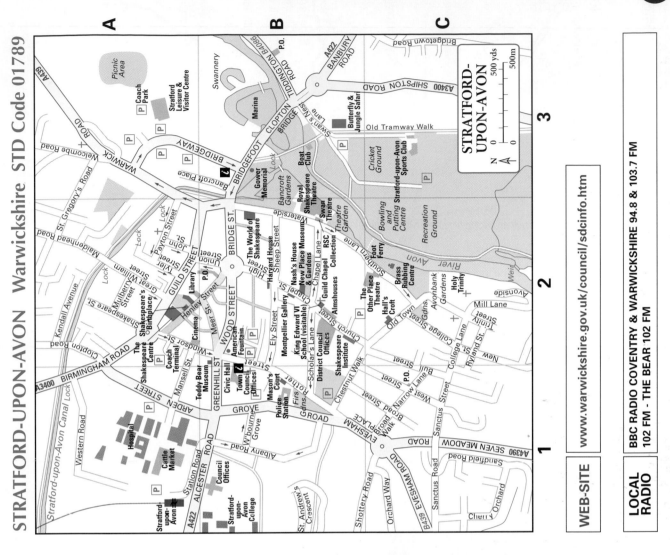

INDEX TO STREET NAMES

Albany Road	B1	Great William Street	A2	Sanctus Street	C1
Alcester Road	A1	Greenhill Street	B1	Sandfield Road	C1
Arden Street	A1	Grove Road	C2	Scholar's Lane	B1
Avonside	C2	Guild Street	B3	Shakespeare Street	A2
Banbury Road	B3	Henley Street	B3	Sheep Street	B2
Bancroft Place	B3	High Street	B2	Shipston Road	C3
Birmingham Road	A1	John Street	B2	Shottery Road	B1
Bridgefoot	B3	Kendall Avenue	A2	Seven Meadow Road	C1
Bridge Street	B2	Maidenhead Road	A2	Southern Lane	C2
Bridgeway	B3	Mansell Street	A1	Station Road	A1
Bridgetown Road	C3	Meer Street	B2	Swans Nest lane	B3
Broad Street	C1	Mill Lane	C2	Tiddington Road	B3
Broad Walk	C1	Mulberry Street	A2	Trinity Street	C2
Bull Street	C1	Narrow Lane	C1	Tyler Street	A2
Chapel Lane	B2	New Street	C2	Union Street	B2
Chapel Street	B2	Old Town	B2	Warwick Road	A3
Cherry Orchard	C1	Old Tramway Walk	C3	Waterside	B2
Chestnut Walk	B1			Welcombe Road	A3
Church Street	B2	Orchard Way	C1	Westbourne Grove	B1
Clopton Bridge	B3	Payton Street	A2	Western Road	A1
Clopton Road	A2	Rother Street	B1	West Street	C1
College Lane	C2	Ryland Street	C2	Windsor Street	B2
College Street	C2	St. Andrews Crescent	B1	Wood Street	B2
Ely Street	B2	St. Gregory's Road	A2		
Evesham Place	C1	Sanctus Road	C1		
Evesham Road	C1				

TOURIST INFORMATION ☎ 01789 293127
BRIDGEFOOT, STRATFORD-UPON-AVON,
WARWICKSHIRE, CV37 6GW

HOSPITAL A & E ☎ 01926 495321
WARWICK HOSPITAL, WAKIN ROAD,
WARWICK, CV34 5BW

COUNCIL OFFICE ☎ 01789 267575
COUNCIL OFFICES, ELIZABETH HOUSE,
CHURCH ST, STRATFORD-UPON-AVON, CV37 6HX

WEB-SITE www.warwickshire.gov.uk/council/sdcinfo.htm

LOCAL RADIO BBC RADIO COVENTRY & WARWICKSHIRE 94.8 & 103.7 FM
102 FM - THE BEAR 102 FM

Stratford-upon-Avon (Also spelled Stratford-on-Avon.) *Warks.* Population: 22,231. Town, on River Avon, 8m/13km SW of Warwick. Tourist centre. Many attractive 16c buildings. Reconstructed Shakespeare's Birthplace. Elizabethan garcen at New Place. Hall's Croft Elizabethan town house and doctor's dispensary. Royal Shakespeare Theatre. Shakespeare's grave at Ho y Trinity Church. Anne Hathaway's Cottage to W, at Shottery.

SWANSEA

STD Code 01792

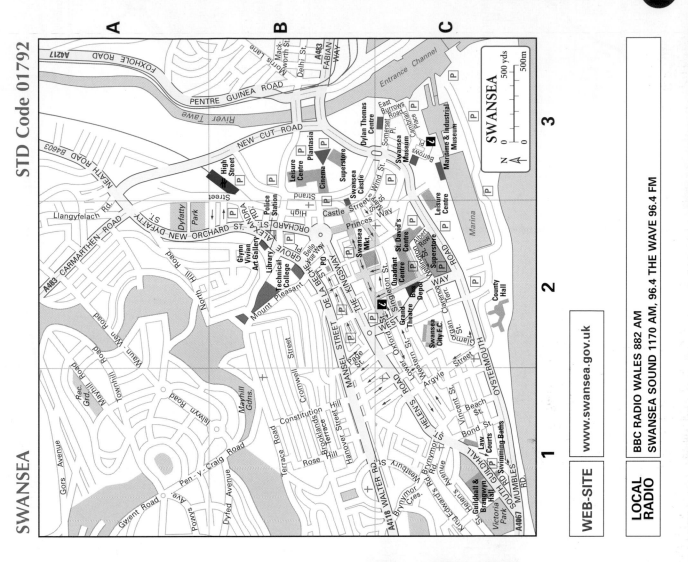

INDEX TO STREET NAMES

Albert Row	C2	Grove Place	B2
Alexandra Road	B2	Gwent Road	A1
Argyle Street	C1	Hanover Street	B1
Beach Street	C1	High Street	B2
Belle Vue Way	B2	Islwyn Road	A1
Bond Street	C1	King Edward's Road	C1
Brooklands Terrace	B1	Llangyfelach Road	A2
Brynmcyr Crescent	C1	Lower Oxford Street	C1
Brynmcyr Road	C3	Mackworth Street	B3
Burrows Place	C3	Mansel Street	A2
Cambrian Place	C3	Mayhill Road	A1
Carmarthen Road	A2	Morris Lane	B3
Castle Street	B2	Mount Pleasant	B2
Clarence Terrace	C2	Mumbles Road	C1
Constitution Hill	B1	Neath Road	A3
Cromwell Street	B1	New Cut Road	B3
De La Beche Street	B2	New Orchard Street	A2
Delhi Street	B3	North Hill Road	C3
Dyfatty Street	A2	Orchard Street	B2
Dyfed Avenue	B1	Oystermouth Road	A3
East Burrows Road	C3	Page Street	B2
Fabian Way	B3	Pentre Guinea Road	A3
Foxhole Road	A3	Pen-y-Craig Road	A1
Glamorgan Street	C2	Powys Avenue	A1
Gors Avenue	A1	Princess Way	B2
		Rose Hill	B1
		St. Helen's Avenue	C1
		St. Helen's Road	C1
		St. Mary Street	B2
		Singleton Street	C2
		Somerset Place	C3
		South Guildhall Road	C1
		Strand	B3
		Terrace Road	B1
		The Kingsway	B2
		Townhill Road	A1
		Vincent Street	C1
		Walter Road	C1
		Waun-Wen Road	A2
		Wellington Street	C2
		Westbu'y Street	B2
		Western Street	C1
		West Way	C2

TOURIST INFORMATION ☎ 01792 702222
WEST WAY CAR PARK,
SWANSEA, SA1 3QG.

HOSPITAL A & E ☎ 01792 702222
MORRISTON HOSPITAL, MORRISTON,
SWANSEA, SA6 6NL.

COUNCIL OFFICE ☎ 01792 636000
THE GUILDHALL, (OFF FRANCIS STREET),
SWANSEA, SA1 4PA.

WEB-SITE www.swansea.gov.uk

LOCAL RADIO
BBC RADIO WALES 882 AM
SWANSEA SOUND 1170 AM, 96.4 THE WAVE 96.4 FM

Swansea (Abertawe). Population: 171,038. City, port on Swansea Bay at mouth of River Tawe, and Wales' second city, 35m/57km W of Cardiff. Settlement developed next to Norman castle built in 1099, but claims made that a Viking settlement existed before this date. Previously a port for local metal smelting industries. Bombed in World War II, and city centre rebuilt. Birthplace of Dylan Thomas, who described it as 'an ugly, lovely town'. Remains of 14c castle (Cadw) or fortified manor house. University of Wales. Tropical plant and wildlife leisure centre, Plantasia. Airport 5m/9km W at Fairwood Common.

SWINDON

STD Code 01793

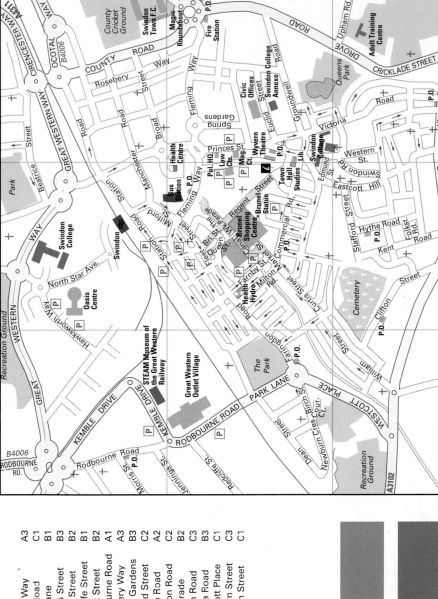

INDEX TO STREET NAMES

Bath Road	C2	Fleet Street	B2
Beatrice Street	A2	Fleming Way	B2
Birch Street	B1	Folkstone Road	C2
Bridge Street	B2	Great Western	A1
Broad Street	A3	Way	
Canal Walk	B2	Groundwell Road	B3
Cirencester Way	A3	Hawksworth Way	A1
Clifton Street	C2	High Street	C3
Commercial Road	B2	Hythe Road	C2
County Road	A3	Jennings Street	B1
Courtsknap Court	B1	Kemble Drive	A1
Cricklade Street	C3	Kent Road	C2
Curtis Street	B2	Manchester Road	A2
Dean Street	B1	Market Street	B2
Drove Road	C3	Milford Street	B2
Eastcott Hill	C2	Milton Road	B2
Edmund Street	B2	Morris Street	A1
Euclid Street	A3	Newburn Crescent	B1
Faringdon Road	B1	North Star	A2
Farnby Street	B2	Avenue	

Ocotal Way	A3
Okus Road	C1
Park Lane	B1
Princes Street	B3
Queen Street	B2
Redcliffe Street	B1
Regent Street	B2
Rodbourne Road	A1
Rosebery Way	A3
Spring Gardens	B3
Stafford Street	C2
Station Road	A2
Swindon Road	B2
The Parade	C3
Upham Road	B3
Victoria Road	C1
Westcott Place	C3
Western Street	C1

TOURIST INFORMATION ☎ 01793 530328
37 REGENT STREET,
SWINDON, SN1 1JL

HOSPITAL A & E ☎ 01793 530328
PRINCESS MARGARET HOSPITAL, OKUS ROAD,
SWINDON, SN1 4JU

COUNCIL OFFICE ☎ 01793 463000
CIVIC OFFICES, EUCLID STREET,
SWINDON, SN1 2JH

Swindon *Swin.* Population: 145,236. Town, industrial and commercial centre, 70m/113km W of London. Large, modern shopping centre. Town expanded considerably in 19c with arrival of the railway. The Museum of the Great Western Railway exhibits Swindon built locomotives and documents the history of the railway works.

WEB-SITE www.swindon.gov.uk

LOCAL RADIO
BBC WILTSHIRE SOUND 103.6 FM
BRUNEL CLASSIC GOLD 936 AM, GWR FM WILTSHIRE 97.2 FM

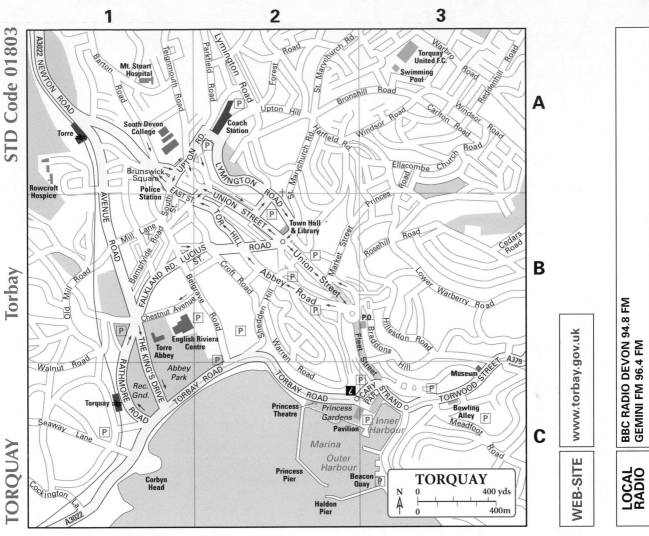

STD Code 01803

Torbay

TORQUAY

WEB-SITE www.torbay.gov.uk

LOCAL RADIO BBC RADIO DEVON 94.8 FM GEMINI FM 96.4 FM

INDEX TO STREET NAMES

Abbey Road	B2	East Street	A1	Old Mill Road	B1	Torbay Road	C1
Avenue Road	B1	Ellacombe Church Road	A3	Parkfield Road	A2	Tor Hill Road	B2
Bampfylde Road	B1	Falkland Road	B1	Prince's Road	B3	Torwood Street	C3
Barton Road	A1	Fleet Street	B2	Rathmore Road	C1	Union Street	B2
Belgrave Road	B1	Forest Road	A2	Reddenhill Road	A3	Upton Hill	A2
Braddons Hill	B3	Hatfield Road	A2	Rosehill Road	B3	Upton Road	A1
Bronshill Road	A2	Hillesdon Road	B3	St. Marychurch Road	B2	Walnut Road	C1
Brunswick Square	B1	Lower Warberry Road	B3	Seaway Lane	C1	Warbro Road	A3
Carlton Road	A3	Lucius Street	B1	Shedden Hill	B2	Warren Road	B2
Cary Parade	C3	Lymington Road	A2	Shiphay Lane	A1	Westhill Road	A2
Cedars Road	B3	Market Street	B2	South Street	B1	Windsor Road	A3
Chestnut Avenue	B1	Meadfoot Road	C3	Strand	C3		
Cockington Lane	C1	Mill Lane	B1	Teignmouth Road	A1		
Croft Road	B2	Newton Road	A1	The King's Drive	B1		

TOURIST INFORMATION ☎ 01803 297428
VAUGHAN PARADE,
TORQUAY, TQ2 5JG

HOSPITAL A & E ☎ 01803 614567
TORBAY HOSPITAL, LAWES BRIDGE,
TORQUAY, TQ2 7AA

COUNCIL OFFICE ☎ 01803 201201
CIVIC OFFICES, CASTLE CIRCUS,
TORQUAY, TQ1 3DR

Torquay *Torbay* Population: 59,587. Town, 18m/30km S of Exeter. Chief town and resort of Torbay English Riviera district, with harbour and several beaches. Noted for mild climate. Torre Abbey with 15c gatehouse, is a converted monastery housing a collecion of furniture and glassware. Torquay Museum has display on crimewriter Agatha Christie born in Torquay. Kent's Cavern showcaves are an important prehistoric site. Babbacombe Model village 2m/3km N.

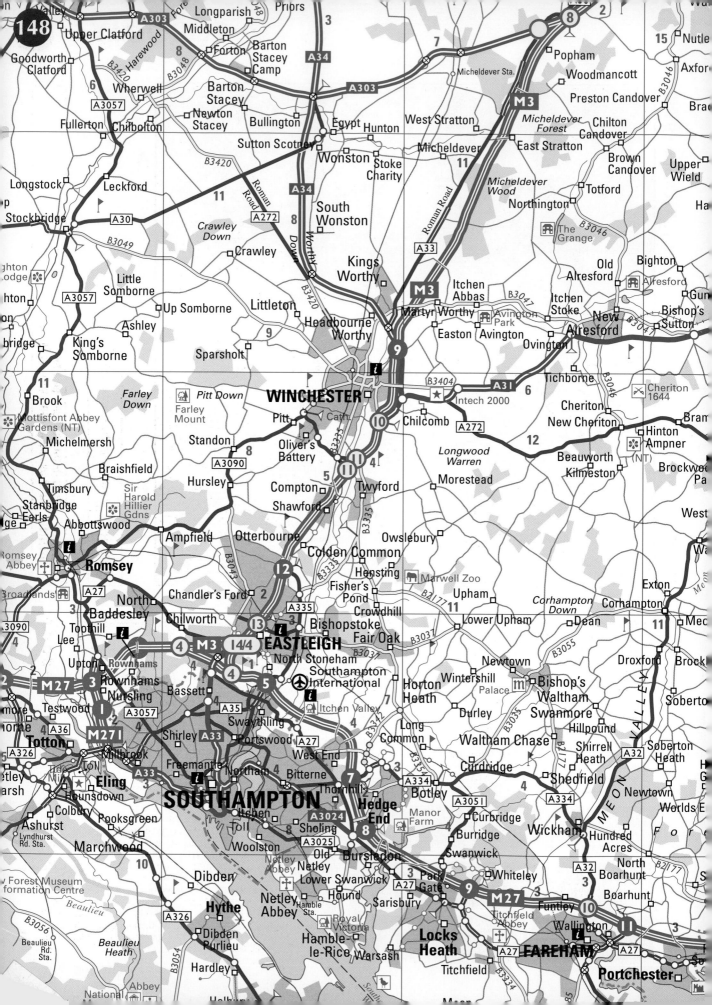

STD Code 01962

Hampshire

WINCHESTER

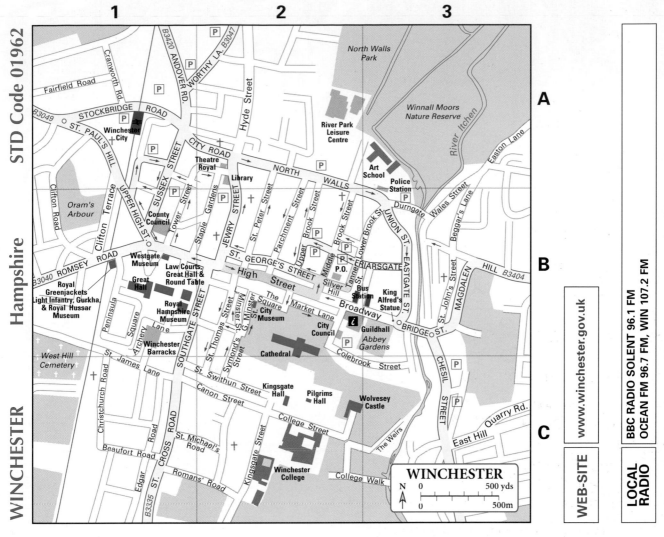

WEB-SITE — www.winchester.gov.uk

LOCAL RADIO — BBC RADIO SOLENT 96.1 FM, OCEAN FM 96.7 FM, WIN 107.2 FM

INDEX TO STREET NAMES

Andover Road	A1	College Street	C2	Jewry Street	B2	St. Cross Road	C1	Sussex Street	B1
Archery Lane	B1	College Walk	C2	Kingsgate Street	C2	St. George's Street	B2	Symond's Street	C2
Beaufort Road	C1	Cranworth Road	A1	Little Minster Street	B2	St. James Lane	B1	Tanner Street	B2
Beggar's Lane	B3	Durngate	B3	Lower Brook Street	B2	St. John's Street	B3	The Square	B2
Bridge Stret	B3	Eastgate Street	B3	Magdalen Hill	B3	St. Michael's Road	C1	Tower Street	B2
Broadway	B2	Easton Lane	A3	Market Lane	B2	St. Paul's Hill	A1	Union Street	B3
Canon Street	C2	East Hill	C3	Middle Brook Street	B2	St. Peter Street	B2	Upper Brook Street	B2
Chesil Street	C3	Edgar Road	C1	North Walls	A1	St. Swithun Street	C2	Upper High Street	B1
Christchurch Road	C1	Fairfield Road	A1	Parchment Street	B2	St. Thomas Street	C2	Wales Street	B3
City Road	A1	Friarsgate	B2	Peninsula Square	B1	Silver Hill	B2	Worthy Lane	A1
Clifton Road	A1	Great Minster Street	B2	Quarry Road	C3	Southgate Street	C1		
Clifton Terrace	B1	High Street	B2	Romans' Road	C1	Staple Gardens	B2		
Colebrook Street	B2	Hyde Street	A2	Romsey Road	B1	Stockbridge Road	A1		

TOURIST INFORMATION ☎ 01962 840500
GUILDHALL, THE BROADWAY, WINCHESTER
HAMPSHIRE, SO23 9LJ

HOSPITAL A & E ☎ 01962 863535
ROYAL HAMPSHIRE COUNTY HOSPITAL,
ROMSEY ROAD, WINCHESTER, SO22 5DG

COUNCIL OFFICE ☎ 01962 840222
CITY OFFICES, COLEBROOK STREET,
WINCHESTER, SO23 9LJ

Winchester *Hants.* Population: 36,121. City, county town on River Itchen on site of Roman town of Venta Belgarum, 12m/19km N of Southampton. Ancient capital of Wessex and of Anglo-Saxon England. 11c cathedral, longest in Europe with carved Norman font and England's oldest complete choir-stalls. Winchester College, boys' public school founded 1382. 13c Great Hall is only remaining part of Winchester Castle. Westgate Museum is in 12c gatehouse in medieval city wall, once a debtors' prison. 12c hospital of St. Cross. City Mill (National Trust), built over river in 18c. To S across river, St. Catherine's Hill, Iron Age fort. Extensive ruins of medieval Wolvesey Castle, also known as Old Bishop's Palace (English Heritage), 1m/2km SE.

WINDSOR   Windsor & Maidenhead   STD Code 01753

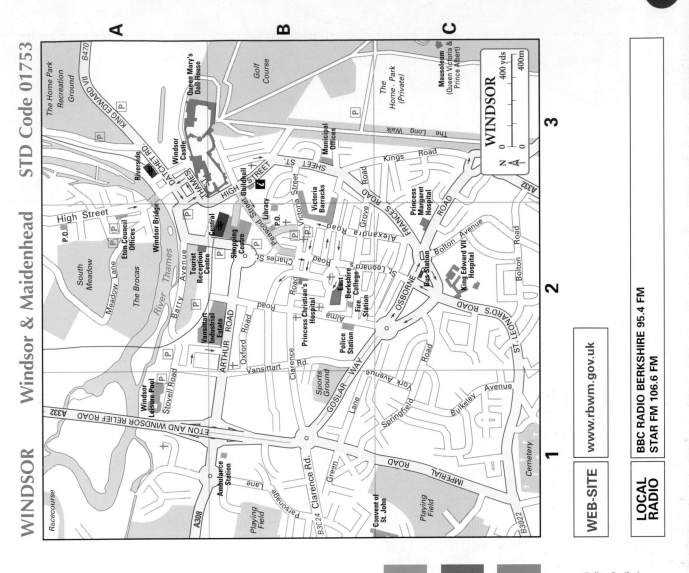

INDEX TO STREET NAMES

Alexandra Road	C2
Alma Road	B2
Arthur Road	B2
Barry Avenue	A2
Bolton Avenue	C2
Bolton Road	C2
Bulkeley Avenue	C1
Charles Street	B2
Clarence Road	B1
Datchet Road	A3
Eton & Windsor Relief Road	B1
Frances Road	C2
Goslar Way	B1
Green Lane	B1
Grove Road	B2
High Street (Eton)	A2
High Street (Windsor)	B3

Imperial Road	C1
King Edward VII Avenue	A3
Kings Road	C3
Meadow Lane	A2
Osborne Road	C2
Oxford Road	B2
Parsonage Lane	B1
Peascod Street	B2
St. Leonards Road	C2
Sheet Street	B3
Springfield Road	C1
Stovell Road	A1
Thames Street	A3
The Long Walk	C3
Vansittart Road	B2
Victoria Street	B2
York Avenue	C1

TOURIST INFORMATION ☎ 01753 743900
24 HIGH STREET,
WINDSOR, SL4 1LH

HOSPITAL A & E ☎ 01753 633000
WEXHAM PARK HOSPITAL, WEXHAM STREET,
SLOUGH, SL2 4HL

COUNCIL OFFICE ☎ 01753 810525
COUNCIL OFFICES, YORK HOUSE, SHEET STREET,
WINDSOR, SL4 1DD

WEB-SITE | www.rbwm.gov.uk

LOCAL RADIO | BBC RADIO BERKSHIRE 95.4 FM
STAR FM 106.6 FM

Windsor *W. & M.* Population: 26,339. Town, attractive market town on S bank of River Thames, 2m/3km S of Slough and 21m/34km W of London. Castle is royal residence. Great Park to S of town is open to public; Home Park bordering river is private. St. George's Chapel is impressive. Many Georgian houses, and guildhall designed by Sir Christopher Wren.

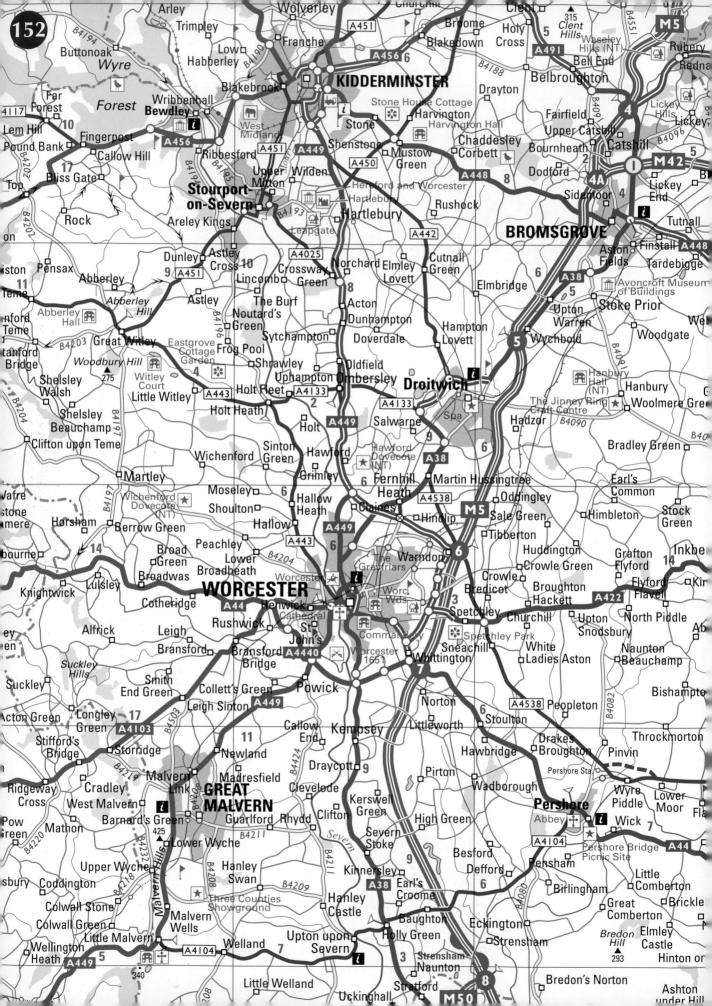

STD Code 01905

Worcestershire

WORCESTER

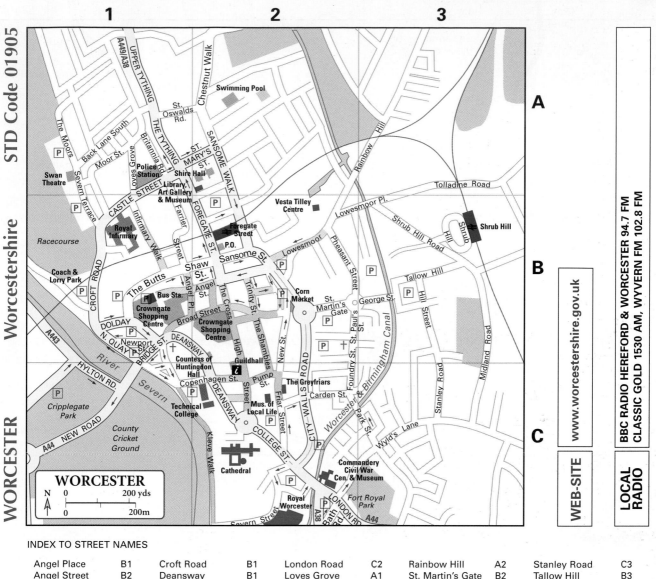

www.worcestershire.gov.uk

WEB-SITE

BBC RADIO HEREFORD & WORCESTER 94.7 FM
CLASSIC GOLD 1530 AM, WYVERN FM 102.8 FM

LOCAL RADIO

INDEX TO STREET NAMES

Angel Place	B1	Croft Road	B1	London Road	C2	Rainbow Hill	A2	Stanley Road	C3
Angel Street	B2	Deansway	B1	Loves Grove	A1	St. Martin's Gate	B2	Tallow Hill	B3
Back Lane South	A1	Dolday	B1	Lowesmoor	B2	St. Mary's Street	A1	The Butts	B1
Bath Road	C2	Farrier Street	B1	Lowesmoor Place	B2	St. Oswalds Road	A1	The Cross	B2
Bridge Street	B1	Foregate Street	B2	Midland Road	C3	St. Paul's Street	B2	The Moors	A1
Britannia Road	A1	Foundry Street	C2	Moor Street	A1	Sansome Street	B2	The Shambles	B2
Broad Street	B1	Friar Street	C2	Newport Street	B1	Sansome Walk	A2	The Tything	A1
Carden Street	C2	George Street	B3	New Road	C1	Severn Street	C2	Tolladine Road	A3
Castle Street	B1	High Street	B2	New Street	B2	Severn Terrace	A1	Trinity Street	B2
Chestnut Walk	A2	Hill Street	B3	North Quay	B1	Shaw Street	B1	Upper Tything	A1
City Walls Road	C2	Hylton Road	B1	Park Street	C3	Shrub Hill	B3	Wyld's Lane	C3
College Street	C2	Infirmary Walk	B1	Pheasant Street	B2	Shrub Hill Road	B3		
Copenhagen Street	C1	Kleve Walk	C2	Pump Street	C2	Sidbury	C2		

TOURIST INFORMATION ☎ 01905 726311
THE GUILDHALL, HIGH STREET,
WORCESTER, WR1 2EY

HOSPITAL A & E ☎ 01905 763333
WORCESTER ROYAL INFIRMARY, RONKSWOOD
HOSPITAL, NEWTOWN ROAD, WR5 1HN

COUNCIL OFFICE ☎ 01905 763763
COUNTY HALL, SPETCHLEY ROAD,
WORCESTER, WR1 2EY

Worcester *Worcs.* Population: 82,661. City, on River Severn, 24m/38km SW of Birmingham. Shopping, cultural, sports and industrial centre; industries include porcelain and sauces and condiments. 18c guildhall. Cathedral mainly Early English includes England's largest Norman crypt, 13c choir and Lady Chapel and tomb of King John. Three Choirs Festival held here every third year. Civil War Centre at the Commandery, headquarters for Charles II during Battle of Worcester. Factory tours and museum at Royal Worcester Porcelain. Elgar's Birthplace, home of composer Sir Edward Elgar, in Broadheath, 3m/5km W.

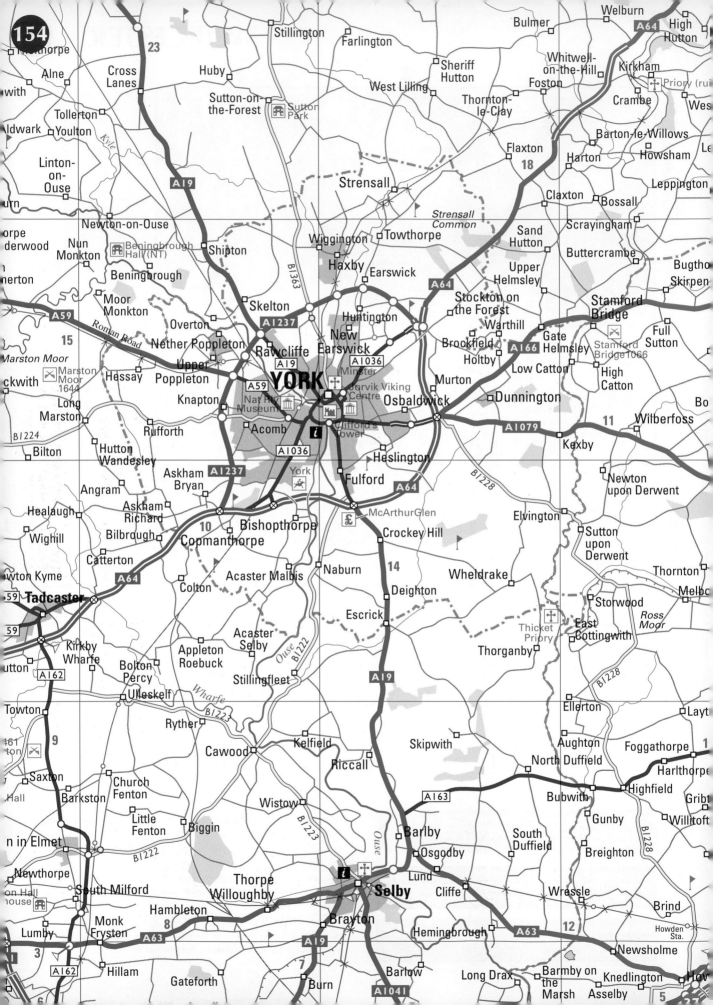

STD Code 01904

YORK

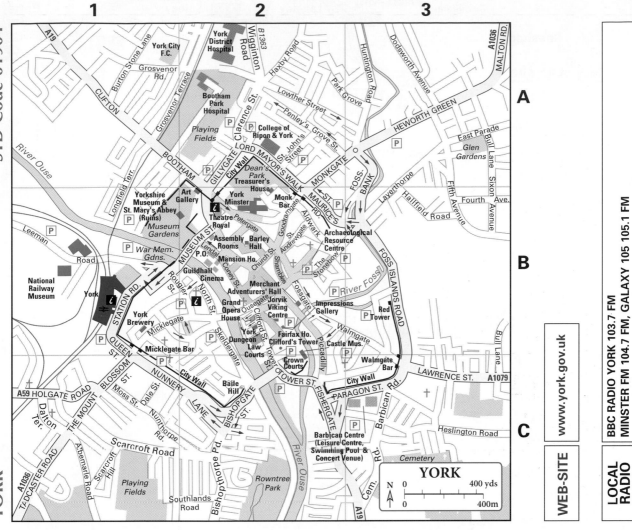

www.york.gov.uk

WEB-SITE

BBC RADIO YORK 103.7 FM
MINSTER FM 104.7 FM, GALAXY 105 105.1 FM

LOCAL RADIO

YORK

N
0   400 yds
0   400m

INDEX TO STREET NAMES

Albermarle Road	C1	Dale Street	C1	Heslington Road	C3	Museum Street	B2	Scarcroft Hill	C1
Aldwark	B2	Dalton Terrace	C1	Heworth Green	A3	North Street	B2	Scarcroft Road	C1
Barbican Road	C3	Dodsworth Avenue	A3	Holgate Road	C1	Nunnery Lane	C1	Shambles	B2
Bishopthorpe Road	C2	East Parade	A3	Huntington Road	A3	Nunthorpe Road	C1	Sixon Avenue	A3
Bishopgate Street	C2	Fifth Avenue	A3	Lawrence Street	C3	Ousegate	B2	Sixth Avenue	A3
Blossom Street	C1	Fishergate	C2	Layerthorpe	B3	Paragon Street	C2	Skeldergate	B2
Bootham	A1	Foss Bank	B3	Leeman Road	B1	Park Grove	A2	Southlands Road	C1
Bull Lane	A3/B3	Fossgate	B2	Lendal	B2	Penley's Grove		Station Road	B1
Burton Stone	A1	Foss Islands Road	B3	Longfield Terrace	B3	Street	A2	Tadcaster Road	C1
Lane		Fourth Avenue	B3	Lord Mayor's Walk	A2	Petergate	B2	The Mount	C1
Cemetery Road	C3	Gillygate	A2	Lowther Street	A2	Piccadilly	B2	The Stonebow	B2
Church Street	B2	Goodramgate	B2	Malton Road	A3	Queen Street	B1	Tower Street	B2
Clarence Street	A2	Grosvenor Road	A1	Maurices Road	B2	Rougier Street	B1	Walmgate	B2
Clifford Street	B2	Grosvenor Terrace	A1	Micklegate	B1	St. Andrewgate	B2	Wigginton Road	A2
Clifton	A1	Hallfield Road	B3	Monkgate	A2	St. John's Street	A2		
Coney Street	B2	Haxby Road	A2	Moss Street	C1	St. Maurice's Road	B2		

TOURIST INFORMATION ☎ 01904 554488
TIC TRAVEL OFFICE, 20 GEORGE HUDSON ST.,
YORK, YO1 6WR

HOSPITAL A & E ☎ 01904 631313
YORK DISTRICT HOSPITAL, WIGGINTON ROAD,
YORK, YO31 8HE

COUNCIL OFFICE ☎ 01904 613161
THE GUILDHALL,
YORK, YO1 9QN

York Population: 124,609. City, ancient city and archiepiscopal see on River Ouse, 22m/36km NE of Leeds. On site of Roman Eboracum. Constantine the Great proclaimed Roman Emperor in York in AD 306; only emperor to be enthroned in Britain. City fell to Danes in AD 867 and became known as Jorvik. Medieval wall largely intact, other fortifications including Clifford's Tower (English Heritage). York Minster has largest Medieval stained glass window in country. Previously a wool trading, craft and railway centre. Home to National Railway Museum. Jorvik Viking Centre in Coppergate. Merchant Adventurers' Hall in Fossgate is finest remaining guildhall in Europe. University of York at Heslington. Racecourse at Knavesmire.

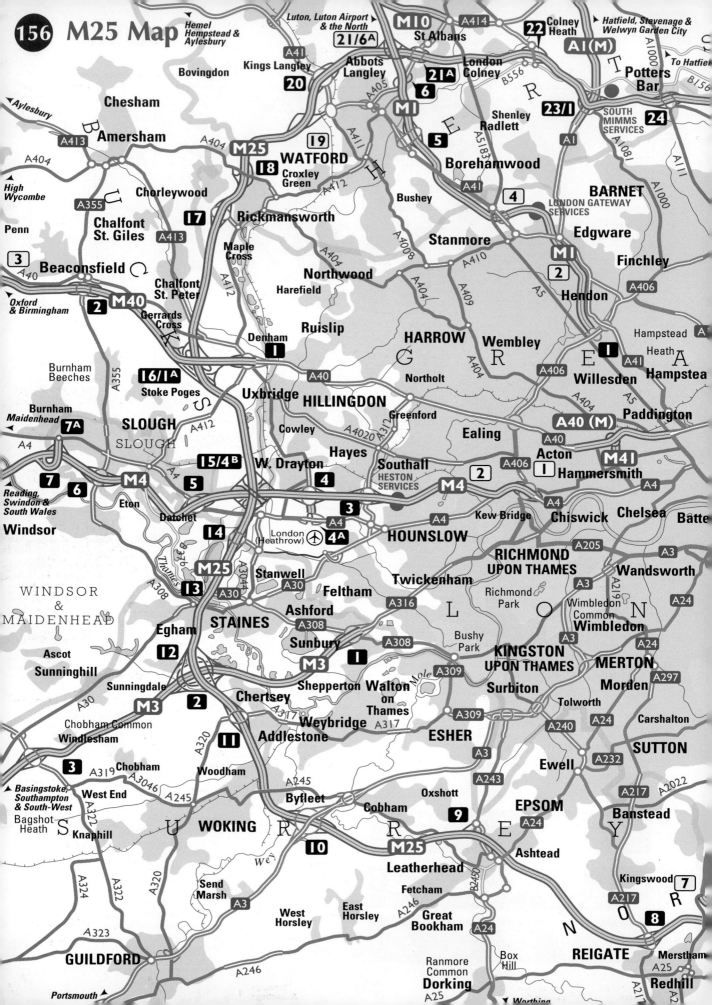

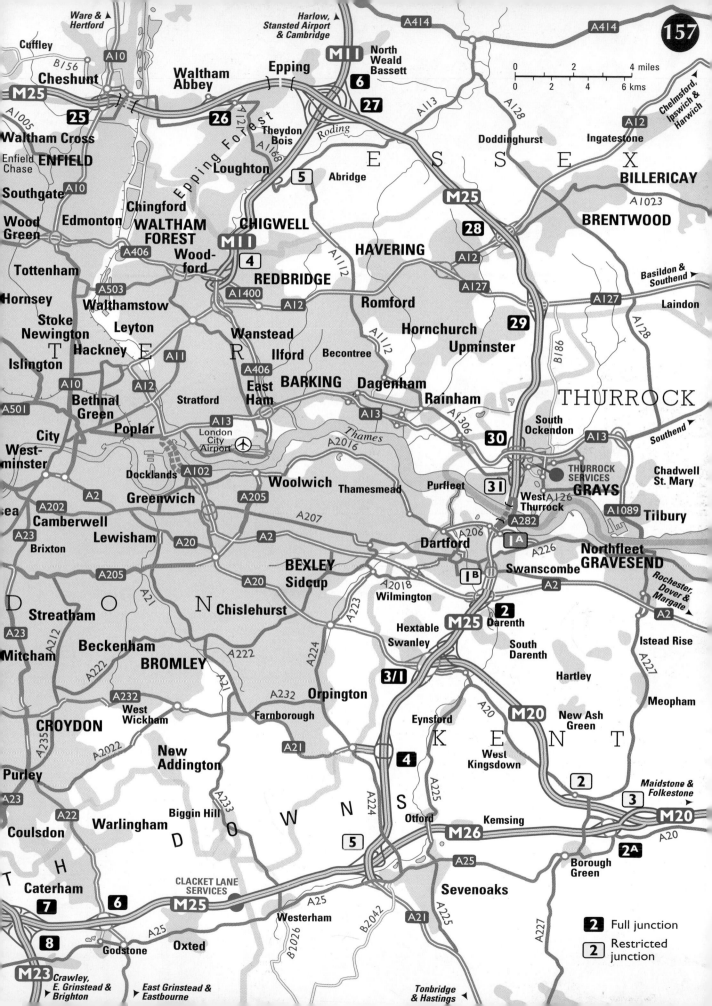

Abbreviations

All.	Alley	Church		Embk.	Embankment	Mkt.	Market
App.	Approach	Chyd.	Churchyard	Est.	Estate	Mkts.	Markets
Arc.	Arcade	Circ.	Circus	Flds.	Fields	Ms.	Mews
Ave.	Avenue	Clo.	Close	Gdn.	Garden	Pas.	Passage
Bdy.	Broadway	Cor.	Corner	Gdns.	Gardens	Pk.	Park
Bldgs.	Buildings	Cres.	Crescent	Grd.	Ground	Pl.	Place
Bri.	Bridge	Ct.	Court	Gro.	Grove	Rd.	Road
Cen.	Centre,	Ct.	Courtyard	Ho.	House	Ri.	Rise
Central Ch.		E.	East	La.	Lane	Sq.	Square

St.	Street, Saint
Ter.	Terrace
Twr.	Tower
Wf.	Wharf
Wk.	Walk
Yd.	Yard

Adam & Eve Ct. W1 158 B2
Adam St. WC2 158 F5
Addington St. SE1 159 H9
Addle Hill EC4 159 M4
Addle St. EC2 159 P1
Adelaide St. WC2 158 E5
Adeline Pl. WC1 158 D1
Adelphi Ter. WC2 158 F5
Agar St. WC2 158 E5
Air St. W1 158 B5
Alaska St. SE1 159 J7
Albany W1 158 A5
Albany Ctyd. W1 158 B5
Albion Way EC1 159 N1
Aldermanbury EC2 159 P2
Aldermanbury Sq. EC2 159 P1
Aldersgate St. EC1 159 N2
Aldwych WC2 158 G4
Ambassador's Ct. SW1 158 B7
Amen Cor. EC4 159 M3
Amen Ct. EC4 159 M2
America St. SE1 159 N7
Andrew Borde St. WC2 158 D2
Andrews Crosse WC2 159 J3
Angel Ct. SW1 158 B7
Angel St. EC1 159 N2
Apothecary St. EC4 159 L3
Apple Tree Yd. SW1 158 B6
Aquinas St. SE1 159 K7
Archer St. W1 158 C4
Arches, The WC2 158 F6
Argent St. SE1 159 M8
Argyll St. W1 158 A3
Arlington St. SW1 158 A6
Arne St. WC2 158 F3
Arundel Great Ct. WC2 159 H4
Arundel St. WC2 159 H4
Ashentree Ct. EC4 159 K3
Ave Maria La. EC4 159 M3
Avon Pl. SE1 159 P9
Ayres St. SE1 159 P8

B

Babmaes St. SW1 158 B5
Bainbridge St. WC1 158 D2
Banbury Ct. WC2 158 E4
Bank End SE1 159 P6
Bankside SE1 159 N5
Barge Ho. St. SE1 159 K6
Barley Mow Pas. EC1 159 M1
Barnard's Inn EC1 159 K2
Barons Pl. SE1 159 K9
Barter St. WC1 158 F1
Bartholomew Clo. EC1 159 N1
Bartholomew Pl. EC1 159 N1
Bartlett Ct. EC4 159 K2
Bartletts Pas. EC4 159 K2
Bateman St. W1 158 C3
Bateman's Bldgs. W1 158 C3
Bayley St. WC1 158 C1

Baylis Rd. SE1 159 J9
Beak St. W1 158 B4
Bear All. EC4 159 L2
Bear Gdns. SE1 159 N6
Bear La. SE1 159 M6
Bear St. WC2 158 D4
Beauchamp St. EC1 159 J1
Bedford Ave. WC1 158 D1
Bedford Ct. WC2 158 E5
Bedford Sq. WC1 158 D1
Bedford St. WC2 158 E4
Bedfordbury WC2 158 E4
Bell Wf. La. EC4 159 P4
Bell Yd. WC2 159 J2
Belvedere Bldgs. SE1 159 M9
Belvedere Pl. SE1 159 M9
Belvedere Rd. SE1 159 H8
Bennet's Hill EC4 159 M4
Bennett St. SW1 158 A6
Berners Ms. W1 158 B1
Berners Pl. W1 158 B2
Berners St. W1 158 B1
Berwick St. W1 158 C3
Betterton St. WC2 158 E3
Birdcage Wk. SW1 158 B9
Bishop's Ct. EC4 159 L2
Bishop's Ct. WC2 159 J2
Bittern St. SE1 159 N9
Black Friars Ct. EC4 159 L4
Black Friars La. EC4 159 L4
Blackfriars Bri. EC4 159 L4
Blackfriars Bri. SE1 159 L4
Blackfriars Pas. EC4 159 L4
Blackfriars Rd. SE1 159 L9
Bleeding Heart Yd. EC1 159 K1
Bloomsbury Ct. WC1 158 F1
Bloomsbury Sq. WC1 158 F1
Bloomsbury St. WC1 158 D1
Bloomsbury Way WC1 158 E2
Blore Ct. W1 158 C3
Blue Ball Yd. SW1 158 A7
Bolt Ct. EC4 159 K3
Book Ms. WC2 158 D3
Booth's Pl. W1 158 B1
Borough High St. SE1 159 N9
Borough Sq. SE1 159 N9
Boundary Row SE1 159 L8
Bourchier St. W1 158 C4
Bourlet Clo. W1 158 A1
Bouverie St. EC4 159 K3
Bow Chyd. EC4 159 P3
Bow La. EC4 159 P3
Bow St. WC2 158 F3
Boyce St. SE1 159 H7
Boyfield St. SE1 159 M9
Boyle St. W1 158 A4
Brad St. SE1 159 K7
Bread St. EC4 159 P3
Bream's Bldgs. EC4 159 J2
Brewer St. W1 158 B4
Brewers Hall Gdns. EC2 159 P1

Brick Ct. EC4 159 J3
Bride Ct. EC4 159 L3
Bride La. EC4 159 L3
Bridewell Pl. EC4 159 L3
Bridge St. SW1 158 E9
Bridle La. W1 158 B4
Brinton Wk. SE1 159 L7
Broad Ct. WC2 158 F3
Broad Sanctuary SW1 158 D9
Broadwall SE1 159 K6
Broadwick St. W1 158 B4
Broken Wf. EC4 159 N4
Brooke St. EC1 159 J1
Brownlow St. WC1 159 H1
Brydges Pl. WC2 158 E5
Buckingham Arc. WC2 158 F5
Buckingham Gate SW1 158 A9
Buckingham St. WC2 158 F5
Buckley St. SE1 159 J7
Bucknall St. WC2 158 D2
Bull Inn Ct. WC2 158 F5
Bull Wf. La. EC4 159 P4
Burgon St. EC4 159 M3
Burleigh St. WC2 158 G4
Burlington Arc. W1 158 A5
Burlington Gdns. W1 158 A5
Burrell St. SE1 159 L6
Burrows Ms. SE1 159 L8
Bury Pl. WC1 158 E1
Bury St. SW1 158 A6
Bywell Pl. W1 158 A1

C

Caleb St. SE1 159 N8
Cambridge Circ. WC2 158 D3
Candover St. W1 158 A1
Cannon St. EC4 159 N3
Canon Row SW1 158 E9
Canvey St. SE1 159 M6
Carey La. EC2 159 N2
Carey St. WC2 159 H3
Carlisle St. W1 158 C3
Carlton Gdns. SW1 158 C7
Carlton Ho. Ter. SW1 158 C7
Carlton St. SW1 158 C5
Carmelite St. EC4 159 K4
Carnaby St. W1 158 A3
Carter La. EC4 159 M3
Carteret St. SW1 158 C9
Carting La. WC2 158 F5
Castle Baynard St. EC4 159 M4
Castle Yd. SE1 159 M6
Cathedral Pl. EC4 159 N2
Catherine St. WC2 158 G4
Catherine Wheel Yd. SW1 158 A7
Catton St. WC1 158 G1
Cecil Ct. WC2 158 D5
Central Mkts. EC1 159 M1
Chancel St. SE1 159 L6
Chancery La. WC2 159 J2

Chandos Pl. WC2 158 E5
Chaplin Clo. SE1 159 K8
Chapone Pl. W1 158 C3
Chapter Ho. Ct. EC4 159 N3
Charing Cross SW1 158 E6
Charing Cross Rd. WC2 158 D2
Charles II St. SW1 158 C6
Charlotte Pl. W1 158 B1
Charlotte St. W1 158 B1
Charterhouse St. EC1 159 K1
Cheapside EC2 159 P3
Cheshire Ct. EC4 159 K3
Chicheley St. SE1 159 H8
Chichester Rents WC2 159 J2
Ching Ct. WC2 158 E3
Christ Ch. Pas. EC1 159 M2
Church Entry EC4 159 M3
Church Pl. SW1 158 B5
Clare Mkt. WC2 158 G3
Clement's Inn WC2 159 H3
Clement's Inn Pas. WC2 159 H3
Clennam St. SE1 159 P8
Cleveland Pl. SW1 158 B6
Cleveland Row SW1 158 A7
Clifford St. W1 158 A5
Clifford's Inn Pas. EC4 159 J3
Clink St. SE1 159 P6
Cloak La. EC4 159 P4
Cloth Ct. EC1 159 M1
Cloth Fair EC1 159 M1
Coach & Horses Yd. W1 158 A4
Cock La. EC1 159 L1
Cockpit Steps SW1 158 D9
Cockspur Ct. SW1 158 D6
Cockspur St. SW1 158 D6
Coin St. SE1 159 J6
Cole St. SE1 159 P9
College Hill EC4 159 P4
Collinson St. SE1 159 N9
Collinson Wk. SE1 159 N9
Colombo St. SE1 159 L7
Colville Pl. W1 158 B1
Concert Hall App. SE1 159 H7
Conduit Ct. WC2 158 E4
Cons St. SE1 159 K8
Cooper Clo. SE1 159 K9
Copperfield St. SE1 159 M8
Coptic St. WC1 158 E1
Coral St. SE1 159 K9
Cork St. W1 158 A5
Cork St. Ms. W1 158 A5
Corner Ho. St. WC2 158 E6
Cornwall Rd. SE1 159 J6
Covent Gdn. WC2 158 F4
Coventry St. W1 158 C5
Craigs Ct. SW1 158 E6
Cranbourn All. WC2 158 D4
Cranbourn St. WC2 158 D4
Crane Ct. EC4 159 K3
Craven Pas. WC2 158 E6
Craven St. WC2 158 E6
Creed La. EC4 159 M3

Cross Keys Sq. EC1 159 N1
Crown Ct. EC2 159 P3
Crown Ct. WC2 158 F3
Crown Office Row EC4 159 J4
Crown Pas. SW1 158 B7
Cubitts Yd. WC2 158 F4
Cursitor St. EC4 159 J2
Cut, The SE1 159 K8

D

Dane St. WC1 158 G1
Dansey Pl. W1 158 C4
D'Arblay St. W1 158 B3
Dartmouth St. SW1 158 C9
Davidge St. SE1 159 L9
Dean St. W1 158 C2
Deans Ct. EC4 159 M3
Denman St. W1 158 C5
Denmark Pl. WC2 158 D2
Denmark St. WC2 158 D3
Derby Gate SW1 158 E8
Devereux Ct. WC2 159 J3
Diadem Ct. W1 158 C3
Disney Pl. SE1 159 P8
Disney St. SE1 159 P8
Distaff La. EC4 159 N4
Dodson St. SE1 159 K9
Dolben St. SE1 159 L7
Dolby Ct. EC4 159 P4
Doon St. SE1 159 J7
Dorset Bldgs. EC4 159 L3
Dorset Ri. EC4 159 L3
Dover Yd. W1 158 A6
Downing St. SW1 158 E8
Doyce St. SE1 159 N8
Drake St. WC1 158 G1
Drury La. WC2 158 F3
Dryden St. WC2 158 F3
Duchy St. SE1 159 K6
Duck La. W1 158 C3
Dufour's Pl. W1 158 B3
Duke of York St. SW1 158 B6
Duke St. SW1 158 B6
Duncannon St. WC2 158 E5
Dunns Pas. WC1 158 F2
Durham Ho. St. WC2 158 F5
Dyer's Bldgs. EC1 159 J1
Dyott St. WC1 158 E2

E

Eagle Pl. SW1 158 B5
Eagle St. WC1 158 G1
Earlham St. WC2 158 D3
Earnshaw St. WC2 158 D2
East Harding St. EC4 159 K2
East Poultry Ave. EC1 159 L1
Eastcastle St. W1 158 A2
Elm Ct. EC4 159 J4
Ely Ct. EC1 159 K1
Ely Pl. EC1 159 K1
Embankment Pl. WC2 158 F6
Emerson St. SE1 159 N6
Endell St. WC2 158 E2

Essex Ct. EC4 159 J3
Essex St. WC2 159 J4
Evelyn Yd. W1 158 C2
Ewer St. SE1 159 N7
Excel Ct. WC2 158 D5
Exchange Ct. WC2 158 F5
Exeter St. WC2 158 F4
Exton St. SE1 159 J7

F
Falcon Clo. SE1 159 M6
Falcon Ct. EC4 159 J3
Falconberg Ct. W1 158 D2
Falconberg Ms. W1 158 C2
Fareham St. W1 158 C2
Farnham Pl. SE1 159 M7
Farringdon St. EC4 159 L2
Fetter La. EC4 159 K3
Field Ct. WC1 159 H1
Finck St. SE1 159 H9
Fisher St. WC1 158 G1
Flaxman Ct. W1 158 C3
Fleet St. EC4 159 J3
Flitcroft St. WC2 158 D2
Floral St. WC2 158 E4
Foley St. W1 158 A1
Fore St. EC2 159 P1
Foster La. EC2 159 N2
Foubert's Pl. W1 158 A3
Fountain Ct. EC4 159 J4
Frazier St. SE1 159 J9
Friar St. EC4 159 M3
Friary Ct. SW1 158 B7
Friday St. EC4 159 N3
Frith St. W1 158 C3
Fulwood Pl. WC1 159 H1
Furnival St. EC4 159 J2

G
Galen Pl. WC1 158 F1
Gambia St. SE1 159 M7
Ganton St. W1 158 A4
Garden Ct. EC4 159 J4
Gardners La. EC4 159 N4
Garlick Hill EC4 159 P4
Garrick St. WC2 158 E4
Gate St. WC2 158 G2
George Ct. WC2 158 F5
Gerrard Pl. W1 158 D4
Gerrard St. W1 158 C4
Gerridge St. SE1 159 K9
Gilbert Pl. WC1 158 E1
Giltspur St. EC1 159 M2
Glasshill St. SE1 159 M8
Glasshouse All. EC4 159 K3
Glasshouse St. W1 158 B5
Godliman St. EC4 159 N3
Golden Sq. W1 158 B4
Goldsmith St. EC2 159 P2
Goodge Pl. W1 158 B1
Goodge St. W1 158 B1
Goodwins Ct. WC2 158 E4
Gosfield St. W1 158 A1
Goslett Yd. WC2 158 D3
Gough Sq. EC4 159 K2
Gower Ms. WC1 158 C1
Grange Ct. WC2 159 H3
Grape St. WC2 158 E2
Gray St. SE1 159 K9
Gray's Inn Pl. WC1 159 H1
Great Chapel St. W1 158 C2
Great Dover St. SE1 159 P9
Great George St. SW1 158 D9
Great Guildford St. SE1 159 N6
Great Marlborough St. W1 158 A3
Great New St. EC4 159 K2
Great Pulteney St. W1 158 B4
Great Queen St. WC2 158 F3
Great Russell St. WC1 158 D2

Great St. Thomas Apostle EC4 159 P4
Great Scotland Yd. SW1 158 E7
Great Suffolk St. SE1 159 M7
Great Titchfield St. W1 158 A2
Great Trinity La. EC4 159 P4
Great Turnstile WC1 159 H1
Great Windmill St. 158 C4
Greek Ct. W1 158 D3
Greek St. W1 158 D3
Greek Yd. WC2 158 E4
Green Arbour Ct. EC1 159 L2
Greenham Clo. SE1 159 J9
Green's Ct. W1 158 C4
Greet St. SE1 159 K7
Gresham St. EC2 159 N2
Gresse St. W1 158 C1
Greville St. EC1 159 K1
Greyfriars Pas. EC1 159 M2
Greystoke Pl. EC4 159 J2
Grindal St. SE1 159 J9
Groveland Ct. EC4 159 P3
Gunpowder Sq. EC4 159 K2
Gutter La. EC2 159 P2

H
Half Moon Ct. EC1 159 N1
Ham Yd. W1 158 C4
Hand Ct. WC1 159 H1
Hanover Pl. WC2 158 F3
Hanway Pl. W1 158 C2
Hanway St. W1 158 C2
Hare Ct. EC4 159 J3
Hare Pl. EC4 159 K3
Harp All. EC4 159 L2
Hatfields SE1 159 K6
Haymarket SW1 158 C5
Haymarket Arc. SW1 158 C5
Heddon St. W1 158 A4
Henrietta St. WC2 158 F4
High Holborn WC1 158 F2
High Timber St. EC4 159 N4
Hills Pl. W1 158 A3
Hind Ct. EC4 159 K3
Holborn EC1 159 J1
Holborn Circ. EC1 159 K1
Holborn Pl. WC1 158 G1
Holborn Viaduct EC1 159 K1
Holland St. SE1 159 M6
Hollen St. W1 158 C2
Holmes Ter. SE1 159 J8
Honey La. EC2 159 P3
Hood Ct. EC4 159 K3
Hop Gdns. WC2 158 E5
Hopkins St. W1 158 B3
Hopton Gdns. SE1 159 M6
Hopton St. SE1 159 M6
Horse and Dolphin Yd. W1 158 D4
Horse Guards Ave. SW1 158 E7
Horse Guards Rd. SW1 158 D7
Horse Ride SW1 158 C7
Hosier La. EC1 159 L1
Houghton St. WC2 159 H3
Huggin Ct. EC4 159 P4
Huggin Hill EC4 159 P4
Hungerford Bri. SE1 158 F6
Hungerford Bri. WC2 158 F6
Hungerford La. WC2 158 E6
Hunt's Ct. WC2 158 D5
Hutton St. EC4 159 K3

I
India Pl. WC2 158 G4

Ingestre Pl. W1 158 B3
Inigo Pl. WC2 158 E4
Inner Temple La. EC4 159 J3
Invicta Plaza SE1 159 L6
Ireland Yd. EC4 159 M3
Irving St. WC2 158 D4
Isabella St. SE1 159 L7
Ivybridge La. WC2 158 F5

J
James St. WC2 158 F4
Jermyn St. SW1 158 A6
Joan St. SE1 159 L7
Johanna St. SE1 159 J9
John Adam St. WC2 158 F5
John Carpenter St. EC4 159 L4

K
Kean St. WC2 158 G3
Keeley St. WC2 158 G3
Kemble St. WC2 158 G3
Kemp's Ct. W1 158 B3
Kennet Wf. La. EC4 159 P4
Keppel Row SE1 159 N7
King Charles St. SW1 158 D8
King Edward St. EC1 159 N2
King James St. SE1 159 M9
King St. EC2 159 P3
King St. SW1 158 B7
King St. WC2 158 E4
Kinghorn St. EC1 159 N1
Kingly Ct. W1 158 A4
Kingly St. W1 158 A3
Kings Bench St. SE1 159 M8
Kings Bench Wk. EC4 159 K3
Kings Pl. SE1 159 N9
King's Reach Twr. SE1 159 K6
Kingscote St. EC4 159 L4
Kingsway WC2 158 G2
Kirkman Pl. W1 158 C1
Knightrider Ct. EC4 159 N4

L
Lambeth Hill EC4 159 N4
Lancaster Pl. WC2 158 G4
Lancaster St. SE1 159 M9
Langham St. W1 158 A1
Langley Ct. WC2 158 E4
Langley St. WC2 158 E3
Lant St. SE1 159 N8
Launcelot St. SE1 159 J9
Lavington St. SE1 159 M7
Lawrence La. EC2 159 P3
Laytons Bldgs. SE1 159 P8
Leake Ct. SE1 159 H9
Leake St. SE1 159 H8
Leather La. EC1 159 K1
Leicester Ct. WC2 158 D4
Leicester Pl. WC2 158 D4
Leicester Sq. WC2 158 D5
Leicester St. WC2 158 D4
Leigh Hunt St. SE1 159 N8
Lewisham St. SW1 158 D9
Lexington St. W1 158 B3
Library St. SE1 159 L9
Limeburner La. EC4 159 L3
Lincoln's Inn WC2 159 H2
Lincoln's Inn Flds. WC2 158 G2
Lisle St. WC2 158 D4
Litchfield St. WC2 158 D4
Little Argyll St. W1 158 A3
Little Britain EC1 159 M1
Little Dorrit Ct. SE1 159 P8
Little Essex St. WC2 159 J4
Little George St. SW1 158 E9
Little Marlborough St. W1 158 A3

Little New St. EC4 159 K2
Little Newport St. WC2 158 D4
Little Portland St. W1 158 A2
Little Russell St. WC1 158 E1
Little St. James's St. SW1 158 A7
Little Sanctuary SW1 158 D9
Little Titchfield St. W1 158 A1
Little Trinity La. EC4 159 P4
Little Turnstile WC1 158 G1
Livonia St. W1 158 B3
Loman St. SE1 159 M8
Lombard La. EC4 159 K3
London Wall EC2 159 P1
Long Acre WC2 158 E4
Long's Ct. WC2 158 C4
Love La. EC2 159 P2
Lower James St. W1 158 B4
Lower John St. W1 158 B4
Lowndes Ct. W1 158 A3
Ludgate Bdy. EC4 159 L3
Ludgate Circ. EC4 159 L3
Ludgate Hill EC4 159 L3
Ludgate Sq. EC4 159 M3
Lumley Ct. WC2 158 F5

M
Macclesfield St. W1 158 D4
Macklin St. WC2 158 F2
Magpie All. EC4 159 K3
Maiden La. SE1 159 P6
Maiden La. WC2 158 F5
Maidstone Bldgs. SE1 159 P7
Mall, The SW1 158 B8
Maltravers St. WC2 159 H4
Manette St. W1 158 D3
Margaret Ct. W1 158 A2
Marigold All. SE1 159 L5
Market Ct. W1 158 A2
Market Pl. W1 158 A2
Marlborough Ct. W1 158 A3
Marlborough Rd. SW1 158 B7
Marshall St. W1 158 B3
Marshalsea Rd. SE1 159 P8
Mart St. WC2 158 F3
Martlett Ct. WC2 158 F3
Marylebone Pas. W1 158 B2
Mason's Yd. SW1 158 B6
Matthew Parker St. SW1 158 D9
Matthews Yd. WC2 158 E3
Mays Ct. WC2 158 E5
McCoid Way SE1 159 N9
Meard St. W1 158 C3
Melbourne Pl. WC2 159 H4
Mepham St. SE1 159 H7
Mercer St. WC2 158 E3
Meymott St. SE1 159 L7
Middle Temple EC4 159 J4
Middle Temple La. EC4 159 J3
Middlesex Pas. EC1 159 M1
Middleton Bldgs. W1 158 A1
Milcote St. SE1 159 L9
Milford La. WC2 159 H4
Milk St. EC2 159 P3
Mill St. W1 158 A4
Millennium Mile SE1 158 G7
Miller Wk. SE1 159 K7
Milroy Wk. SE1 159 L6
Mint St. SE1 159 N8
Mitre Ct. EC2 159 P2
Mitre Ct. EC4 159 K3
Mitre Rd. SE1 159 K8

Monkwell Sq. EC2 159 P1
Monmouth St. WC2 158 E3
Montague St. EC1 159 N1
Montreal Pl. WC2 158 G4
Moor St. W1 158 D3
Mortimer St. W1 158 A1
Morwell St. WC1 158 D1
Mumford Ct. EC2 159 P2
Murphy St. SE1 159 J9
Museum St. WC1 158 E1

N
Nassau St. W1 158 A1
Neal St. WC2 158 E3
Neal's Yd. WC2 158 E3
Nelson Sq. SE1 159 L8
New Bri. St. EC4 159 L3
New Burlington Ms. W1 158 A4
New Burlington Pl. W1 158 A4
New Burlington St. W1 158 A4
New Change EC4 159 N3
New Compton St. WC2 158 D3
New Ct. EC4 159 J4
New Coventry St. WC2 158 D5
New Fetter La. EC4 159 K2
New Globe Wk. SE1 159 N6
New Inn Pas. WC2 159 H3
New Oxford St. WC1 158 D2
New Row WC2 158 E4
New Sq. WC2 159 H2
New St. Sq. EC4 159 K2
New Turnstile WC1 158 G1
Newburgh St. W1 158 A3
Newbury St. EC1 159 N1
Newcastle Clo. EC4 159 L2
Newgate St. EC1 159 M2
Newman Pas. W1 158 B1
Newman St. W1 158 B1
Newman Yd. W1 158 C2
Newman's Row WC2 159 H1
Newport Ct. WC2 158 D4
Newport Pl. WC2 158 D4
Newton St. WC2 158 F2
Nicholson St. SE1 159 L7
Noble St. EC2 159 N2
Noel St. W1 158 B3
Norris St. SW1 158 C5
Northumberland Ave. WC2 158 E6
Northumberland St. WC2 158 E6
Norwich St. EC4 159 J2
Nottingham Ct. WC2 158 E3

O
Oat La. EC2 159 N2
Odhams Wk. WC2 158 E3
Old Bailey EC4 159 M3
Old Barge Ho. All. SE1 159 J6
Old Bond St. W1 158 A5
Old Brewers Yd. WC2 158 E3
Old Bldgs. WC2 159 J2
Old Burlington St. W1 158 A4
Old Compton St. W1 158 C4
Old Fish St. Hill EC4 159 N4
Old Fleet La. EC4 159 L2
Old Queen St. SW1 158 D9
Old Seacoal La. EC4 159 L2
Old Sq. WC2 159 H2
O'Meara St. SE1 159 P7
Orange St. WC2 158 C5
Orange Yd. W1 158 D3
Ormond Yd. SW1 158 B6

Oxendon St. SW1 158 C5
Oxford Circ. Ave. 158 A3
W1
Oxford St. W1 158 B2

P

Pageantmaster Ct. 159 L3
EC4
Pall Mall SW1 158 B7
Pall Mall E. SW1 158 D6
Pall Mall Pl. SW1 158 B7
Palmer St. SW1 158 C9
Pancras La. EC4 159 P3
Panton St. SW1 158 C5
Panyer All. EC4 159 N2
Paris Gdn. SE1 159 L6
Park Pl. SW1 158 A7
Park St. SE1 159 N6
Parker Ms. WC2 158 F2
Parker St. WC2 158 F2
Parliament Sq. SW1 158 E9
Parliament St. SW1 158 E9
Paternoster Row 159 N3
EC4
Paternoster Sq. EC4 159 M2
Paul's Wk. EC4 159 M4
Peabody Est. SE1 159 K7
Peabody Sq. SE1 159 L9
Peabody Trust SE1 159 N7
Pear Pl. SE1 159 J8
Pemberton Row 159 K2
EC4
Pepper St. SE1 159 N8
Percy Ms. W1 158 C1
Percy Pas. W1 158 B1
Percy St. W1 158 C1
Perkins Sq. SE1 159 P6
Perrys Pl. W1 158 C2
Peter St. W1 158 B4
Peters Hill EC4 159 N4
Phoenix St. WC2 158 D3
Piccadilly Arc. SW1 158 A6
Piccadilly Circ. W1 158 C5
Piccadilly Pl. W1 158 B5
Pickering Pl. SW1 158 B7
Pickwick St. SE1 159 N9
Pilgrim St. EC4 159 L3
Playhouse Yd. EC4 159 L3
Pleydell Ct. EC4 159 K3
Pleydell St. EC4 159 K3
Plough Pl. EC4 159 K2
Plumtree Ct. EC4 159 K2
Pocock St. SE1 159 L8
Poland St. W1 158 B3
Pollen St. W1 158 A3
Pontypool Pl. SE1 159 L8
Poppins Ct. EC4 159 L3
Porter St. SE1 159 P6
Portland Ms. W1 158 B3
Portsmouth St. 158 G3
WC2
Portugal St. WC2 158 G3
Priest Ct. EC2 159 N2
Primrose Hill EC4 159 K3
Prince's Arc. SW1 158 B6
Princes Pl. SW1 158 B6
Printer St. EC4 159 K2
Printers Inn Ct. EC4 159 J2
Procter St. WC1 158 G1
Prudent Pas. EC2 159 P2
Puddle Dock EC4 159 M4
Pump Ct. EC4 159 J3

Q

Quadrant Arc. W1 158 B5
Quality Ct. WC2 159 J2
Queen Anne's Gate 158 C9
SW1
Queen St. EC4 159 P4
Queen St. Pl. EC4 159 P5
Queen Victoria St. 159 M4
EC4
Queenhithe EC4 159 P4
Queen's Wk. SW1 158 A7
Quilp St. SE1 159 N8

R

Ramillies Pl. W1 158 A3
Ramillies St. W1 158 A3
Rathbone Pl. W1 158 C2
Rathbone St. W1 158 B1
Red Lion Ct. EC4 159 K2
Red Lion Sq. WC1 158 G1
Redcross Way SE1 159 P8
Regent Pl. W1 158 B4
Regent St. SW1 158 C5
Remnant St. WC2 158 G2
Rennie St. SE1 159 L6
Richmond Bldgs. 158 C3
W1
Richmond Ms. W1 158 C3
Richmond Ter. SW1 158 E8
Riding Ho. St. W1 158 A1
Risborough St. SE1 159 M8
Rising Sun Ct. EC1 159 M1
Riverside Wk. SE1 158 G7
Robert St. WC2 158 F5
Rolls Bldgs. EC4 159 J2
Rolls Pas. EC4 159 J2
Romilly St. W1 158 C4
Rose All. SE1 159 P6
Rose & Crown Ct. 159 N2
EC2
Rose & Crown Yd. 158 B6
SW1
Rose St. WC2 158 E4
Rotherham Wk. SE1 159 L7
Roupell St. SE1 159 K7
Royal Arc. W1 158 A5
Royal Opera Arc. 158 C6
SW1
Royalty Ms. W1 158 C3
Rupert Ct. W1 158 C4
Rupert St. W1 158 C4
Rushworth St. SE1 159 M8
Russell Ct. SW1 158 B7
Russell St. WC2 158 F4
Russia Ct. EC2 159 P2
Russia Row EC2 159 P3
Ryder Ct. SW1 158 B6
Ryder St. SW1 158 B6
Ryder Yd. SW1 158 B6

S

Sackville St. W1 158 B5
St. Albans St. SW1 158 C5
St. Alphage Gdns. 159 P1
EC2
St. Andrew St. EC4 159 K1
St. Andrew's Hill 159 M4
EC4
St. Anne's Ct. W1 158 C3
St. Bride St. EC4 159 L2
St. Bride's Pas. EC4 159 L3
St. Clement's La. 159 H3
WC2
St. Georges Ct. EC4 159 L2
St. Giles High St. 158 D2
WC2
St. Giles Pas. WC2 158 D3
St. James's Mkt. 158 C5
SW1
St. James's Palace 158 B8
SW1
St. James's Pk. SW1 158 C8
St. James's Pl. SW1 158 A7
St. James's Sq. SW1 158 B6
St. James's St. SW1 158 A6
St. Margaret's Ct. 159 P7
SE1
St. Margaret's St. 158 E9
SW1
St. Martin's La. WC2 158 E4
St. Martin's Ms. 158 E5
WC2
St. Martin's Pl. WC2 158 E5
St. Martin's St. WC2 158 D5
St. Martin's-le- 159 N2
Grand EC1
St. Paul's Chyd. EC4 159 M3
Salisbury Ct. EC4 159 L3

Salisbury Sq. EC4 159 K3
Sanctuary, The SW1 158 D9
Sanctuary St. SE1 159 P9
Sandell St. SE1 159 J8
Sandland St. WC1 159 H1
Sardinia St. WC2 158 G3
Savile Row W1 158 A4
Savoy Bldgs. WC2 158 G5
Savoy Ct. WC2 158 F5
Savoy Hill WC2 158 G5
Savoy Pl. WC2 158 F5
Savoy Row WC2 158 G4
Savoy St. WC2 158 G4
Savoy Way WC2 158 G5
Sawyer St. SE1 159 N8
Scoresby St. SE1 159 L7
Scotland Pl. SW1 158 E6
Scovell Cres. SE1 159 N9
Scovell Rd. SE1 159 N9
Secker St. SE1 159 J7
Serjeants Inn EC4 159 K3
Serle St. WC2 159 H2
Sermon La. EC4 159 N3
Shaftesbury Ave. 158 C4
W1
Shaftesbury Ave. 158 C4
WC2
Shavers Pl. SW1 158 C5
Sheffield St. WC2 158 G3
Shelton St. WC2 158 E3
Sheraton St. W1 158 C3
Sherwood St. W1 158 B4
Shoe La. EC4 159 K2
Short St. SE1 159 K8
Shorts Gdns. WC2 158 E3
Sicilian Ave. WC1 158 F1
Silex St. SE1 159 M9
Silver Pl. W1 158 B4
Silvester St. SE1 159 P9
Skinners La. EC4 159 P4
Slingsby Pl. WC2 158 E4
Smart's Pl. WC2 158 F2
Smithfield St. EC1 159 L1
Smith's Ct. W1 158 B4
Snow Hill EC1 159 L1
Snow Hill Ct. EC1 159 M2
Soho Sq. W1 158 C2
Soho St. W1 158 C2
South Cres. WC1 158 C1
South Sq. WC1 159 J1
Southampton 159 J2
Bldgs. WC2
Southampton Pl. 158 F1
WC1
Southampton St. 158 F4
WC2
Southwark Bri. EC4 159 P6
Southwark Bri. SE1 159 P6
Southwark Gro. SE1 159 N7
Southwark St. SE1 159 M6
Spring Gdns. SW1 158 D6
Spur Rd. SE1 159 J8
Spur Rd. SW1 158 A9
Stable Yd. SW1 158 A8
Stable Yd. Rd. SW1 158 A7
Stacey St. WC2 158 D3
Stafford St. W1 158 A6
Staining La. EC2 159 P2
Stamford St. SE1 159 J7
Staple Inn WC1 159 J1
Staple Inn Bldgs. 159 J1
WC1
Star Yd. WC2 159 J2
Station App. SE1 159 H9
Stedham Pl. WC1 158 E2
Stephen Ms. W1 158 C1
Stephen St. W1 158 C1
Stew La. EC4 159 N4
Stone Bldgs. WC2 159 H1
Stonecutter St. EC4 159 L2
Stones End St. SE1 159 N9
Store St. WC1 158 C1
Storey's Gate SW1 158 D9
Strand WC2 158 E5
Strand La. WC2 159 H4

Streatham St. WC1 158 D2
Stukeley St. WC2 158 F2
Sturge St. SE1 159 N8
Sudrey St. SE1 159 N9
Suffolk Pl. SW1 158 D6
Suffolk St. SW1 158 D6
Sumner St. SE1 159 M6
Surrey Row SE1 159 L8
Surrey St. WC2 159 H4
Sutton Row W1 158 D2
Swallow St. W1 158 B5

T

Tallis St. EC4 159 K4
Tanswell Est. SE1 159 K9
Tanswell St. SE1 159 J9
Tavistock St. WC2 158 F4
Temple Ave. EC4 159 K4
Temple La. EC4 159 K3
Temple Pl. WC2 159 H4
Tenison Ct. W1 158 A4
Tenison Way SE1 159 J7
Thames Path SE1 159 K5
Thavies Inn EC1 159 K2
Theed St. SE1 159 J7
Thrale St. SE1 159 P7
Three Barrels Wk. 159 P4
EC4
Three Cups Yd. 159 H1
WC1
Took's Ct. EC4 159 J2
Tothill St. SW1 158 C9
Tottenham St. W1 158 B1
Toulmin St. SE1 159 N9
Tower Ct. WC2 158 E3
Tower Royal EC4 159 P4
Tower St. WC2 158 D3
Trafalgar Sq. SW1 158 D6
Trafalgar Sq. WC2 158 D6
Treveris St. SE1 159 L7
Trig La. EC4 159 N4
Trinity St. SE1 159 P9
Trio Pl. SE1 159 P9
Trump St. EC2 159 P3
Trundle St. SE1 159 N8
Tudor Pl. W1 158 C2
Tudor St. EC4 159 K4
Turnagain La. EC4 159 L2
Tweezer's All. WC2 159 J4
Twyford Pl. WC2 158 G2
Tyler's Ct. W1 158 C3

U

Ufford St. SE1 159 K8
Union St. SE1 159 M7
Upper Grd. SE1 159 J6
Upper James St. 158 B4
W1
Upper John St. W1 158 B4
Upper St. Martin's 158 E4
La. WC2
Upper Thames St. 159 M4
EC4

V

Valentine Pl. SE1 159 L8
Valentine Row SE1 159 L9
Vernon Pl. WC1 158 F1
Victoria Embk. EC4 158 G5
Victoria Embk. SW1 158 F8
Victoria Embk. WC2 158 G5
Vigo St. W1 158 A5
Villiers St. WC2 158 E5
Vine St. W1 158 B5
Vine Yd. SE1 159 P8

W

Waithman St. EC4 159 L3
Walkers Ct. W1 158 C4
Wallis All. SE1 159 P9
Wardens Gro. SE1 159 N7
Wardour Ms. W1 158 B3
Wardour St. W1 158 C4
Wardrobe Pl. EC4 159 M4
Wardrobe Ter. EC4 159 M4

Warwick Ct. WC1 159 H1
Warwick Ho. St. 158 D6
SW1
Warwick La. EC4 159 M3
Warwick Pas. EC4 159 M2
Warwick Sq. EC4 159 M2
Warwick St. W1 158 B4
Water St. WC2 159 H4
Watergate EC4 159 K4
Watergate Wk. WC2 158 F6
Waterhouse Sq. 159 J1
EC1
Waterloo Bri. SE1 158 G5
Waterloo Bri. WC2 158 G5
Waterloo Pl. SW1 158 C6
Waterloo Rd. SE1 159 J8
Watling Ct. EC4 159 P3
Watling St. EC4 159 N3
Waxwell Ter. SE1 159 H9
Webber St. SE1 159 K8
Wedgwood Ms. W1 158 D3
Well Ct. EC4 159 P3
Weller St. SE1 159 N8
Wellington St. WC2 158 F4
Wells Ms. W1 158 B2
Wells St. W1 158 A1
West Cen. St. WC1 158 E2
West Harding St. 159 K2
EC4
West Poultry Ave. 159 L1
EC1
West Smithfield EC1 159 L1
West St. WC2 158 D3
Westminster Bri. 158 F9
SE1
Westminster Bri. 158 F9
SW1
Westminster Bri. 159 H9
Rd. SE1
Whetstone Pk. WC2 158 G2
Whichcote St. SE1 159 J7
Whitcomb St. WC2 158 D5
White Lion Hill EC4 159 M4
Whitefriars St. EC4 159 K3
Whitehall SW1 158 E6
Whitehall Ct. SW1 158 E7
Whitehall Gdns. 158 E7
SW1
Whitehall Pl. SW1 158 E7
Whitfield St. W1 158 C1
Whittlesey St. SE1 159 J7
Wild Ct. WC2 158 G2
Wild St. WC2 158 F3
William IV St. WC2 158 E5
Willoughby St. WC1 158 E1
Windmill St. W1 158 C1
Windmill Wk. SE1 159 K8
Wine Office Ct. EC4 159 K2
Winnett St. W1 158 C4
Winsley St. W1 158 B2
Wood St. EC2 159 P3
Wootton St. SE1 159 K8

Y

York Bldgs. WC2 158 F5
York Pl. WC2 158 F5
York Rd. SE1 159 H9
Yorkshire Grey 158 G1
Yd. WC1

Z

Zoar St. SE1 159 N6

Abbreviations

Aber.	Aberdeenshire	Glos.	Gloucestershire	Northumb.	Northumberland	Stir.	Stirling
Arg. & B.	Argyll & Bute	Gt.Lon.	Greater London	Norf.	Norfolk	Suff.	Suffolk
B'burn.	Blackburn with Darwen	Gt.Man.	Greater Manchester	Northants.	Northamptonshire	Surr.	Surrey
Beds.	Bedfordshire	Hants.	Hampshire	Notts.	Nottinghamshire	Swan.	Swansea
Brack.F.	Bracknell Forest	Here.	Herefordshire	Ork.	Orkney	Swin.	Swindon Borough
Bucks.	Buckinghamshire	Herts.	Hertfordshire	Oxon.	Oxfordshire	T. & W.	Tyne & Wear
Caerp.	Caerphilly	High.	Highland	P. & K.	Perth & Kinross	Tel. & W.	Telford & Wrekin
Cambs.	Cambridgeshire	I.o.M.	Isle of Man	Pembs.	Pembrokeshire	Thur.	Thurrock
Ches.	Cheshire	I.o.W.	Isle of Wight	Peter.	Peterborough	V. of Glam.	Vale of Glamorgan
Cornw.	Cornwall	Lancs.	Lancashire	R.C.T.	Rhondda Cynon Taff	W'ham	Wokingham
Cumb.	Cumbria	Leics.	Leicestershire	Renf.	Renfrewshire	W. & M.	Windsor & Maidenhead
D. & G.	Dumfries & Galloway	Lincs.	Lincolnshire	S.Ayr.	South Ayrshire	W.Isles	Western Isles (Na h-Eileanan an Iar)
Derbys.	Derbyshire	M.K.	Milton Keynes	S.Glos.	South Gloucestershire	W.Loth.	West Lothian
Dur.	County Durham	Med.	Medway	S.Lan.	South Lanarkshire	W.Mid.	West Midlands
E.Ayr.	East Ayrshire	Mersey.	Merseyside	S.Yorks.	South Yorkshire	W.Suss.	West Sussex
E.Loth.	East Lothian	Midloth.	Midlothian	Sc.Bord.	Scottish Borders	W.Yorks.	West Yorkshire
E.Riding	East Riding of Yorkshire	Mon.	Monmouthshire	Shet.	Shetland	Warks.	Warwickshire
		N.Lan.	North Lanarkshire	Shrop.	Shropshire	Warr.	Warrington
E.Suss.	East Sussex	N.Lincs.	North Lincolnshire	Slo.	Slough	Wilts.	Wiltshire
Edin.	City of Edinburgh	N.P.T.	Neath & Port Talbot	Som.	Somerset	Worcs.	Worcestershire
Flints.	Flintshire	N.Yorks.	North Yorkshire	Staffs.	Staffordshire	Wrex.	Wrexham

Abbeytown	29	E2	Adderbury	15	D2	Altrincham	25	E4	
Abbots Bromley	20	C3	Addingham	25	F2	Alva	38	B4	
Abbotsbury	8	A4	Addlestone	10	A2	Alvechurch	14	B1	
Aberaeron	12	B3	Adlington	25	D3	Alveley	20	A4	
Aberaman	7	D1	Adwick le Street	26	B3	Alves	42	B2	
Aberavon	6	C1	Ainsdale	24	C3	Alveston	14	A4	
Abercanaid	7	E1	Aintree	24	C4	Alvie	42	A4	
Aberchirder	43	D2	Aird Asaig	47	D3	Alyth	39	D2	
Abercynon	7	E1	Aird of Sleat	40	B4	Ambergate	21	D2	
Aberdare	7	D1	Airdrie	34	A2	Amble	35	F4	
Aberdaron	18	A3	Airidh a'Bhruaich	47	E2	Amblecote	20	B4	
Aberdeen	43	F4	Airth	34	A1	Ambleside	29	F4	
Aberdeen Airport	43	E4	Airton	25	E1	Ambrosden	15	E3	
Aberdour	34	B1	Aith Ork.	49	F2	Amersham	15	F3	
Aberdyfi	12	C1	Aith Shet.	48	B3	Amesbury	8	C2	
Aberfeldy	38	B2	Akeld	35	E3	Amlwch	18	B1	
Abertffraw	18	A2	Albrighton	20	B3	Ammanford	6	C1	
Aberfoyle	38	A4	Alcester	14	C1	Ampthill	15	F2	
Abergavenny	7	E1	Aldbourne	14	C4	Amulree	38	B3	
Abergele	19	D1	Aldbrough	27	D2	An t-Ob	47	D4	
Abergynolwyn	12	C1	Aldeburgh	17	F2	An Tairbeart	47	E3	
Aberkenfig	7	D2	Aldenham	16	A4	Ancaster	21	F2	
Aberlady	34	C1	Alderbury	8	C2	Ancroft	35	E2	
Aberlemno	39	E2	Alderholt	8	C3	Ancrum	35	D3	
Aberlour	42	C3	Alderley Edge	20	B1	Andover	9	D1	
Abernethy	38	C4	Aldershot	9	F1	Andreas	24	B2	
Aberporth	12	A3	Aldingham	24	C1	Angle	12	A2	
Abersoch	18	A3	Aldington	11	E3	Angmering	10	A4	
Abersychan	7	E1	Aldridge	20	B4	Anlaby	27	D3	
Abertillery	7	E1	Alexandria	33	E1	Annan	29	E1	
Aberuthven	38	C4	Alford Aber.	43	D4	Annbank	33	E3	
Aberystwyth	12	C2	Alford Lincs.	22	B1	Annfield Plain	30	C2	
Abhainnsuidhe	47	D3	Alfreton	21	D1	Anstey	21	D3	
Abingdon	15	D4	Allanton N.Lan.	34	A2	Anstruther	39	E4	
Abington	34	A3	Allendale Town	30	B2	Aoradh	32	A2	
Aboyne	43	D4	Allenheads	30	B2	Appleby Magna	20	C3	
Abram	25	D4	Allhallows	11	D1	Appleby	30	A3	
Accrington	25	E3	Allnabad	44	C2	-in-Westmorland			
Achadh Mór	47	E2	Alloa	34	A1	Applecross	40	C3	
Achahoish	32	C1	Allonby	29	E2	Appledore Devon	6	B4	
Acharacle	36	C2	Alloway	33	E3	Appledore Kent	11	E3	
Achavanich	45	E2	Almondsbury	14	A4	Appleton Thorn	19	F1	
Achfary	44	B2	Alness	42	A2	Appley Bridge	25	D3	
Achiltibuie	44	A3	Alnmouth	35	F4	Arbirlot	39	E3	
Achintee	41	D1	Alnwick	35	F4	Arbroath	39	E3	
Achnacroish	37	D3	Alresford	17	D3	Ardchiavaig	36	B4	
Achnasheen	41	E2	Alrewas	20	C3	Arden	33	E1	
Achosnich	36	C2	Alsager	20	A1	Ardentinny	33	E1	
Achriesgill	44	B2	Alston	30	A2	Ardeonaig	38	A3	
Ackworth Moor Top	26	A3	Altnafeadh	37	F2	Ardersier	42	A2	
			Altnaharra	44	C2	Ardfern	37	D4	
Acle	23	F3	Alton Hants.	9	F2	Ardgay	44	C4	
Acomb	30	B1	Alton Staffs.	20	C2	Ardleigh	17	D3	

Ardlui	37	F4	Attleborough Norf.	23	D4				
Ardlussa	32	B1	Attlebridge	23	E3				
Ardmair	41	D1	Auchallater	38	C1				
Ardminish	32	B2	Auchenblae	39	E1				
Ardmolich	37	D1	Auchenbreck	33	D1				
Ardrishaig	32	C1	Auchencairn	29	D2				
Ardrossan	33	E3	Auchencrow	35	E2				
Ardtalnaig	38	A3	Auchindrain	37	E4				
Ardtoe	36	C2	Auchinleck	33	F3				
Ardvasar	40	C4	Auchmull	39	E1				
Arinagour	36	B2	Auchnagatt	43	F3				
Arisaig	36	C1	Aucholzie	39	D1				
Armadale	34	A1	Auchterarder	38	B4				
Armitage	20	C3	Auchtermuchty	39	D4				
Armthorpe	26	B4	Auchtertool	34	B1				
Arncliffe	25	E1	Audlem	20	A2				
Arnisdale	40	C4	Audley	20	A2				
Arnol	47	E1	Aughton Lancs.	24	C4				
Arnold	21	E2	Aughton S.Yorks.	26	A4				
Arnprior	38	A4	Auldearn	42	B2				
Arrochar	37	F4	Aultbea	41	D1				
Arundel	10	A4	Aultguish Inn	41	E2				
Ascot	9	F1	Aveley	10	C1				
Asfordby	21	E3	Aviemore	42	B4				
Ash Kent	11	F2	Avoch	42	A2				
Ash Surr.	9	F1	Avonbridge	34	A1				
Ashbourne	20	C2	Avonmouth	7	F2				
Ashburton	5	D2	Awre	14	A3				
Ashbury	14	C4	Awsworth	21	D2				
Ashby de la Zouch	21	D3	Axminster	5	F1				
Ashchurch	14	B2	Aycliffe	31	D3				
Ashcott	7	F3	Aylesbury	15	E3				
Ashford Kent	11	E2	Aylesford	11	D2				
Ashford Surr.	10	A1	Aylesham	11	F2				
Ashington	31	D1	Aylsham	23	E3				
Ashkirk	34	C3	Ayr	33	E3				
Ashley Cambs.	16	C1	Aysgarth	30	C4				
Ashton	19	F2							
Ashton-in-Makerfield	25	D4							
Ashton-under-Lyne	25	E4	**B**						
Ashurst E.Suss.	10	C3	Babworth	26	B4				
Ashurst Hants.	9	D3	Backaland	49	E2				
Ashwick	8	A1	Backwell	7	F2				
Askern	26	B3	Bacup	25	E3				
Aspatria	29	E2	Badcaul	41	D1				
Aston Clinton	15	F3	Badenscoth	43	E3				
Aston on Trent	21	D2	Badlipster	45	F2				
Astwood Bank	14	B1	Badsey	14	B2				
Atherington	6	C4	Bagh a'Chaisteil (Castlebay)	46	A4				
Atherstone	20	C4	Bagillt	19	E1				
Atherton	25	D4	Baglan	6	C1				
Attadale	41	D3	Bagshot	9	F1				

Name	Pg	Grid
Baildon	25	F2
Baile Ailein	47	E2
Baile a'Mhanaich	46	A2
Baile Mhartainn	46	A1
Baile Mòr	36	B3
Bainbridge	30	B4
Bainton	26	C2
Bala	19	D3
Balbeggie	38	C3
Balblair	42	A2
Balcombe	10	B3
Balderton	21	E2
Baldock	16	A2
Baldslow	11	D4
Balemartine	36	A3
Balephuil	36	A3
Balfour	49	E3
Balfron	33	F1
Balgown	40	B2
Balgray	39	D3
Balintore	42	A2
Ballabeg	24	A3
Ballachulish	37	E2
Ballantrae	28	A1
Ballasalla	24	A3
Ballater	39	D1
Ballaugh	24	A2
Ballingry	38	C4
Ballinluig	38	C2
Ballintuim	38	C2
Balloch	33	E1
Ballochroy	32	C2
Ballygrant	32	A2
Balmacara	40	C3
Balmaha	33	E1
Balmedie	43	F4
Balnacra	41	D3
Balnahard	36	C3
Balnapaling	42	A2
Balquhidder	38	A3
Baltasound	48	C1
Balvicar	37	D4
Bamburgh	35	F3
Bampton *Devon*	7	D4
Bampton *Oxon.*	14	C3
Banbury	15	D2
Banchory	39	E1
Banff	43	E2
Bangor	18	B1
Banham	23	D4
Bankfoot	38	C3
Bannockburn	34	A1
Banstead	10	B2
Banwell	7	F3
Bar Hill	16	B1
Barabhas	47	E1
Barassie	33	E3
Barbaraville	42	A2
Barbon	25	D1
Barby	15	D1
Bardney	22	A1
Bardsea	24	C1
Bargoed	7	E1
Bargrennan	28	B1
Barham	11	F2
Barkston	21	F2
Barkway	16	B2
Barlaston	20	B2
Barlborough	21	D1
Barley	16	B2
Barmouth	12	C1
Barnard Castle	30	C3
Barningham	17	D1
Barnoldswick	25	E2
Barnsley	26	A4
Barnstaple	6	C4
Barnton	20	A1
Barr	33	E4
Barrapol	36	A3
Barrhead	33	F2
Barrhill	28	B1
Barrock	45	F1
Barrow upon Humber	27	D3
Barrow upon Soar	21	E3
Barrow-in-Furness	24	B1
Barrowford	25	E2
Barry	7	E2
Barton (Preston) *Lancs.*	25	D2
Barton-le-Clay	16	A3
Barton-under-Needwood	20	C3
Barton-upon-Humber	27	D3
Baschurch	19	F3
Basildon	11	D1
Basingstoke	9	E1
Baslow	20	C1
Bassingham	21	F1
Bath	8	B1
Batheaston	8	B1
Bathford	8	B1
Bathgate	34	A1
Batley	25	F3
Battle	11	D4
Bawdeswell	23	D3
Bawdsey	17	E2
Bawtry	26	B4
Baycliff	24	C1
Bayston Hill	13	F1
Beaconsfield	10	A1
Beadnell	35	F3
Beaminster	5	F1
Bearsden	33	F1
Bearsted	11	D2
Beattock	34	B4
Beauly	41	F3
Beaumaris	18	B1
Bebington	19	E1
Beccles	23	F4
Beckingham	26	C4
Bedale	31	D4
Beddau	7	D2
Beddgelert	18	B2
Beddingham	10	C4
Bedford	15	F2
Bedlington	30	C1
Bedwas	7	E2
Bedworth	21	D4
Beeford	27	D2
Beer	5	E1
Beeston *Notts.*	21	D2
Beighton *S.Yorks.*	26	A4
Beith	33	E2
Belbroughton	20	B4
Belford	35	F3
Bellingham	30	B1
Bellshill *N.Lan.*	33	F2
Belmont *Shet.*	48	C1
Belper	21	D2
Belsay	30	C1
Bembridge	9	E4
Bempton	27	D1
Benenden	11	D3
Benllech	18	B1
Benson	15	E4
Bentley *S.Yorks.*	26	B4
Bere Alston	4	B2
Bere Ferrers	4	B2
Bere Regis	8	B3
Berinsfield	15	D4
Berkeley	14	A3
Berkhamsted	15	F3
Berkswell	20	C4
Bernisdale	40	B2
Berriedale	45	E3
Berrow	7	E3
Bersham	19	E2
Berwick-upon-Tweed	35	E2
Bessacarr	26	B4
Bethersden	11	E3
Bethesda	18	B2
Bettyhill	44	C1
Betws-y-coed	18	C2
Beverley	27	D2
Bewdley	20	A4
Bexhill	11	D4
Bibury	14	C3
Bicester	15	E3
Bickleigh (Plymouth) *Devon*	4	C2
Bickleigh (Tiverton) *Devon*	5	D1
Bicknacre	16	C4
Biddenden	11	D3
Biddulph	20	B1
Bideford	6	B4
Bidford-on-Avon	14	C1
Bigbury-on-Sea	4	C3
Biggar	34	A3
Biggin Hill	10	C2
Biggleswade	16	A2
Bilbster	45	F2
Billericay	16	C4
Billinge	25	D4
Billingham	31	D3
Billinghay	22	A2
Billingshurst	10	A3
Billockby	23	F3
Billy Row	30	C2
Bilston *Midloth.*	34	B2
Bilton	27	D3
Bimbister	49	E3
Binbrook	27	D4
Binfield	9	F1
Bingham	21	E2
Bingley	25	F2
Birchgrove *N.P.T.*	6	C1
Birchington	11	F1
Bircotes	26	B4
Birkenhead	19	E1
Birmingham	20	C4
Birmingham International Airport		
Birsay	49	D2
Birstall	21	E3
Birtley *T. & W.*	31	D2
Bishop Auckland	30	C3
Bishopbriggs	33	F1
Bishop's Castle	13	F2
Bishop's Cleeve	14	B2
Bishop's Hull	7	E4
Bishop's Itchington	15	D1
Bishop's Lydeard	7	E4
Bishop's Stortford	16	B3
Bishop's Tawton	6	C4
Bishop's Waltham	9	E3
Bishopston	6	C1
Bishopton *Renf.*	33	F1
Bisley	14	B3
Bitton	8	A1
Bixter	48	B3
Blaby	21	D4
Black Bourton	14	C3
Black Notley	16	C3
Blackburn *Aber.*	43	E4
Blackburn *B'burn.*	25	D3
Blackburn *W.Loth.*	34	A2
Blackford	38	B4
Blackhall Colliery	31	D2
Blacklunans	38	C2
Blackmoor Gate	6	C3
Blackpool	24	C2
Blackpool Airport	24	C3
Blackridge	34	A1
Blackwaterfoot	32	C3
Blackwood	7	E1
Blaenau Ffestiniog	18	C2
Blaenavon	7	E1
Blaengarw	7	D1
Blaengwrach	7	D1
Blagdon	7	F3
Blaich	37	E1
Blaina	7	E1
Blair Atholl	38	B2
Blairgowrie	38	C3
Blakeney *Glos.*	14	A3
Blakeney *Norf.*	23	D2
Blandford Forum	8	B3
Blaydon	30	C1
Blean	11	E2
Bletchley	15	F2
Blewbury	15	D4
Blisworth	15	E1
Blockley	14	C2
Bloxham	15	D2
Blubberhouses	25	F2
Blyth *Northumb.*	31	D1
Blyth *Notts.*	26	B4
Blyth Bridge	34	B2
Blyton	26	C4
Boat of Garten	42	B4
Boath	41	F2
Boddam *Aber.*	43	F3
Boddam *Shet.*	48	B4
Bodelwyddan	19	D1
Bodenham	13	F3
Bodicote	15	D2
Bodmin	4	A2
Bogniebrae	43	D3
Bognor Regis	9	F3
Boldon	31	D2
Boldre	9	D3
Bollington (Macclesfield) *Ches.*	20	B1
Bolnhurst	16	A1
Bolsover	21	D1
Boltby	31	D4
Bolton *E.Loth.*	34	C1
Bolton *Gt.Man.*	25	D3
Bolton-le-Sands	24	C1
Bolventor	4	A2
Bonar Bridge	44	C4
Bonawe	37	E3
Bonawe Quarries	37	E3
Bonchester Bridge	35	D4
Bo'ness	34	A1
Bonjedward	35	D3
Bonnybridge	34	A1
Bonnyrigg	34	C2
Bonvilston	7	E2
Bootle *Cumb.*	29	E4
Bootle *Mersey.*	19	E1
Boreham	16	C3
Borehamwood	16	A4
Boreland	34	B4
Boreraig	40	A2
Borgh	46	A4
Borgue *D. & G.*	28	C2
Borgue *High.*	45	E3
Borough Green	10	C2
Boroughbridge	26	A1
Borrowash	21	D2
Borrowdale	29	F3
Borth	12	C2
Borve	40	B3
Bosbury	14	A2
Boscastle	4	A1
Bosham	9	F3
Boston	22	A2
Boston Spa	26	A2
Botesdale	17	D1
Bothel	29	E2
Bothenhampton	5	F1
Bottesford *Leics.*	21	E2
Bottesford *N.Lincs.*	26	C3
Boughton	21	E1
Bourne	22	A3
Bourne End *Bucks.*	15	F4
Bournemouth	8	C3
Bournemouth International Airport		
Bournmoor	31	D2
Bourton	8	B2
Bourton-on-the-Water	14	C3
Bovey Tracey	5	D2
Bow	49	E4
Bowburn	31	D2
Bowes	30	B3
Bowmore	32	A2
Bowness-on-Solway	29	E1
Bowness-on-Windermere	29	F4
Box	8	B1
Bozeat	15	F1
Braaid	24	A3
Bracadale	40	A3
Bracebridge Heath	21	F1
Brackley	15	E2
Bracknell	9	F1
Braco	38	B4
Bracora	37	D1
Bradford *W.Yorks.*	25	F2
Bradford-on-Avon	8	B1
Brading	9	E4
Bradninch	5	E1
Bradpole	5	F1
Bradshaw	25	D3
Bradwell *Derbys.*	25	F4
Bradwell *Norf.*	23	F4
Bradwell Waterside	17	D3
Brae	48	B2
Braeantra	41	F1
Braemar	38	C1
Bragar	47	E1
Brailsford	20	C2
Braintree	16	C3
Braithwaite	29	E3
Braithwell	26	B4
Bramford	17	E2
Bramhall	25	E4
Bramley *S.Yorks.*	26	A4
Brampton *Cambs.*	16	A1
Brampton *Cumb.*	30	A2
Brampton *Suff.*	17	F1
Brancaster	22	C2
Brandesburton	27	D2
Brandon *Dur.*	30	C2
Brandon *Suff.*	22	C4
Branston	21	F1
Brantham	17	E2
Bratton	8	B1
Braunston	15	D1
Braunstone	21	D3
Braunton	6	B4
Bray	10	A1
Brayton	26	B3
Breage	3	E3
Breakish	40	C4
Bream	14	A3
Breanais	47	D2
Breascleit	47	E2
Breaston	21	D2
Brechfa	12	B4
Brechin	39	E2
Brecon	13	D4
Bredbury	25	E4
Bredon	14	B2
Brentwood	10	C1
Bretton	19	E2
Brewood	20	B3
Bridge	11	E2
Bridge of Allan	38	B4
Bridge of Balgie	38	A2
Bridge of Cally	38	C2
Bridge of Craigisla	39	D2
Bridge of Don	43	F4
Bridge of Dun	39	E2
Bridge of Dye	39	E1
Bridge of Earn	38	C4
Bridge of Orchy	37	F3
Bridge of Walls	48	B3
Bridge of Weir	33	E2
Bridgend Angus	39	E2
Bridgend *Bridgend*	7	D2
Bridgend Moray	42	C3
Bridgend (Islay) *Arg. & B.*	32	A2
Bridgend (Lochgilphead) *Arg. & B.*	32	C1
Bridgnorth	20	A4
Bridgwater	7	E4

Place	Page	Grid
Bridlington	27	D1
Bridport	5	F1
Brierfield	25	E2
Brig o'Turk	38	A4
Brigg	26	C3
Brigham	29	E3
Brighouse	25	F3
Brighstone	9	D4
Brightlingsea	17	D3
Brighton	10	B4
Brigstock	21	F4
Brimington	21	D1
Brinian	49	E2
Brinsley	21	D2
Brinsworth	26	A4
Bristol	14	A4
Bristol International Airport	7	F2
Briston	23	D3
Briton Ferry	6	C1
Brixham	5	D3
Brixworth	15	E1
Broad Haven	12	A2
Broad Oak	11	D3
Broadclyst	5	D1
Broadford	40	C4
Broadheath	14	A1
Broadmayne	8	B4
Broadstairs	11	F2
Broadway	14	C2
Broadwey	8	A4
Broadwindsor	5	F1
Brochel	40	B3
Brockenhurst	9	D3
Brockworth	14	B3
Brodick	33	D3
Bromham *Beds.*	15	F1
Bromham *Wilts.*	8	C1
Brompton	31	D4
Brompton on Swale	30	C4
Bromsgrove	14	B1
Bromyard	14	A1
Bronaber	18	C3
Brooke	23	E4
Brookmans Park	16	A4
Broomfield	16	C3
Brora	45	D4
Broseley	20	A4
Brotton	31	E3
Brough *Cumb.*	30	B3
Brough *E.Riding*	26	C3
Brough *High.*	45	E1
Brough *Shet.*	48	C2
Broughton *Flints.*	19	E2
Broughton *N.Lincs.*	26	E3
Broughton *Northants.*	21	F4
Broughton *Sc.Bord.*	34	B3
Broughton Astley	21	D4
Broughton in Furness	29	E4
Broughtown	49	F2
Broughty Ferry	39	E3
Brownhills *W.Mid.*	20	B3
Broxburn	34	B1
Brundall	23	E3
Brundish	17	E1
Bruton	8	A2
Brynamman	6	C1
Brynford	19	E1
Brynmawr	7	E1
Bubwith	26	B2
Buchlyvie	33	F1
Buckden *Cambs.*	16	A1
Buckden *N.Yorks.*	25	E1
Buckfastleigh	4	C2
Buckhaven	39	D4
Buckie	43	D2
Buckingham	15	E2
Bucklebury	9	E1
Buckley	19	E2
Bucksburn	43	E4
Bude	4	A1
Budleigh Salterton	5	E2
Bugbrooke	15	E1
Builth Wells	13	D3
Buldoo	45	E1
Bulford	8	C2
Bulkington *Warks.*	21	D4
Bulmer Tye	17	D2
Bunessan	36	B3
Bungay	23	E4
Buntingford	16	B3
Burbage	9	D1
Bures	17	D2
Burford	14	C3
Burgess Hill	10	B3
Burgh by Sands	29	F2
Burgh le Marsh	22	B1
Burghead	42	B2
Burghfield Common	9	E1
Burghill	13	F3
Burley	9	D3
Burley in Wharfdale	25	F2
Burness	49	F2
Burnham *Bucks.*	10	A1
Burnham Market	22	C2
Burnham-on-Crouch	17	D4
Burnham-on-Sea	7	E3
Burnhouse	33	E2
Burniston	31	F4
Burnley	25	E2
Burnmouth	35	E2
Burnopfield	30	C2
Burntisland	34	B1
Burntwood Green	20	C3
Burravoe	48	C2
Burrelton	38	C3
Burry Port	6	B1
Burscough	24	C3
Burscough Bridge	24	C3
Bursledon	9	E3
Burslem	20	B2
Burton Bradstock	5	F1
Burton Joyce	21	E2
Burton Latimer	15	F1
Burton Leonard	26	A1
Burton upon Stather	26	C3
Burton upon Trent	20	C3
Burton-in-Kendal	25	D1
Burwardsley	19	F2
Burwarton	20	A4
Burwash	11	D3
Burwell	16	B1
Burwick	49	E4
Bury	25	E3
Bury St. Edmunds	17	D1
Bushey	16	A4
Buttermere	29	E3
Butterwick	26	C1
Buxted	10	C3
Buxton	20	B1
Byfield	15	D1
Byfleet	10	A2
Bylchau	19	D2

C

Place	Page	Grid
Caerau *Cardiff*	7	E2
Caergwrle	19	E2
Caerhun	18	C1
Caerleon	7	F1
Caernarfon	18	B2
Caerphilly	7	E2
Caerwent	7	F1
Cairnbaan	32	C1
Cairndow	37	E4
Cairneyhill	34	A1
Cairnryan	28	A1
Caister-on-Sea	23	F3
Caistor	27	D4
Calanais	47	E2
Caldbeck	29	F2
Caldecott	21	F4
Caldercruix	34	A1
Caldicot	7	F2
Caldwell	30	C3
Calfsound	49	E2
Calgary	36	B2
Callander	38	A4
Callington	4	B2
Calne	14	B4
Calver	20	C1
Calverton	21	E2
Calvine	38	B2
Cam	14	A3
Camasnacroise	37	D2
Camberley	9	F1
Camborne	3	E3
Cambridge	16	B2
Cambridge Airport	16	B2
Camelford	4	A2
Campbeltown	32	C3
Camptown	35	D4
Camrose	12	A1
Cannich	41	E3
Cannington	7	E3
Cannock	20	B3
Canonbie	29	F1
Canterbury	11	E2
Canton	7	E2
Canvey Island	11	D1
Caolas	36	A2
Caolas Scalpaigh	47	E3
Capel	10	B3
Capel Curig	18	C2
Capel St. Mary	17	D2
Cappercleuch	34	B3
Capplegill	34	B4
Caputh	38	C3
Carbost (Loch Harport) *High.*	40	B3
Carbost (Loch Snizort Beag) *High.*	40	B3
Carcroft	26	B3
Cardenden	39	D4
Cardiff	7	E2
Cardiff International Airport	7	D2
Cardigan	12	A3
Cardross	33	E1
Cargenbridge	29	D1
Cargill	38	C3
Carlabhagh	47	E1
Carlisle	29	F2
Carlops	34	B2
Carlton *Notts.*	21	E2
Carlton Colville	23	F4
Carlton in Lindrick	26	B4
Carlton-on-Trent	21	E1
Carluke	34	A2
Carmarthen	12	B4
Carmyllie	39	E3
Carnbee	39	E4
Carnbo	38	C4
Carnforth	24	C1
Carno	13	D1
Carnoustie	39	E3
Carnwath	34	A2
Carradale	32	C3
Carrbridge	42	B4
Carronbridge	34	A4
Carsaig	36	C3
Carsluith	28	C2
Carspairn	33	F4
Carstairs	34	A2
Carterton	14	C3
Cartmel	24	C1
Castle Bromwich	20	C4
Castle Carrock	30	A2
Castle Cary	8	A2
Castle Donnington	21	D3
Castle Douglas	29	D2
Castle Kennedy	28	A2
Castlebay (Bagh a Chaisteil)	46	A4
Castleford	26	A3
Castlemartin	12	A2
Castleside	30	C2
Castleton *N.Yorks.*	31	E4
Castletown *High.*	45	E1
Castletown *I.o.M.*	24	A3
Caterham	10	B2
Caton	25	D1
Catrine	33	F3
Catshill	14	B1
Catterick	30	C4
Catterick Camp	30	C4
Caverswall	20	B2
Cawdor	42	A2
Cawood	26	B2
Cawston	23	E3
Caythorpe	21	F2
Cayton	27	D1
Ceann a'Bháigh	46	A1
Cearsiadar	47	E2
Cefn-mawr	19	E2
Ceres	39	D4
Cerrigydrudion	19	D2
Chadderton	25	E4
Chagford	4	C1
Chailey	10	B3
Chalfont St. Giles	10	A1
Chalford	14	B3
Chalgrove	15	E4
Champany	34	A1
Chapel St. Leonards	22	B1
Chapel-en-le-Frith	25	F4
Chapelhall	34	A2
Chapeltown *S.Yorks.*	26	A4
Chard	5	F1
Chardstock	5	F1
Charfield	14	A4
Charing	11	E2
Charlbury	15	D3
Charlestown	43	F4
Charlesworth	25	E4
Charlton *Hants.*	9	D1
Charlton *Wilts.*	14	B4
Charlton Kings	14	B3
Charlwood	10	B3
Charminster	8	A3
Charmouth	5	F1
Chartham	11	E2
Chatham	11	D2
Chatteris	22	B4
Chatton	35	E3
Cheadle *Gt.Man.*	25	E4
Cheadle *Staffs.*	20	B2
Checkley *Staffs.*	20	B2
Chedburgh	16	C2
Cheddar	7	F3
Cheddleton	20	B2
Chelmorton	20	C1
Chelmsford	16	C3
Cheltenham	14	B3
Chepstow	7	F1
Cherlton	9	E2
Chertsey	10	A2
Chesham	15	F3
Cheshunt	16	B4
Chester	19	F2
Chester-le-Street	31	D2
Chesterfield *Derbys.*	21	D1
Chesters	35	D4
Chew Magna	8	A1
Chichester	9	F3
Chickerell	8	A4
Chiddingfold	9	F2
Chieveley	15	D4
Chigwell	10	C1
Chilcompton	8	A1
Childrey	15	D4
Chilham	11	E2
Chilton	31	D3
Chingford	10	B1
Chinnor	15	E3
Chippenham	14	B4
Chipping Campden	14	C2
Chipping Norton	14	C2
Chipping Ongar	16	B4
Chipping Sodbury	14	A4
Chirbury	13	E1
Chirk	19	E3
Chirnside	35	E2
Chiseldon	14	C4
Chopwell	30	C2
Chorley	25	D3
Chorleywood	15	F4
Christchurch *Dorset*	8	C4
Christon Bank	35	F3
Chryston	33	F1
Chudleigh	5	D2
Chulmleigh	6	C4
Church Aston	20	A3
Church Lawton	20	B1
Church Stretton	13	F1
Churchdown	14	B3
Cilcain	19	E2
Cille Bhrighde	46	A3
Cinderford	14	A3
Cirencester	14	B3
Clabhach	36	A2
Clachan (Kintyre) *Arg. & B.*	32	C2
Clachan (Loch Fyne) *Arg. & B.*	37	E4
Clachan (Raasay) *High.*	40	B3
Clachan of Glendaruel	33	D1
Clachtoll	44	A3
Clackmannan	34	A1
Clacton-on-Sea	17	E3
Cladich	37	E3
Claggan	37	D2
Clanfield *Oxon.*	14	C3
Claonaig	32	C2
Clapham *Beds.*	15	F1
Clapham *N.Yorks.*	25	D1
Clarborough	26	B4
Clare	16	C2
Clashmore	42	A1
Clashnessie	44	A3
Clavering	16	B3
Clay Cross	21	D1
Claydon	17	E2
Claypole	21	F2
Clayton *W.Suss.*	10	B4
Clayton West	25	F3
Clayton-le-Moors	25	D3
Clayton-le-Woods	25	D3
Cleadale	36	C1
Cleadon	31	D1
Cleat	49	E4
Cleator Moor	29	E3
Cleckheaton	25	F3
Cleehill	14	A1
Cleethorpes	27	E3
Clehonger	13	F4
Cleland	34	A2
Clenchwarton	22	B3
Clent	20	B4
Cleobury Mortimer	14	A1
Clestrain	49	D3
Clevedon	7	F2
Cleveleys	24	C2
Cliffe	11	D1
Cliffe Woods	11	D1
Clipstone	21	E1
Clitheroe	25	D2
Closeburn	34	A4
Cloughton	31	F4
Clova	39	D1
Clovelly	6	B4
Clovenfords	34	C3
Clovullin	37	E2
Clowne	21	D1
Clun	13	E2
Clunes	37	E1
Clutton	8	A1

Clydach	6	C1
Clydach Vale	7	D1
Clydebank	33	F1
Clynderwen	12	A4
Clyro	13	E3
Coalburn	34	A3
Coalville	21	D3
Coast	41	D1
Coatbridge	33	F2
Cobham *Surr.*	10	A2
Cock Bridge	42	C4
Cockburnspath	35	D1
Cockenzie & Port Seton	34	C1
Cockerham	24	C2
Cockermouth	29	E3
Cockett	6	C1
Cockfield	30	C3
Coddenham	17	E2
Coddington	21	F1
Codicote	16	A3
Codnor	21	D2
Codsall	20	B3
Coggeshall	17	D3
Colchester	17	D3
Colden Common	9	E2
Coldingham	35	E2
Coldstream	35	E3
Coleford	14	A3
Colehill	8	C3
Coleshill *Warks.*	20	C4
Colintraive	33	D1
Collafirth	48	B2
Collieston	43	F3
Collin	29	E1
Collingham	21	F1
Colmonell	28	A1
Colnabaichin	42	C4
Colnbrook	10	A1
Colne	25	E2
Colney Heath	16	A4
Colquhar	34	C2
Colsterworth	21	F3
Coltishall	23	E3
Colwich	20	B3
Colwick	21	E2
Colwyn Bay	18	C1
Colyford	5	E1
Colyton	5	E1
Combe Martin	6	C3
Combe St. Nicholas	7	E4
Comberton	16	B2
Comrie	38	B3
Congdon's Shop	4	B2
Congleton	20	B1
Congresbury	7	F2
Coningsby	22	A2
Conisbrough	26	A4
Coniston	29	F4
Connah's Quay	19	E1
Connel	37	D3
Conon Bridge	41	F2
Consett	30	C2
Constantine	3	E3
Contin	41	F2
Conwy	18	C1
Cookham	15	F4
Cookley *Worcs.*	20	B4
Coombe Bissett	8	C2
Copley	30	C3
Copplestone	5	D1
Coppull	25	D3
Copythorne	9	D3
Corbridge	30	B1
Corby	21	F4
Corfe Castle	8	C4
Corfe Mullen	8	C3
Cornhill	43	D2
Cornhill-on-Tweed	35	E3
Cornholme	25	E3
Corpach	37	E1
Corrie	33	D3
Corringham	11	D1
Corsham	8	B1
Corsock	29	D1
Corton	23	F4
Corwen	19	D2
Coryton	11	D1
Cosby	21	D4
Coshieville	38	B2
Cotgrave	21	E2
Cottenham	16	B1
Cottesmore	21	F3
Cottingham *E.Riding*	27	D2
Cottingham *Northants.*	21	F4
Coulport	33	E1
Coundon	30	C3
Coupar Angus	39	D3
Cove *Arg. & B.*	33	E1
Cove *High.*	40	C1
Cove Bay	43	F4
Coventry	21	D4
Coverack	3	F4
Cowbit	22	A3
Cowbridge	7	D2
Cowdenbeath	34	B1
Cowes	9	E3
Cowfold	10	B3
Cowie	34	A1
Cowling	25	E2
Cowshill	30	B2
Coxheath	11	D2
Coxwold	26	B1
Coychurch	7	D2
Coylton	33	E3
Coylumbridge	42	B4
Cradley *Here.*	14	A2
Craichie	39	E2
Craig	41	D3
Craigandaive	33	D1
Craigdarroch	33	F4
Craigellachie	42	C3
Craigendoran	33	E1
Craighat	33	F1
Craignure	37	D3
Crail	39	E4
Cramlington	31	D1
Cramond	34	B1
Cranage	20	A1
Cranfield	15	F2
Cranleigh	10	A3
Cranshaws	35	D2
Cranwell	21	F2
Crask Inn	44	C3
Craster	35	F3
Crathie	39	D1
Craven Arms	13	F2
Crawfordjohn	34	A3
Crawley	10	B3
Creag Ghoraidh	46	B2
Credenhill	13	F3
Crediton	5	D1
Creetown	28	C2
Cregneash	24	A3
Creswell	21	D1
Crewe	20	A1
Crewkerne	5	F1
Crianlarich	37	F3
Criccieth	18	B3
Crickhowell	13	E4
Cricklade	14	C4
Crieff	38	B3
Crigglestone	26	A3
Crimond	43	F2
Crinan	37	D4
Cringleford	23	E4
Cripp's Corner	11	D3
Crocketford or Ninemile Bar	29	D1
Croeserw	7	D1
Crofton	26	A3
Crofty	6	B1
Cromarty	42	A2
Cromer	23	E2
Cromford	20	C1
Cromhall	14	A4
Crondall	9	F1
Crook	30	C3
Crookham	35	E3
Crosbost	47	E2
Crosby *Mersey.*	24	C4
Crosby *N.Lincs.*	26	C3
Crosby Ravensworth	30	A3
Cross Inn	12	C3
Crossaig	32	C2
Crosscanonby	29	E2
Crossford *Fife*	34	B1
Crossford *S.Lan.*	34	A2
Crossgates *Fife*	34	B1
Crossgates *Powys*	13	E3
Crosshands	33	F3
Crosshill	33	E4
Crosshouse	33	E3
Crossmichael	28	C1
Crossway	13	D3
Croston	24	C3
Croughton	15	D2
Crow Hill	14	A2
Crowborough	10	C3
Crowland	22	A3
Crowle	26	C3
Crowthorne	9	F1
Croy *High.*	42	A3
Croy *N.Lan.*	33	F1
Croyde	6	B3
Cruden Bay	43	F3
Crulabhig	47	E2
Crumlin	7	E1
Crymych	12	A4
Crynant	6	C1
Cubbington	15	D1
Cuckfield	10	B3
Cuddington *Ches.*	19	F1
Cudworth	26	A3
Cuffley	16	A4
Culbokie	41	F2
Culcheth	19	F1
Culdrain	43	D3
Cullen	43	D2
Cullicudden	42	A2
Cullingworth	25	F2
Cullipool	37	D4
Cullivoe	48	C1
Cullompton	5	E1
Culmstock	7	E4
Culnacraig	44	A4
Culnaknock	40	B2
Culross	34	A1
Culswick	48	B3
Cults	43	E4
Cumbernauld	34	A1
Cuminestown	43	E2
Cumnock	33	F3
Cumnor	15	D3
Cunningsburgh	48	B4
Cupar	39	D4
Curry Rivel	7	F4
Cwm	7	E1
Cwmafan	6	C1
Cwmbran	7	E1
Cwmllynfell	6	C1
Cydweli (Kidwelly)	6	B1
Cymmer	7	D1
Cynghordy	13	D4
Cynwyl Elfed	12	B4
D		
Dacre	29	F3
Dail Bho Thuath	47	F1
Dailly	33	E4
Dairsie	39	D4
Dalabrog	46	A3
Dalbeattie	29	D2
Dalby	24	A3
Dale *Pembs.*	12	A2
Dalgety Bay	34	B1
Dalham	16	C1
Dalkeith	34	C2
Dallas	42	B2
Dalmally	37	E3
Dalmellington	33	F4
Dalnavie	42	A2
Dalry	33	E2
Dalrymple	33	E4
Dalston	29	F2
Dalton *S.Yorks.*	26	A4
Dalton-in-Furness	24	B1
Dalwhinnie	38	A1
Damerham	8	C3
Danbury	16	C4
Danby	31	E4
Danehill	10	B3
Darfield	26	A4
Darlington	31	D3
Darra	43	E3
Dartford	10	C1
Dartington	5	D2
Dartmeet	4	C2
Dartmouth	5	D3
Darton	26	A3
Darvel	33	F3
Darwen	25	D3
Dava	42	B3
Davenham	20	A1
Daventry	15	D1
Daviot	42	A3
Dawlish	5	D2
Deal	11	F2
Dearham	29	E3
Debenham	17	E1
Dechmont	34	A1
Deddington	15	D2
Dedham	17	D2
Deeping St. James	22	A3
Deeping St. Nicholas	22	A3
Deganwy	18	C1
Delabole	4	A1
Delamere	19	F2
Denbigh	19	D2
Denby Dale	25	F3
Denham *Bucks.*	10	A1
Denholm	35	D3
Denholme	25	F2
Denmead	9	E3
Dennington	17	E1
Denny	34	A1
Denton	25	E4
Denver	22	C4
Derby	21	D2
Dersingham	22	C3
Dervaig	36	C2
Desborough	21	E4
Devil's Bridge	12	C2
Devizes	8	C1
Dewsbury	25	F3
Dhoon	24	B2
Dibden	9	D3
Didcot	15	D4
Dinas Powys	7	E2
Dingwall	41	F2
Dinnet	43	D4
Dinnington *S.Yorks.*	26	B4
Dippen	32	C3
Dirleton	34	C1
Diss	17	E1
Distington	29	E3
Ditton *Kent*	11	D2
Dobwalls	4	A2
Dochgarroch	41	F3
Docking	22	C2
Doddington	35	E3
Dodington	14	A4
Dodworth	26	A4
Dogdyke	22	A2
Dolanog	13	E1
Dolbenmaen	18	B3
Dolfor	13	E2
Dolgarrog	18	C2
Dolgellau	12	C1
Dollar	38	B4
Dolphinton	34	B2
Doncaster	26	B4
Donington	22	A2
Donnington *Tel. & W.*	20	A3
Dorchester	8	A4
Dordon	20	C4
Dores	41	F3
Dorking	10	B2
Dornie	41	D3
Dornoch	42	A1
Dougarie	32	C3
Douglas *I.o.M.*	24	B3
Douglas *S.Lan.*	34	A3
Douglastown	39	D2
Dounby	49	D3
Doune	38	B4
Dounreay	45	E1
Dover	11	F3
Doveridge	20	C2
Dowally	38	C2
Downham Market	22	C4
Downton	8	C2
Dowsby	22	A3
Drayton *Norf.*	23	E3
Drayton *Oxon.*	15	D4
Drefach	6	B1
Dreghorn	33	E3
Drem	34	C1
Driffield	27	D2
Drimnin	36	C2
Droitwich	14	B1
Dronfield	21	D1
Drongan	33	F3
Droylsden	25	E4
Druid	19	D3
Druimdrishaig	32	C1
Drumbeg	44	A3
Drumclog	33	F3
Drumlithie	39	F1
Drummore	28	A2
Drumnadrochit	41	F3
Drybrook	14	A3
Drymen	33	F1
Duddo	35	E2
Dudley *W.Mid.*	20	B4
Duffield	21	D2
Dufftown	42	C3
Duirinish	40	C3
Dullingham	16	C2
Dulnain Bridge	42	B3
Dulverton	7	D4
Dumbarton	33	E1
Dumfries	29	D1
Dunbar	35	D1
Dunbeath	45	E3
Dunblane	38	B4
Dunchurch	15	D1
Dundee	39	D3
Dundonald	33	E3
Dundreggan	41	E4
Dundrennan	29	D2
Dunecht	43	E4
Dunfermline	34	B1
Dunholme	21	F1
Dunkeld	38	C3
Dunkirk	11	E2
Dunlop	33	E2
Dunnet	45	E1
Dunning	38	C4
Dunoon	33	D1
Dunragit	28	A2
Duns	35	D2
Dunscore	29	D1
Dunstable	15	F3
Dunster	7	D3
Dunure	33	E4
Dunvant	6	C1
Dunvegan	40	A3
Durham	31	D2
Durness	44	B1
Durrington	8	C1
Dursley	14	A3

Name	Page	Grid
Dyce	43	E4
Dyke	42	B2
Dykehead	39	D2
Dymchurch	11	E3
Dymock	14	A2
Dyserth	19	D1

E

Name	Page	Grid
Eaglescliffe	31	D3
Eaglesfield	29	E1
Eaglesham	33	F2
Earby	25	E2
Eardisley	13	E3
Earith	16	B1
Earl Shilton	21	D4
Earl Stonham	17	E2
Earls Barton	15	F1
Earls Colne	17	D3
Earlston	35	D3
Earsairidh	46	A4
Easdale	37	D4
Easebourne	9	F2
Easington Dur.	31	D2
Easington E.Riding	27	E3
Easington Colliery	31	D2
Easingwold	26	B1
East Bergholt	17	D2
East Bridgford	21	E2
East Calder	34	B1
East Dereham	23	D3
East Goscote	21	E3
East Grinstead	10	B3
East Hanney	15	D4
East Harling	23	D4
East Haven	39	E3
East Horsley	10	A2
East Huntspill	7	F3
East Keal	22	B1
East Kilbride	33	F2
East Leake	21	D3
East Linton	35	D1
East Malling	11	D2
East Markham	21	E1
EastMidlands International Airport	21	D2
East Preston	10	A4
East Retford (Retford)	21	E1
East Wemyss	39	D4
East Wittering	9	F3
Eastbourne E.Suss.	10	C4
Easter Lednathie	39	D2
Easter Quarff	48	B4
Eastfield	27	D1
Eastgate	30	B2
Eastleigh Hants.	9	D3
Eastoft	26	C3
Easton	8	A4
Easton on the Hill	21	F3
Easton-in-Gordano	7	F2
Eastriggs	29	F1
Eastry	11	F2
Eastwood Notts.	21	D2
Eaton Socon	16	A1
Ebbw Vale	7	E1
Ecclaw	35	D1
Ecclefechan	29	E1
Eccles Sc.Bord.	35	D2
Ecclesfield	26	A4
Eccleshall	20	B2
Eccleston Lancs.	25	D3
Echt	43	E4
Eckford	35	D3
Eckington Derbys.	21	D1
Eckington Worcs.	14	B2
Edderton	42	A1
Eddleston	34	B2
Edenbridge	10	C2
Edenfield	25	E3
Edgworth	25	D3
Edinburgh	34	B1
Edinburgh Airport	34	B1
Edlingham	35	F4
Edmundbyers	30	C2
Edwinstowe	21	E1
Edzell	39	E2
Egglescliffe	31	D3
Egham	10	A1
Eglingham	35	F3
Eglwys Fach	12	C1
Eglwyswrw	12	A4
Egremont	29	E3
Egton	31	F4
Einacleit	47	D2
Elgin	42	C2
Elgol	40	B4
Elham	11	E2
Elie	39	E4
Eling	9	D3
Elland	25	F3
Ellesmere	19	E3
Ellesmere Port	19	F1
Ellingham	35	F3
Ellington	35	F4
Ellon	43	F3
Elloughton	26	C3
Elm	22	B4
Elmswell	17	D1
Elmton	21	D1
Elphin	44	B3
Elsdon	35	E4
Elsrickle	34	B2
Elstead	9	F2
Elstree	16	A4
Elswick	24	C2
Elton Cambs.	22	A4
Elton Ches.	19	F1
Elvanfoot	34	A3
Elvington	26	B2
Ely Cambs.	16	B3
Ely Cardiff	7	E2
Embleton	35	F3
Emsworth	9	F3
Enderby	21	D4
Endon	20	B2
Enstone	15	D2
Enterkinfoot	34	A4
Eoropaidh	47	F1
Epping	16	B4
Epsom	10	B2
Epworth	26	C4
Eriboll	44	B2
Eriswell	16	C1
Errogie	41	F4
Errol	39	D3
Esh Winning	30	C2
Esher	10	A2
Eskdalemuir	34	B4
Eston	31	E3
Eton	10	A1
Etteridge	38	A1
Ettington	14	C2
Ettrick	34	B4
Ettrickbridge	34	C3
Euxton	25	D3
Evanton	41	F2
Evercreech	8	A2
Evesham	14	B2
Ewell	10	B2
Ewhurst	10	A3
Exebridge	7	D4
Exeter	5	D1
Exminster	5	D1
Exmouth	5	E2
Eye Peter.	22	A4
Eye Suff.	17	E1
Eyemouth	35	E2
Eynsford	10	C2
Eynsham	15	D3

F

Name	Page	Grid
Failsworth	25	E4
Fair Oak Hants.	9	E3
Fairford	14	C3
Fairlie	33	E2
Fairlight	11	D4
Fakenham	23	D3
Falkirk	34	A1
Falkland	39	D4
Fallin	34	A1
Falmouth	3	F3
Falstone	30	A1
Fareham	9	E3
Faringdon	14	C4
Farington	25	D3
Farmborough	8	A1
Farnborough Hants.	9	F1
Farndon	21	E2
Farnham	9	F1
Farnham Royal	10	A1
Farnsfield	21	E1
Farnworth Gt.Man.	25	D3
Farr	42	A3
Fauldhouse	34	A2
Faversham	11	E2
Fawley Hants.	9	D3
Fazeley	20	C4
Fearnhead	19	F1
Fearnmore	40	C2
Featherstone Staffs.	20	B3
Featherstone W.Yorks.	26	A3
Felindre	13	E2
Felixstowe	17	E2
Felling	31	D1
Felsted	16	C3
Felton	35	F4
Feltwell	22	C4
Feniton	5	E1
Fenstanton	16	A1
Fenwick E.Ayr.	33	F2
Fenwick Northumb.	35	F2
Feochaig	32	C4
Feolin Ferry	32	B2
Fern	39	E2
Ferndale	7	D1
Ferndown	8	C3
Ferness	42	B3
Fernhill Heath	14	B1
Fernhurst	9	F2
Ferryden	39	E2
Ferryhill	31	D3
Feshiebridge	42	A4
Fettercairn	39	E1
Ffestiniog	18	C3
Ffostrasol	12	B3
Filey	27	D1
Fillongley	20	C4
Filton	14	A4
Fimber	26	C1
Finavon	39	E2
Finchampstead	9	F1
Finchingfield	16	C3
Findern	20	C2
Findhorn	42	B2
Findochty	43	D2
Findon	10	A4
Finedon	15	F1
Finningham	17	D1
Finningley	26	B4
Finnygaud	43	D2
Finstown	49	E3
Fintry	33	F1
Fionnphort	36	B3
Fishburn	31	D3
Fishguard	12	B1
Fishnish	36	C3
Fiunary	36	C2
Flackwell Heath	15	F4
Flamborough	27	D1
Fleet	9	F1
Fleetwood	24	C2
Flempton	16	C1
Flimby	29	E3
Flimwell	11	D3
Flint	19	E1
Flitwick	15	F2
Flodden	35	E3
Flookburgh	24	C1
Fochabers	42	C2
Folkestone	11	F3
Folkingham	21	F2
Folly Gate	4	C1
Ford Arg. & B.	37	D4
Ford Northumb.	35	E3
Fordham	16	C1
Fordingbridge	8	C3
Fordoun	39	F1
Fordyce	43	D2
Forest Row	10	C3
Forfar	39	D2
Forgandenny	38	C3
Forgie	42	C2
Formby	24	C3
Forres	42	B2
Forsbrook	20	B2
Forsinard	45	D2
Fort Augustus	41	E4
Fort William	37	E1
Forth	34	A2
Fortingall	38	B2
Fortrose	42	A2
Fortuneswell	8	A4
Fotherby	27	E4
Foulden	35	E2
Foulridge	25	E2
Four Elms	10	C2
Four Marks	9	E2
Four Oaks E.Suss.	11	D3
Fowey	4	A3
Fownhope	14	A2
Foxdale	24	A3
Foyers	41	F4
Framfield	10	C3
Framlingham	17	E1
Frampton Cotterell	14	A4
Frampton on Severn	14	A3
Frankley	20	B4
Fraserburgh	43	F2
Freckleton	24	C3
Fremington	6	B4
Freshwater	9	D4
Freshwater East	12	B2
Fressingfield	17	E1
Freswick	45	F1
Freuchie	39	D4
Fridaythorpe	26	C1
Frimley	9	F1
Frinton-on-Sea	17	E3
Friockheim	39	E2
Frithelstock Stone	6	B4
Frizington	29	E3
Frodsham	19	F1
Frogmore Hants.	9	F1
Frome	8	B1
Fulbourn	16	B2
Fulford Staffs.	20	B2
Fulford York	26	B2
Fulham	10	B1
Fulwood Lancs.	25	D2
Funzie	48	C1
Furnace	37	E4
Fyfield Essex	16	B3
Fyvie	43	E3

G

Name	Page	Grid
Gaer	13	E4
Gainford	30	C3
Gainsborough	20	C4
Gairloch	40	C1
Galashiels	34	C3
Galmisdale	36	C1
Galston	33	F3
Gamlingay	16	A2
Gardenstown	43	E2
Garderhouse	48	B3
Garelochhead	33	E1
Garforth	26	A2
Gargrave	25	E2
Garlieston	28	C2
Garsdale Head	30	B4
Garstang	24	C2
Garth	13	D3
Garthmyl	13	E1
Gartocharn	33	E1
Garvald	35	D1
Garvamore	38	A1
Garvard	32	A1
Garve	41	F2
Gatehouse of Fleet	28	C2
Gateshead	31	D2
Gatley	25	E4
Gatwick (London) Airport	10	B3
Gawthrop	30	A4
Gayton	22	C3
Gearraidh na h-Aibhne	47	E2
Geddington	21	F4
Gedney	22	B3
Gelligaer	7	E1
Georgeham	6	B3
Gerrards Cross	10	A1
Giffnock	33	F2
Gifford	34	C1
Gilberdyke	26	C3
Gillamoor	31	E4
Gilling West	30	C4
Gillingham Dorset	8	B2
Gillingham Medway	11	D2
Gilmerton	38	B3
Gilsland	30	A1
Gilston	34	C2
Gilwern	7	E1
Girlsta	48	B3
Girvan	33	E4
Gisburn	25	E2
Glamis	39	D2
Glanaman	6	C1
Glanton	35	E3
Glasbury	13	E4
Glasgow	33	F2
Glasgow Airport	33	F2
Glassford	33	F2
Glastonbury	7	F3
Glemsford	16	C2
Glen Vine	24	A3
Glenbarr	32	B3
Glenbeg	36	C2
Glenborrodale	36	C2
Glenbreck	34	B3
Glenbrittle	40	B4
Glencaple	29	E1
Glencarse	38	C3
Glencoe	37	E2
Gleneagles	38	B4
Glenegedale	32	A2
Glenelg	40	C4
Glenfarg	38	C4
Glenfield	21	D3
Glenfinnan	37	D1
Glengarnock	33	E2
Glenkindie	43	D4
Glenluce	28	A2
Glenrothes	39	D4
Glinton	22	A4
Glossop	25	F4
Gloucester	14	B3
Glusburn	25	E2
Glyn Ceiriog	19	E3
Glyn-Neath	7	D1
Glyncorrwg	7	D1
Gnosall	20	B3
Gobowen	19	E3
Godalming	10	A2
Godmanchester	16	A1
Godstone	10	B2
Golborne	25	D4
Goldcliff	7	F2
Golden Pot	9	F2
Golspie	45	D4
Goodwick	12	A1

Goole 26 B3
Goonhavern 3 F2
Gordon 35 D2
Gorebridge 34 C2
Goring 15 E4
Gorseinon 6 C1
Gosberton 22 A3
Gosfield 16 C3
Gosforth *Cumb.* 29 E4
Gosforth *T. & W.* 30 C1
Gosport 9 E3
Gotham 21 D2
Goudhurst 11 D3
Gourdon 39 F2
Goxhill 27 D3
Grabhair 47 E2
Grain 11 D1
Grampound 3 F3
Grandtully 38 B2
Grange-over-Sands 24 C1
Grangemouth 34 A1
Grantham 21 F2
Grantown-on-Spey 42 B3
Grantshouse 35 D2
Grasmere 29 F4
Grassington 25 E1
Gravesend 10 C1
Grayrigg 30 A4
Grays 10 C1
Grayshott 9 F2
Greasby 19 E1
Great Ayton 31 E3
Great Baddow 16 C3
Great Barton 17 D1
Great Bircham 22 C3
Great Broughton 31 E4
Great Clifton 29 E3
Great Cornard 17 D2
Great Dunmow 16 C3
Great Eccleston 24 C2
Great Ellingham 23 D4
Great Glen 21 E4
Great Gonerby 21 F2
Great Gransden 16 A2
Great Harwood 25 D2
Great Horkesley 17 D3
Great Linford 15 F2
Great Malvern 14 A2
Great Marton 24 C2
Great Missenden 15 F3
Great Ponton 21 F2
Great Salkeld 30 A2
Great Sampford 16 C2
Great Sankey 19 F1
Great Shelford 16 B2
Great Torrington 6 B4
Great Wakering 11 E1
Great Wyrley 20 B3
Great Yarmouth 23 F4
Great Yeldham 16 C2
Greatham *Hants.* 9 F2
Greatstone-on-Sea 11 E3
Greengairs 34 A1
Greenham 9 E1
Greenhead 30 A1
Greenigo 49 E3
Greenlaw 35 D2
Greenloaning 38 B4
Greenock 33 E1
Greenodd 24 C1
Greenway 12 A4
Gresford 19 E2
Gretna 29 F1
Greystoke 29 F3
Griais 47 F1
Grimoldby 22 B1
Grimsby 27 D3
Grimston 22 C3
Gringley on the Hill 26 B4
Gritley 49 E3
Grizebeck 29 E4
Grove 15 D4
Grudie 41 E2
Grutness 48 B4

Guide Post 30 C1
Guildford 10 A2
Guildtown 38 C3
Guisborough 31 E3
Guiseley 25 F2
Guist 23 D3
Gullane 34 C1
Gunness 26 C3
Gunnislake 4 B2
Gurnos 6 C1
Gutcher 48 C1
Gwaun-Cae-Gurwen 6 C1
Gwithian 3 E3
Gwytherin 18 C2

H
Hackleton 15 E1
Hacklinge 11 F2
Hackness 31 F4
Haddenham 16 B1
Haddington 34 C1
Haddiscoe 23 F4
Hadleigh 17 D2
Hadley 20 A3
Hagley *Here.* 14 A2
Hagley *Worcs.* 20 B4
Hailsham 10 C4
Hale *Gt.Man.* 25 E4
Hales 23 F4
Halesowen 20 B4
Halesworth 17 F1
Halewood 19 F1
Halifax 25 F3
Halkirk 45 E2
Halkyn 19 E1
Hall 33 E2
Halland 10 C4
Hallow 14 B1
Hallworthy 4 A1
Halstead *Essex* 16 C3
Halton Gill 25 E1
Haltwhistle 30 A1
Halwell 5 D3
Ham *Shet.* 48 A3
Hamble-le-Rice 9 E3
Hambleton 24 C2
Hamilton 33 F2
Hamnavoe (Mainland) *Shet.* 48 B4
Hamnavoe (Yell) *Shet.* 48 C2
Hampreston 8 C3
Hamstreet 11 E3
Handsacre 20 C3
Hanham 14 A4
Hanley Castle 14 B2
Hanwood 13 F1
Happisburgh 23 F3
Harbledown 11 E2
Harbury 15 D1
Hardingstone 15 E1
Hardwicke 14 A3
Hare Street 16 B3
Harefield 10 A1
Harewood 26 A2
Harlech 18 B3
Harleston 23 E4
Harlington 15 F2
Harlow 16 B3
Harmston 21 F1
Haroldswick 48 C1
Harpenden 16 A3
Harpole 15 E1
Harrietfield 38 C3
Harrietsham 11 D2
Harrogate 26 A2
Harston 16 B2
Hartfield 10 C3
Harthill *N.Lan.* 34 A2
Hartland 6 A4
Hartlebury 14 B1
Hartlepool 31 E3

Hartley *Kent* 10 C2
Hartley Wintney 9 F1
Hartpury 14 A2
Hartshill 21 D4
Hartshorne 21 D3
Harvington *Worcs.* 14 B2
Harwell 15 D4
Harwich 17 E3
Harworth 26 B4
Hasland 21 D1
Haslemere 9 F2
Haslingden 25 E3
Hassendean 34 C3
Hastings 11 D4
Haswell 31 D2
Hatfield *Herts.* 16 A3
Hatfield *S.Yorks.* 26 B3
Hatfield Broad Oak 16 B3
Hatfield Peverel 16 C3
Hatherleigh 4 C1
Hathern 21 D3
Hathersage 25 F4
Hatton *Aber.* 43 F3
Hatton *Derbys.* 20 C2
Haugh of Urr 29 D1
Haughton 20 B3
Havant 9 F3
Haverfordwest 12 A2
Haverhill 16 C2
Hawarden 19 E2
Hawes 30 B4
Hawick 34 C3
Hawkhurst 11 D3
Hawkinge 11 F3
Hawkshead 29 F4
Hawkwell 11 D1
Hawley *Hants.* 9 F1
Haworth 25 F2
Haxby 26 B1
Haxey 26 C4
Hay-on-Wye 13 E3
Haydock 25 D4
Haydon Bridge 30 B1
Haydon Wick 14 C4
Hayfield 25 F4
Hayle 3 E3
Hayton 26 C2
Haywards Heath 10 B3
Hazel Grove 25 E4
Hazlemere 15 F4
Heacham 22 C2
Headcorn 11 D2
Headley 9 F2
Healeyfield 30 C2
Healing 27 D3
Heanor 21 D2
Heath 21 D1
Heathfield 10 C3
Hebburn 31 D1
Hebden Bridge 25 E3
Heckington 22 A2
Hedge End 9 E3
Hedon 27 D3
Heglibister 48 B3
Heighington 21 F1
Helensburgh 33 E1
Helhoughton 23 D3
Hellifield 25 E2
Helmsdale 45 E3
Helmsley 31 E4
Helpringham 22 A2
Helsby 19 F1
Helston 3 E3
Hemel Hempstead 16 A3
Hemingford Grey 16 A1
Hempnall 23 E4
Hempstead 16 C2
Hemsby 23 F3
Hemsworth 26 A3
Hemyock 7 E4
Hendon *Gt.Lon.* 10 B1
Henfield 10 B4
Hengoed 7 E1
Henley-in-Arden 14 C1

Henley-on-Thames 15 E4
Henlow 16 A2
Henstridge 8 B2
Hereford 13 F4
Heriot 34 C2
Herne Bay 11 E2
Herstmonceux 10 C4
Herston 49 E4
Hertford 16 B3
Heswall 19 E1
Hethersett 23 E4
Hetton 25 E1
Hetton-le-Hole 31 D2
Hexham 30 B1
Hextable 10 C1
Heybridge (Maldon) 17 D3 *Essex*
Heysham 24 C1
Heywood 25 E3
Hibaldstow 26 C4
High Bentham 25 D1
High Blantyre 33 F2
High Bradfield 26 A4
High Etherley 30 C3
High Garrett 16 C3
High Halden 11 D3
High Hawsker 31 F4
High Hesket 29 F2
High Legh 25 D4
High Lorton 29 E3
High Wycombe 15 F4
Higham 11 D1
Higham Ferrers 15 F1
Highampton 4 B1
Highbridge 7 E3
Highclere 9 D1
Higher Walton *Lancs.* 25 D3
Highley 20 A4
Highnam 14 A3
Highworth 14 C4
Hildenborough 10 C2
Hilgay 22 C4
Hill End 38 C4
Hill of Fearn 42 A1
Hillside Angus 39 E2
Hillside *Shet.* 48 B2
Hillswick 48 B2
Hilperton 8 B1
Hilton *Derbys.* 20 C2
Hinckley 21 D4
Hinderwell 31 F3
Hindhead 9 F2
Hindley 25 D4
Hindon 8 B2
Hingham 23 D4
Hirwaun 7 D1
Histon 16 B1
Hitchin 16 A3
Hockley 11 D1
Hockley Heath 14 C1
Hoddesdon 16 B3
Hodnet 19 F3
Hogsthorpe 22 B1
Holbeach 22 B3
Holbrook *Suff.* 17 E2
Holden 25 E2
Holland-on-Sea 17 E3
Hollington 11 D4
Hollingworth 25 F4
Hollybush *E.Ayr.* 33 E4
Hollybush *Worcs.* 14 A2
Holme-on-Spalding-Moor 26 C2
Holmes Chapel 20 A1
Holmesfield 20 C1
Holmfirth 25 F3
Holsworthy 4 B1
Holt *Norf.* 23 D2
Holt *Wilts.* 8 B1
Holt *Wrex.* 19 F2
Holyhead 18 A1
Holywell 19 E1
Holywood 29 D1

Homersfield 23 E4
Honiton 5 E1
Honley 25 F3
Hoo 11 D1
Hook *E.Riding* 26 B3
Hook *Hants.* 9 F1
Hook Norton 15 D2
Hope 19 E2
Hopeman 42 B2
Hopton *Norf.* 23 F4
Hopton *Suff.* 17 D1
Horam 10 C3
Horbling 22 A3
Horbury 26 A3
Horden 31 D2
Horeb 12 B3
Horley 10 B2
Hornby 25 D1
Horncastle 22 A1
Horndean *Hants.* 9 E3
Horning 23 E3
Hornsea 27 D2
Horrabridge 4 C2
Horringer 16 C1
Horsehouse 25 F1
Horsford 23 E3
Horsforth 25 F2
Horsham 10 B3
Horsmonden 11 D3
Horstead 23 E3
Horton Heath 9 E3
Horton in Ribblesdale 25 E1
Horwich 25 D3
Houbie 48 C1
Houghton le Spring 31 D2
Houghton Regis 15 F2
Hounslow 35 D2
Houston 33 E2
Houton 49 E3
Hove 10 B4
Hoveton 23 E3
Hovingham 26 B1
Howden 26 B3
Howwood 33 E2
Hoylake 19 E1
Hoyland 26 A4
Hucknall 21 D2
Huddersfield 25 F3
Huggate 26 C2
Huish Episcopi 7 F4
Huisinis 47 D3
Hullavington 14 B4
Hullbridge 11 D1
Humberside International Airport 27 D3
Humberston 27 E4
Humbie 34 C2
Hundleby 22 B1
Hundleton 12 A2
Hungerford 9 D1
Hunmanby 27 D1
Hunstanton 22 C2
Hunter's Quay 33 E1
Huntingdon 16 A1
Huntly 43 D3
Hurlford 33 F3
Hursley 9 D2
Hurst Green 11 D3
Hurstbourne Tarrant 9 D1
Hurstpierpoint 10 B3
Hurworth-on-Tees 31 D3
Husbands Bosworth 21 E4
Huttoft 22 B1
Hutton Cranswick 27 D2
Hutton Rudby 31 D4
Huyton 19 F1
Hyde 25 E4
Hythe *Hants.* 9 D3
Hythe *Kent* 11 E3

I

Ibstock 21 D3
Icklesham 11 D4
Icklingham 16 C1
Idrigil 40 B2
Ilchester 7 F4
Ilford 10 C1
Ilfracombe 6 B3
Ilkeston 21 D2
Ilkley 25 F2
Ilminster 7 F4
Immingham 27 D3
Inchbare 39 E2
Inchnadamph 44 B3
Inchture 39 D3
Ingatestone 16 C4
Ingleton Dur. 30 C3
Ingleton N.Yorks. 25 D1
Inglewhite 25 D2
Ingoldmells 22 B1
Inkberrow 14 B1
Innellan 33 D2
Innerleithen 34 C3
Insch 43 D3
Inveralligan 40 C2
Inverallochy 43 F2
Inveraray 37 E4
Inverarity 39 D3
Inverarnan 37 F4
Inverbervie 39 F1
Invercassley 44 C4
Invercharnan 37 E2
Inverey 38 C1
Invergarry 41 E4
Invergordon 42 A2
Inverinan 37 E4
Inverkeilor 39 E2
Inverkeithing 34 B1
Inverkirkaig 44 A3
Inverlael 41 E1
Invermoriston 41 F4
Inverneil 32 C1
Inverness 42 A3
Inverness Airport 42 A2
Invernoaden 37 E4
Inverurie 43 E4
Ipplepen 5 D2
Ipstones 20 B2
Ipswich 17 E2
Irchester 15 F1
Irlam 25 D4
Ironbridge 20 A3
Irthlingborough 15 F1
Irvine 33 E3
Isbister (Mainland) 48 B1 Shet.
Isbister (Whalsay) 48 C2 Shet.
Isle of Man Airport 24 A3
Isle of Whithorn 28 C2
Isleham 16 C1
Iver 10 A1
Ivinghoe 15 F3
Ivybridge 4 C3
Iwade 11 D2
Ixworth 17 D1

J

Jarrow 31 D1
Jaywick 17 E3
Jedburgh 35 D3
Jemimaville 42 A2
John o' Groats 45 F1
Johnston 12 A2
Johnstone 33 E2
Johnstonebridge 34 B4

K

Kames 33 D1
Kearsley 25 D4
Kedington 16 C2
Keelby 27 D3

Keele 20 A2
Kegworth 21 D3
Keighley 25 F2
Keillmore 32 C1
Keiss 45 F1
Keith 43 D2
Kellas Angus 39 D3
Kellas Moray 42 C2
Kelso 35 D3
Kelty 38 C4
Kelvedon 17 D3
Kelvedon Hatch 16 B4
Kemnay 43 E4
Kempsey 14 B2
Kempston 15 F2
Kendal 30 A4
Kenilworth 14 C1
Kenmore 38 B2
Kennacraig 32 C2
Kennethmont 43 D3
Kennington 15 D3
Kennoway 39 D4
Kensaleyre 40 B2
Kensworth 15 F3
Kentallen 37 E2
Kenton Devon 5 D2
Kesgrave 17 E2
Kessingland 23 F4
Keswick 29 F3
Kettering 21 F4
Kettletoft 49 F2
Kettlewell 25 E1
Ketton 21 F3
Kewstoke 7 F2
Keyingham 27 D3
Keymer 10 B4
Keynsham 8 A1
Keyworth 21 E2
Kibworth Harcourt 21 E4
Kidderminster 20 B4
Kidlington 15 D3
Kidsgrove 20 B2
Kidwelly (Cydweli) 6 B1
Kielder 35 D4
Kilberry 32 C2
Kilbirnie 33 E2
Kilburn Derbys. 21 D2
Kilcadzow 34 A2
Kilchattan 36 B4
Kilchenzie 32 C3
Kilchiaran 32 A2
Kilchoan 36 C2
Kilchoman 32 A2
Kilchrenan 37 E3
Kilconquhar 39 E4
Kilcreggan 33 E1
Kildonan Lodge 45 D3
Kildrummy 43 D4
Kilfinan 33 D1
Kilgetty 6 A1
Kilham E.Riding 27 D1
Kilham Northumb. 35 E3
Kilkhampton 6 A4
Killamarsh 26 A4
Killay 6 C1
Killean 32 C2
Killearn 33 F1
Killichonan 38 A2
Killiecrankie 38 B2
Killin 38 A3
Killinghall 26 A1
Killingworth 31 D1
Killundine 36 C2
Kilmacolm 33 E1
Kilmalieu 37 D2
Kilmaluag 40 B2
Kilmarnock 33 F3
Kilmartin 37 D4
Kilmaurs 33 E3
Kilmelford 37 D4
Kilmington 5 F1
Kilmory Arg. & B. 32 C1
Kilmory (Rum) 40 A4 High.

Kilninian 36 B2
Kilninver 37 D3
Kiloran 36 B4
Kilrenny 39 E4
Kilsyth 33 F1
Kilwinning 33 E2
Kimberley Norf. 23 D4
Kimberley Notts. 21 D2
Kimbolton 16 A1
Kimpton 16 A3
Kinbrace 45 D3
Kincardine 34 A1
Kincardine O'Neil 43 D4
Kincraig 42 A4
Kingarth 33 D2
Kinghorn 34 B1
Kinglassie 39 D4
Kings Langley 15 F3
King's Lynn 22 C3
King's Sutton 15 D2
Kings Worthy 9 E2
Kingsbarns 39 E4
Kingsbridge 4 C3
Kingsbury Warks. 20 C4
Kingsbury Episcopi 7 F4
Kingsclere 9 E1
Kingsdown 11 F2
Kingshouse 38 A3
Kingskerswell 5 D2
Kingsley Ches. 19 F1
Kingsley Staffs. 20 B2
Kingsnorth 11 E3
Kingsteignton 5 D2
Kingsthorne 13 F4
Kingston 42 C2
Kingston Bagpuize 15 D3
Kingston Seymour 7 F2
Kingston upon Hull 27 D3
Kingstone 13 F4
Kingswear 5 D3
Kingswood S.Glos. 14 A4
Kingswood Surr. 10 B2
Kington 13 E3
Kingussie 42 A4
Kinloch 40 B4
Kinloch Hourn 41 D4
Kinloch Rannoch 38 A2
Kinlochard 38 A4
Kinlochbervie 44 B2
Kinlocheil 37 E1
Kinlochewe 41 D2
Kinlochleven 37 E2
Kinloss 42 B2
Kinmel Bay 19 D1
Kinross 38 C4
Kintbury 9 D1
Kintore 43 E4
Kintour 32 B2
Kintra 32 A2
Kinver 20 B4
Kippax 26 A3
Kippen 38 A4
Kirby Muxloe 21 D3
Kirk Michael 24 A2
Kirk Sandall 26 B3
Kirk Yetholm 35 E3
Kirkbean 29 D2
Kirkbride 29 E2
Kirkburton 25 F3
Kirkby Mersey. 24 C4
Kirkby in Ashfield 21 D1
Kirkby Lonsdale 25 D1
Kirkby Malzeard 25 F1
Kirkby Stephen 30 B4
Kirkbymoorside 31 E4
Kirkcaldy 34 B1
Kirkcolm 28 A1
Kirkconnel 34 A4
Kirkcowan 28 B2
Kirkcudbright 28 C2
Kirkham 28 B2
Kirkinner 28 B2
Kirkintilloch 33 F1
Kirkliston 34 B1

Kirkmichael P. & K. 38 C2
Kirkmichael S.Ayr. 33 E4
Kirkmuirhill 34 A2
Kirknewton 35 E3 Northumb.
Kirknewton 34 B2 W.Loth.
Kirkoswald Cumb. 30 A2
Kirkoswald S.Ayr. 33 E4
Kirkpatrick 29 D1 Durham
Kirkpatrick-Fleming 29 F1
Kirkton 37 D4
Kirkton of 43 D3 Culsalmond
Kirkton of Durris 39 F1
Kirkton of Glenisla 39 D2
Kirkton of 39 D2 Kingoldrum
Kirkton of Menmuir 39 E2
Kirkton of Skene 43 E4
Kirktown of 43 E3 Auchterless
Kirktown of 43 D2 Deskford
Kirkwall 49 E3
Kirriemuir 39 D2
Kirtlington 15 D3
Kirton Lincs. 22 A2
Kirton Suff. 17 E2
Kirton in Lindsey 26 C4
Knaresborough 26 A2
Knayton 31 D4
Knebworth 16 A3
Knighton 13 E2
Knock 36 C3
Knockandhu 42 C4
Knottingley 26 A3
Knowle W.Mid. 20 C4
Knucklas 13 E2
Knutsford 20 A1
Kyle of Lochalsh 40 C3
Kyleakin 40 C3
Kylerhea 40 C4
Kylestrome 44 B2

L

Laceby 27 D4
Lacock 8 B1
Ladybank 39 D4
Ladykirk 35 E2
Ladysford 43 E2
Lagg 33 D3
Laggan 37 F1 (Invergarry) High.
Laggan 38 A1 (Newtonmore) High.
Lagganulva 36 C3
Laide 41 D1
Lairg 44 C4
Lakenheath 16 C1
Laleston 7 D2
Lamberhurst 11 D3
Lambourn 15 D4
Lamlash 33 D3
Lampeter 12 C3
Lamport 15 E1
Lanark 34 A2
Lancaster 24 C1
Lanchester 30 C2
Landore 6 C1
Lane End Bucks. 15 E4
Langford 16 A2
Langham 21 F3
Langholm 29 F1
Langold 26 B4
Langport 7 F4
Langtoft 26 C1
Langwathby 30 A3
Lanivet 4 A2
Lapworth 14 C1
Larbert 34 A1
Largoward 39 D4

Largs 33 E2
Larkhall 34 A2
Larkhill 8 C1
Larling 23 D4
Latchingdon 17 D4
Latheron 45 E2
Latheronwheel 45 E3
Lauder 34 C2
Laugharne 6 B1
Launceston 4 B1
Laurencekirk 39 E2
Laurieston 28 C1
Lavenham 17 D2
Law 34 A2
Lawers 38 A3
Lawford 17 D3
Laxey 24 B2
Laxford Bridge 44 B2
Laxo 48 B2
Layer de la Haye 17 D3
Lazonby 30 A2
Leadburn 34 B2
Leadenham 21 F2
Leadgate 30 C2
Leadhills 34 A3
Leasingham 21 F2
Leatherhead 10 A2
Leavening 26 C1
Lechlade 14 C3
Leckhampton 14 B3
Leckmelm 41 E1
Ledaig 37 D3
Ledbury 14 A2
Ledmore 44 B3
Lee Lancs. 25 D2
Lee Moor 4 C2
Lee-on-the-Solent 9 E3
Leeds W.Yorks. 26 A2
Leeds Bradford 25 F2 International Airport
Leedstown 3 D2
Leek 20 B1
Leeming 31 D4
Leicester 21 E3
Leigh Gt.Man. 25 D4
Leighton Buzzard 15 F2
Leiston 17 F1
Leith 34 B1
Lenham 11 D2
Lennoxtown 33 F1
Leominster 13 F3
Lerwick 48 B3
Lesbury 35 F4
Leslie 39 D4
Lesmahagow 34 A3
Leswalt 28 A1
Letchworth 16 A2
Letheringsett 23 D2
Letterston 12 B1
Leuchars 39 D3
Leumrabhagh 47 E3
Leven E.Riding 27 D2
Leven Fife 39 D4
Levenwick 48 B4
Lewes 10 B4
Leyburn 30 C4
Leyland 25 D3
Leysdown-on-Sea 11 E1
Lhanbryde 42 C2
Libberton 34 A2
Lichfield 20 C3
Lightwater 9 F1
Lilleshall 20 A3
Lilliesleaf 34 C3
Limekilns 34 B1
Lincoln 21 F1
Lindfield 10 B3
Lindores 39 D4
Linford Thur. 11 D1
Lingfield 10 B2
Linksness 49 D3
Linlithgow 34 A1
Linsidemore 41 F1

Linton 16 B2
Liphook 9 F2
Liskeard 4 B2
Liss 9 F2
Liswerry 7 F2
Litherland 24 C4
Little Clacton 17 E3
Little Common 11 D4
Little Downham 16 B1
Little Eaton 21 D2
Little Missenden 15 F3
Little Oakley 17 E3
Little Paxton 16 A1
Little Plumstead 23 E3
Littleborough 25 E3
Littlebourne 11 F2
Littledean 14 A3
Littlehampton 10 A4
Littlemill E.Ayr. 33 F4
Littlemill High. 42 B2
Littlemore 15 D3
Littleport 22 B4
Littlestone-on-Sea 11 E3
Liverpool 19 E1
Liversedge 25 F3
Livingston 34 B1
Lizard 3 E4
Llanaelhaearn 18 B2
Llanarth 12 B3
Llanarthney 12 B4
Llanbadarn Fawr 12 C2
Llanbadrig 18 A1
Llanbedr 18 B3
Llanbedrog 18 A3
Llanberis 18 B2
Llanbister 13 E2
Llanblethian 7 D2
Llanddarog 12 B4
Llanddeiniolen 18 B2
Llandderfel 19 D3
Llanddowror 6 A1
Llandeilo 12 C4
Llandinam 13 D2
Llandissilio 12 A4
Llandovery 12 C4
Llandrillo 19 D3
Llandrindod Wells 13 E3
Llandudno 18 C1
Llandwrog 18 B2
Llandybie 12 C4
Llandysul 12 B4
Llanegwad 12 B4
Llanelli 6 B1
Llanelltyd 18 C3
Llanelly 13 E4
Llanelwy 19 D1
  (St. Asaph)
Llanerch-y-medd 18 B1
Llanfaelog 18 A1
Llanfair Caereinion 13 E1
Llanfair Talhaiarn 19 D1
Llanfairfechan 18 C1
Llanfairpwll-gwyngyll 18 B1
Llanfihangel ar-arth 12 B4
Llanfyllin 19 D3
Llanfynydd 19 E2
Llangadfan 13 D1
Llangadog 12 C4
Llangefni 18 B1
Llangeler 12 B4
Llangelynin 12 C1
Llangendeirne 6 B1
Llangernyw 18 C2
Llangoed 18 B1
Llangollen 19 E3
Llangranog 12 B3
Llangunnor 12 B4
Llangurig 13 D2
Llangwm 12 B2
Llangynidr 13 E4
Llanharan 7 D2
Llanhilleth 7 E1
Llanidloes 13 D2

Llanilar 12 C2
Llanishen Cardiff 7 E2
Llanllwchaiarn 13 E2
Llanllyfni 18 B2
Llannon 6 B1
Llanon 12 B3
Llanrhaeadr-ym 19 D3
  Mochnant
Llanrhidian 6 B1
Llanrhystud 12 B2
Llanrug 18 B2
Llanrumney 7 E2
Llanrwst 18 C2
Llansamlet 6 C1
Llansannan 19 D2
Llansantffraid Glan 18 C1
  Conwy
Llansawel 12 C4
Llansteffan 6 B1
Llanthony 13 E4
Llantilio Pertholey 13 F4
Llantrisant Mon. 7 F1
Llantrisant R.C.T. 7 D2
Llantwit Major 7 D2
Llanuwchllyn 18 C3
Llanwddyn 19 D3
Llanwnda 18 B2
Llanwnog 13 D1
Llanwrda 12 C4
Llanwrtyd Wells 13 D3
Llanybydder 12 B3
Llanynghenedl 18 A1
Llanystumdwy 18 B3
Lledrod 12 C2
Loanhead 34 B2
Loans 33 E3
Loch Baghasdail 46 B3
  (Lochboisdale)
Loch na Madadh 46 B1
  (Lochmaddy)
Loch Sgioport 46 B2
Lochailort 37 D1
Lochaline 36 C3
Lochans 28 A2
Locharbriggs 29 E1
Lochawe 37 E3
Lochboisdale (Loch 46 B3
  Baghasdail)
Lochcarron 41 D3
Lochdon 37 D3
Lochearnhead 38 A3
Lochend 41 F3
Lochgelly 38 C4
Lochgilphead 32 C1
Lochgoilhead 37 F4
Lochinver 44 A3
Lochmaben 29 E1
Lochmaddy 46 B1
  (Loch na Madadh)
Lochranza 33 D2
Lochwinnoch 33 E2
Lockerbie 29 E1
Locking 7 F3
Locks Heath 9 E3
Lockton 31 F4
Loddiswell 4 C3
Loddon 23 F4
Lofthouse 26 A3
  W.Yorks.
Loftus 31 E3
Logan 33 F3
Loggerheads 20 A2
London 10 B1
London Colney 16 A4
London Heathrow 10 A1
  Airport
London Luton 16 A3
  Airport
Long Ashton 7 F2
Long Bennington 21 F2
Long Buckby 15 E1
Long Compton 14 C2
Long Crendon 15 E3

Long Eaton 21 D2
Long Hanborough 15 D3
Long Itchington 15 D1
Long Lawford 21 D4
Long Melford 17 D2
Long Preston 25 E1
Long Stratton 23 E4
Long Sutton Lincs. 22 B3
Long Sutton Som. 7 F4
Longbenton 31 D1
Longbridge Deverill 8 B2
Longdon 20 C3
Longforgan 39 D3
Longframlington 35 F4
Longhope Glos. 14 A3
Longhope Ork. 49 D4
Longhorsley 35 F4
Longhoughton 35 F3
Longmanhill 43 E2
Longmorn 42 C2
Longniddry 34 C1
Longridge 25 D2
Longside 43 F3
Longton Lancs. 24 C3
Longtown 29 F1
Looe 4 B3
Loose 11 D2
Lopcombe Corner 9 D2
Loscoe 21 D2
Lossiemouth 42 C2
Lostwithiel 4 A2
Loth 49 F2
Lothmore 45 E3
Loughborough 21 D3
Loughor 6 C1
Loughton Essex 16 B4
Louth 22 A1
Low Street 23 E3
Lowdham 21 E2
Lower Beeding 10 B3
Lower Cam 14 A3
Lower Diabaig 40 C2
Lower Killeyan 32 A2
Lowestoft 23 F4
Loweswater 29 E3
Lowick 35 E3
Ludag 46 A3
Ludgershall 9 D1
Ludgvan 3 D3
Ludlow 13 F2
Luib 40 B3
Lumphanan 43 D4
Luncarty 38 C3
Lundin Links 39 D4
Luss 33 E1
Lusta 40 A2
Luton 16 A3
Lutterworth 21 D4
Luxulyan 4 A3
Lybster 45 F2
Lydd 11 E3
Lydd Airport 11 E3
Lydford 4 C1
Lydiate 24 C4
Lydney 14 A3
Lyme Regis 5 F1
Lyminge 11 E3
Lymington 9 D3
Lymm 25 D4
Lympne 11 E3
Lympstone 5 D2
Lyndhurst 9 D3
Lyne of Skene 43 E4
Lyneham 14 B4
Lynemore 42 B3
Lynemouth 35 F4
Lyness 49 D4
Lynmouth 6 C3
Lynton 6 C3
Lytchett Matravers 8 B3
Lytchett Minster 8 C3
Lytham St. Anne's 24 C3

M

Mablethorpe 22 B1
Macclesfield 20 B1
Macduff 43 E2
Macharioch 32 C4
Machen 7 E1
Machrihanish 32 B3
Machynlleth 12 C1
Macmerry 34 C1
Madeley Staffs. 20 A2
Madley 13 F4
Madron 3 D3
Maenclochog 12 A4
Maentwrog 18 C3
Maerdy 7 D1
Maesteg 7 D1
Maghull 24 C4
Maiden Bradley 8 B2
Maiden Newton 8 A3
Maidenhead 15 F4
Maidens 33 E4
Maidstone 11 D2
Maldon 17 D4
Mallaig 36 C1
Mallwyd 13 D1
Malmesbury 14 B4
Malpas 7 E1
Malpas Ches. 19 F2
Maltby S.Yorks. 26 B4
Maltby le Marsh 22 B1
Malton 26 C1
Malvern Link 14 A2
Manby 22 B1
Mancetter 20 C4
Manchester 25 E4
Manchester Airport 25 E4
Manea 22 B4
Mangotsfield 14 A4
Manningtree 17 E3
Manorbier 6 A1
Mansfield 21 D1
Mansfield 21 D1
  Woodhouse
Manston 8 B3
Marazion 3 E3
March 22 B4
Marchwiel 19 E2
Marden Kent 11 D2
Mareham le Fen 22 A2
Maresfield 10 C3
Margam 6 C2
Margate 11 F1
Marham 22 C3
Mark 7 F3
Market Bosworth 21 D3
Market Deeping 22 A3
Market Drayton 20 A2
Market Harborough 21 E4
Market Lavington 8 C1
Market Rasen 27 D4
Market Weighton 26 C2
Markfield 21 D3
Markinch 39 D4
Marks Tey 17 D3
Markyate 15 F3
Marlborough 8 C1
Marldon 5 D2
Marlow 15 F4
Marnhull 8 B2
Marple 25 E4
Marsden W.Yorks. 25 F3
Marshfield S.Glos. 14 A4
Marske-by-the-Sea 31 E3
Marston Oxon. 15 D3
Marston Magna 8 A2
Marston Moreteine 15 F2
Martham 23 F3
Martlesham 17 E2
Martley 14 A1
Martock 7 F4
Marybank 41 F2
Marykirk 39 E2
Marypark 42 C3

Maryport 29 E2
Marywell 39 E1
Masham 25 F1
Matlock 20 C1
Matlock Bath 20 C1
Mauchline 33 F3
Maud 43 F3
Maughold 24 B2
Maybole 33 E4
Mayfield 20 C2
Mealsgate 29 E2
Meare 7 F3
Measham 21 D3
Medstead 9 E2
Meidrim 12 A4
Meigle 39 D3
Meikle Kilmory 33 D2
Meikleour 38 C3
Melbourn 16 B2
Melbourne 21 D3
Melksham 8 B1
Melmerby 30 A2
Melrose 34 C3
Melsonby 30 C4
Meltham 25 F3
Melton 17 E2
Melton Mowbray 21 E3
Melvaig 40 C1
Melvich 45 D1
Memsie 43 F2
Menai Bridge 18 B1
Menston 25 F2
Menstrie 38 B4
Mere Wilts. 8 B2
Meriden 20 C4
Merthyr Tydfil 7 D1
Messingham 26 C4
Metfield 17 E1
Metheringham 21 F1
Methlick 43 E3
Methven 38 C3
Methwold 22 C4
Mevagissey 4 A3
Mexborough 26 A4
Mey 45 F1
Miabhig 47 D2
Mickleton Dur. 30 B3
Mickleton Glos. 14 C2
Mid Ardlaw 43 F2
Mid Yell 48 C1
Midbea 49 E2
Middle Barton 15 D2
Middle Rasen 27 D4
Middleham 30 C4
Middlemarsh 8 A3
Middlesbrough 31 D3
Middlesmoor 25 F1
Middleton 25 E4
  Gt.Man.
Middleton Norf. 22 C3
Middleton Cheney 15 D2
Middleton Stoney 15 D3
Middleton-in- 30 B3
  Teesdale
Middleton-on-Sea 10 A4
Middleton-on-the- 26 C2
  Wolds
Middlewich 20 A1
Midhurst 9 F2
Midlem 34 C3
Midsomer Norton 8 A1
Milborne Port 8 A2
Milborne St. 8 B3
  Andrew
Mildenhall 16 C1
Mile End 17 D3
Milfield 35 E3
Milford Surr. 9 F2
Milford Haven 12 A2
Milford on Sea 9 D4
Millbrook Cornw. 4 B3
Millhouse 33 D1
Millom 24 B1
Millport 33 D2

Place	Page	Grid
Milltown of Rothiemay	43	D3
Milnathort	38	C4
Milngavie	33	F1
Milnrow	25	E3
Milnthorpe	24	C1
Milovaig	40	A2
Milton *High.*	41	F3
Milton *P. & K.*	38	B3
Milton Keynes	15	F2
Milton of Campsie	33	F1
Milverton	7	E4
Minard	37	E4
Minchinhampton	14	B3
Minehead	7	D3
Minera	19	E2
Minnigaff	28	B1
Minster (Sheppey) *Kent*	11	E1
Minster (Thanet) *Kent*	11	F2
Minsterley	13	F1
Mintlaw	43	F3
Mirfield	25	F3
Misterton	26	B4
Mitcheldean	14	A3
Mobberley	20	A1
Modbury	4	C3
Moelfre	18	B1
Moffat	34	B4
Mold	19	E2
Molescroft	27	D2
Moniaive	34	A4
Monifieth	39	E3
Monimail	39	D4
Monkokehampton	4	C1
Monks Eleigh	17	D2
Monmouth (Trefynwy)	7	F1
Monreith	28	B2
Montgomery (Trefaldwyn)	13	E1
Montrose	39	E2
Moorends	26	B3
Morar	36	C1
Morebattle	35	D3
Morecambe	24	C1
Morenish	38	A3
Moresby	29	E3
Moreton *Mersey.*	19	E1
Moreton-in-Marsh	14	C2
Moretonhampstead	5	D1
Morfa Nefyn	18	A3
Morley *W.Yorks.*	26	A3
Morpeth	30	C1
Morriston	6	C1
Mortehoe	6	B3
Mortimer's Cross	13	F3
Morton (Bourne) *Lincs.*	22	A3
Morton (Gainsborough) *Lincs.*	26	C4
Morville	20	A4
Mosborough	26	A4
Moscow	33	F3
Mossat	43	D4
Mossblown	33	E3
Mossley	25	E4
Mosstodloch	42	C2
Motherwell	34	A2
Moulsecoomb	10	B4
Moulton *Lincs.*	22	A3
Moulton *Suff.*	16	C1
Mountain Ash	7	E1
Mountbenger	34	C3
Mountsorrel	21	E3
Moy	42	A3
Much Wenlock	20	A4
Muchalls	39	F1
Muir of Fowlis	43	D4
Muir of Ord	41	F2
Muirdrum	39	E3
Muirhead Angus	39	D3
Muirkirk	33	F3
Mulbarton	23	E4
Mulben	42	C2
Mullion	3	E4
Mundesley	23	E2
Mundford	22	C4
Munlochy	42	A2
Murton	31	D2
Musbury	5	F1
Musselburgh	34	C1
Muthill	38	B4
Mybster	45	E2
Mytholmroyd	25	E3

N

Place	Page	Grid
Nailsea	7	F2
Nailsworth	14	B3
Nairn	42	A2
Nantwich	20	A2
Nantyglo	7	E1
Narberth	6	A1
Narborough *Leics.*	21	D4
Narborough *Norf.*	22	C3
Nateby	30	B4
Nazeing	16	B4
Near Sawrey	29	F4
Neath	6	C1
Necton	23	D4
Needham Market	17	D2
Needingworth	16	B1
Nefyn	18	A3
Neilston	33	F2
Nelson	25	E2
Nenthead	30	B2
Neston	19	E1
Nether Langwith	21	D1
Nether Stowey	7	E3
Netherley	39	F1
Netherton *Northumb.*	35	E4
Netherton *W.Yorks.*	25	F3
Nethy Bridge	42	B4
Nettlebed	15	E4
Nettleham	21	F1
New Abbey	29	D1
New Aberdour	43	E2
New Addington	10	B2
New Alresford	9	E2
New Ash Green	10	C2
New Byth	43	E2
New Cumnock	33	F4
New Deer	43	E3
New Galloway	28	C1
New Leeds	43	F2
New Luce	28	A1
New Mills	25	E4
New Milton	9	D3
New Mistley	17	E3
New Pitsligo	43	E2
New Quay	12	B3
New Radnor	13	E3
New Romney	11	E3
New Rossington	26	B4
New Scone	38	C3
New Tredegar	7	E1
Newark-on-Trent	21	E1
Newbiggin-by-the-Sea	31	D1
Newbigging	34	A2
Newbold Verdon	21	D3
Newborough	22	A4
Newbridge *Caerp.*	7	E1
Newburgh *Aber.*	43	F3
Newburgh *Fife*	39	D4
Newburn	30	C1
Newbury	9	E1
Newby Bridge	29	F4
Newcastle *Shrop.*	13	E2
Newcastle Emlyn	12	B4
Newcastle International Airport	30	C1
Newcastle upon Tyne	30	C1
Newcastle-under-Lyme	20	B2
Newcastleton	29	F1
Newent	14	A2
Newhaven	10	C4
Newick	10	B3
Newington	11	D2
Newlyn	3	D3
Newmachar	43	E4
Newmains	34	A2
Newmarket *Suff.*	16	C1
Newmarket *W.Isles*	47	F2
Newmill	43	D2
Newmilns	33	F3
Newnham	14	A3
Newport *Essex*	16	B2
Newport *High.*	45	E3
Newport *I.o.W.*	9	E4
Newport *Newport*	7	F2
Newport *Pembs.*	12	A4
Newport *Tel. & W.*	20	A3
Newport Pagnell	15	F2
Newport-on-Tay	39	D3
Newquay	3	F2
Newton *Arg. & B.*	37	E4
Newton (Bowland) *Lancs.*	25	D2
Newton Abbot	5	D2
Newton Aycliffe	31	D3
Newton Ferrers	4	C3
Newton Mearns	33	F2
Newton Poppleford	5	E1
Newton St. Cyres	5	D1
Newton Stewart	28	B1
Newton-le-Willows	19	F1
Newtonhill	39	F1
Newtonmore	42	A4
Newtown *Here.*	14	A2
Newtown (Y Drenewydd) *Powys*	13	E2
Newtown St. Boswells	35	D3
Newtyle	39	D3
Neyland	12	B2
Ninemile Bar or Crocketford	29	D1
Ninfield	11	D4
Nisbet	35	D3
Norham	35	E2
Normanton *W.Yorks.*	26	A3
North Baddesley	9	D2
North Ballachulish	37	E2
North Berwick	34	C1
North Cave	26	C2
North Cheriton	8	A2
North Cowton	31	D4
North Duffield	26	B2
North Elmham	23	D3
North Ferriby	26	C3
North Grimston	26	C1
North Hykeham	21	F1
North Kessock	42	A3
North Leigh	15	D3
North Middleton	34	C2
North Molton	6	C4
North Queensferry	34	B1
North Shields	31	D1
North Somercotes	27	E4
North Sunderland	35	F3
North Thoresby	27	E4
North Tidworth	9	D1
North Walsham	23	E3
North Weald Bassett	16	B4
North Wingfield	21	D1
Northallerton	31	D4
Northam *Devon*	6	B4
Northampton	15	E1
Northfleet	10	C1
Northill	16	A2
Northleach	14	C3
Northwich	20	A1
Northwood *I.o.W.*	9	E3
Norton *N.Yorks.*	26	C1
Norton *Suff.*	17	D1
Norton Canes	20	B3
Norton Fitzwarren	7	E4
Norwich	23	E4
Norwich Airport	23	E3
Norwick	48	C1
Nottingham	21	D2
Nuneaton	21	D4

O

Place	Page	Grid
Oadby	21	E4
Oakdale	7	E1
Oakengates	20	A3
Oakham	21	F3
Oakley *Bucks.*	15	E3
Oakley *Fife*	34	A1
Oakley *Hants.*	9	E1
Oban	37	D3
Ochiltree	33	F3
Ockbrook	21	D2
Ockle	36	C2
Oddsta	48	C1
Odiham	9	F1
Ogmore	7	D2
Ogmore Vale	7	D1
Okehampton	4	C1
Old Colwyn	18	C1
Old Dailly	33	E4
Old Felixstowe	17	E2
Old Leake	22	B2
Old Town	25	D1
Oldbury *W.Mid.*	20	B4
Oldham	25	E4
Oldland	8	A1
Oldmeldrum	43	E3
Olgrinmore	45	E2
Ollaberry	48	B2
Ollerton *Notts.*	21	E1
Olney	15	F1
Olveston	14	A4
Ombersley	14	B1
Onchan	24	B3
Onich	37	E2
Orford *Suff.*	17	F2
Ormesby St. Margaret	23	F3
Ormiston	34	C1
Ormskirk	24	C3
Orpington	10	C2
Orrell	25	D3
Orton	30	A4
Orton Longueville	22	A4
Oskaig	40	B3
Ossett	26	A3
Oswaldkirk	26	B1
Oswaldtwistle	25	D3
Oswestry	19	E3
Otford	10	C2
Otley *Suff.*	17	E2
Otley *W.Yorks.*	25	F2
Otter Ferry	33	D1
Otterburn	35	E4
Otterswick	48	C2
Ottery St. Mary	5	E1
Oughtibridge	26	A4
Oulton *Suff.*	23	F4
Oundle	21	F4
Outwell	22	B4
Over Wallop	9	D2
Overbister	49	F2
Overseal	20	C3
Overton *Hants.*	9	E1
Overton *Wrex.*	19	E3
Overtown	34	A2
Oxenhope	25	F2
Oxford	15	D3
Oxnam	35	D3
Oxshott	10	A2
Oxted	10	B2
Oxton *Sc.Bord.*	34	C2
Oykel Bridge	41	F1

P

Place	Page	Grid
Padbury	15	E2
Paddock Wood	11	D2
Padiham	25	E2
Padstow	3	F2
Paignton	5	D2
Painswick	14	B3
Paisley	33	F2
Palnackie	29	D2
Pandy	13	F4
Pangbourne	15	E4
Pant-y-dwr	13	D2
Papworth Everard	16	A1
Par	4	A3
Parbold	24	C3
Parkgate	29	E1
Partington	25	D4
Partney	22	B1
Parton	29	D3
Patchway	14	A4
Pateley Bridge	25	F1
Path of Condie	38	C4
Patna	33	E4
Patrick	24	A2
Patrington	27	E3
Patterdale	29	F3
Paulton	8	A1
Paxton	35	E2
Peacehaven	10	B4
Peasedown St. John	8	B1
Peebles	34	B2
Peel	24	A2
Pegswood	30	C1
Peinchorran	40	B3
Pelsall	20	B3
Pelynt	4	A3
Pembrey	6	B1
Pembridge	13	F3
Pembroke	12	B2
Pembroke Dock	12	B2
Pembury	10	C3
Pen-y-bont-fawr	19	D3
Penally	6	A1
Penarth	7	E2
Pencader	12	B4
Pencaitland	34	C1
Pencoed	7	D2
Pendeen	3	D3
Pendine	6	A1
Pendlebury	25	E4
Penicuik	34	B2
Peninver	32	C3
Penistone	25	F4
Penkridge	20	B3
Penley	19	F3
Penmaenmawr	18	C1
Pennyghael	36	C3
Penpont	34	A4
Penrhiw-pal	12	B3
Penrhyn Bay	18	C1
Penrhyndeudraeth	18	B3
Penrith	30	A3
Penryn	3	F3
Pensilva	4	B2
Pentir	18	B2
Pentraeth	18	B1
Pentre	7	D1
Pentrefoelas	18	C2
Penwortham	25	D3
Penybont	13	E3
Penygraig	7	D1
Penygroes	18	B2
Penywaun	7	D1
Penzance	3	D3
Perranporth	3	E2
Pershore	14	B2
Perth	38	C3
Peterborough	22	A4
Peterculter	43	E4
Peterhead	43	F3

Peterlee	31	D2	Portlethen	39	F1	Ranskill	26	B4	Rockcliffe	29	D2	St. Andrews	39	E4

Peterlee 31 D2
Petersfield 9 F2
Petworth 10 A3
Pevensey 10 C4
Pewsey 8 C1
Pickering 31 F4
Piddletrenthide 8 B3
Pierowall 49 E2
Pilgrims Hatch 16 B4
Pilling 24 C2
Pilning 7 F2
Pimperne 8 B3
Pinchbeck 22 A3
Pinhoe 5 D1
Pinwherry 28 A1
Pirbright 9 F1
Pirnmill 32 C2
Pitagowan 38 B2
Pitlochry 38 B2
Pitmedden 43 E3
Pitscottie 39 D4
Pitt 9 D2
Pittentrail 42 A1
Pittenweem 39 E4
Plean 34 A1
Pleasley 21 D1
Plwmp 12 B3
Plymouth 4 C3
Plymouth City 4 C2
  Airport
Plympton 4 C3
Plymstock 4 C3
Pocklington 26 C2
Polbeth 34 A2
Polegate 10 C4
Polesworth 20 C3
Polloch 37 D2
Polmont 34 A1
Polperro 4 A3
Polwarth 35 D2
Pondersbridge 22 A4
Pontardawe 6 C1
Pontarddulais 6 C1
Pontefract 26 A3
Ponteland 30 C1
Pontesbury 13 F1
Pontllanfraith 7 E1
Pontrhydfendigaid 12 C3
Pontrilas 13 F4
Pontyberem 6 B1
Pontycymer 7 D1
Pontypool 7 E1
Pontypridd 7 E1
Pool 25 F2
Poole 8 C4
Poolewe 40 C1
Pooley Bridge 29 F3
Porlock 7 D3
Port Appin 37 D3
Port Askaig 32 B1
Port Bannatyne 33 D2
Port Driseach 33 D1
Port Ellen 32 A2
Port Erin 24 A3
Port Eynon 6 B2
Port Glasgow 33 E1
Port Henderson 40 C2
Port Logan 28 A2
Port nan Giúran 47 F2
Port nan Long 46 B1
PortNis 47 F1
Port of Menteith 38 A4
Port St. Mary 24 A3
Port Talbot 6 C1
Port William 28 B2
Portchester 9 E3
Portencross 33 D2
Portesham 8 A4
Porth 7 D1
Porthcawl 7 D2
Porthleven 3 E4
Porthmadog 18 B3
Portishead 7 F2
Portknockie 43 D2

Portlethen 39 F1
Portmahomack 42 B1
Portnacroish 37 D2
Portnahaven 32 A2
Portnalong 40 A3
Portnancon 44 B1
Portpatrick 28 A2
Portreath 3 E3
Portree 40 B3
Portsmouth 9 E3
Portsoy 43 D2
Potterne 8 C1
Potters Bar 16 A4
Potton 16 A2
Poulton-le-Fylde 24 C2
Powburn 35 F3
Powick 14 B1
Powmill 38 C4
Poynton 25 E4
Prees 19 F3
Preesall 24 C2
Prescot 19 F1
Prestatyn 19 D1
Prestbury Ches. 20 B1
Prestbury Glos. 14 B3
Presteigne 13 F3
Preston Dorset 8 B4
Preston E.Riding 27 D3
Preston Lancs. 25 D3
Preston Sc.Bord. 35 D2
Prestonpans 34 C1
Prestwich 25 E4
Prestwick 33 E3
Prestwick 33 E3
  International Airport
Prestwood 15 F3
Princes Risborough 15 E3
Princethorpe 15 D1
Princetown 4 C2
Probus 3 F3
Prudhoe 30 C2
Puddletown 8 B3
Pudsey 25 F2
Pulborough 10 A3
Pumsaint 12 C3
Purfleet 10 C1
Puriton 7 F3
Purley 10 B2
Purley on Thames 15 E4
Purton 14 C4
Pwllheli 18 A3
Pyle 7 D2

Q
Quedgeley 14 A3
Queenborough 11 D1
Queensbury 25 F3
Queensferry 19 E2
Queniborough 21 E3
Quernmore 25 D1

R
Rackheath 23 E3
Radcliffe Gt.Man. 25 E3
Radcliffe on Trent 21 E2
Radford Semele 15 D1
Radlett 16 A4
Radstock 8 A1
Radford 42 B2
Raglan 7 F1
Rainford 24 C4
Rainhill 19 F1
Rainow 20 B1
Rainworth 21 E1
Rait 39 D3
Rampside 24 C1
Ramsbottom 25 E3
Ramsbury 14 C4
Ramsey Cambs. 16 A1
Ramsey I.o.M. 24 B2
Ramsey St. Mary's 22 A4
Ramsgate 11 F2

Ranskill 26 B4
Rathillet 39 D3
Ratho 34 B1
Rattray 38 C3
Raunds 15 F1
Ravenglass 29 E4
Ravenshead 21 D2
Rawcliffe E.Riding 26 B3
Rawcliffe York 26 B2
Rawmarsh 26 A4
Rawtenstall 25 E3
Rayleigh 11 D1
Rayne 16 C3
Reading 15 E4
Reay 45 D1
Red Roses 6 A1
Redbourn 16 A3
Redcar 31 E3
Redcastle 41 F3
Redcliff Bay 7 F2
Redditch 14 B1
Redford 39 E3
Redhill Surr. 10 B2
Redlynch 8 C2
Redpoint 40 C2
Redruth 3 E3
Reepham 23 E3
Reigate 10 B2
Reiss 45 F2
Renfrew 33 F2
Rennington 35 F3
Repton 20 C3
Rescobie 39 E2
Resolven 7 D1
Reston 35 E2
Retford (East 21 E1
  Retford)
Reydon 17 F1
Rhayader 13 D2
Rhiconich 44 B2
Rhoose 7 E2
Rhos 6 C1
Rhôs-on-Sea 18 C1
Rhoslanerchrugog 19 E2
Rhossili 6 B2
Rhu 33 E1
Rhuddlan 19 D1
Rhyl 19 D1
Rhymney 7 E1
Rhynie 43 D3
Ribchester 25 D2
Richmond 30 C4
Rickarton 39 F1
Rickinghall 17 D1
Rickmansworth 10 A1
Riding Mill 30 C2
Rigside 34 A3
Ringford 28 C2
Ringmer 10 C4
Ringwood 8 C3
Ripley Derbys. 21 D2
Ripley N.Yorks. 26 A1
Ripon 26 A1
Ripple 14 B2
Ripponden 25 F3
Risca 7 E1
Rishton 25 D3
Risley 21 D2
Roade 15 E1
Roadside 45 E1
Roadside of 39 F1
  Kinneff
Roath 7 E2
Roberton Sc.Bord. 34 C4
Roberton S.Lan. 34 A3
Robin Hood's Bay 31 F4
Rocester 20 C2
Rochdale 25 E3
Roche 4 A2
Rochester Medway 11 D1
Rochester 35 E4
  Northumb.
Rochford 11 D1
Rock 14 A1

Rockcliffe 29 D2
Rockingham 21 F4
Rode Heath 20 A1
Rodney Stoke 7 F3
Rogart 45 D4
Rogate 9 F2
Rogerstone 7 E2
Roghadal 47 D4
Romannobridge 34 B2
Romford Gt.Lon. 10 C1
Romsey 9 D2
Romsley Worcs. 20 B4
Ropley 9 E2
Ropsley 21 F2
Rosedale Abbey 31 E4
Rosehearty 43 F2
Rosemarkie 42 A2
Rosewell 34 B2
Roshven 37 D1
Roskhill 40 A3
Roslin 34 B2
Ross-on-Wye 14 A2
Rossett 19 E2
Rossington 26 B4
Rothbury 35 E4
Rotherfield 10 C3
Rotherham 26 A4
Rothes 42 C3
Rothesay 33 D2
Rothiesholm 49 F3
Rothley 21 E3
Rothwell 21 E4
  Northants.
Rothwell W.Yorks. 26 A3
Rottingdean 10 B4
Roughton 23 E2
Roundway 8 C1
Rowde 8 C1
Rowlands Gill 30 C2
Roxton 16 A2
Royal Leamington 14 C1
  Spa
Royal Tunbridge 10 C3
  Wells
Roybridge 37 F1
Roydon 17 D1
Royston Herts. 16 B2
Royston S.Yorks. 26 A3
Royton 25 E3
Ruabon 19 E3
Ruardean 14 A3
Ruddington 21 E2
Rudgwick 10 A3
Rudston 27 D1
Rufford 24 C3
Rugby 15 D1
Rugeley 20 B3
Rumney 7 E2
Runcorn 19 F1
Runwell 11 D1
Rushall W.Mid. 20 B4
Rushden 15 F1
Rushmere St. 17 E2
  Andrew
Ruskington 22 A2
Ruspidge 14 A3
Rustington 10 A4
Rutherglen 33 F2
Ruthin 19 D2
Ruyton-XI-Towns 19 F3
Ryde 9 E3
Rye 11 E3
Ryhall 21 F3

S
Sacriston 30 C2
Saddell 32 C3
Saffron Walden 16 B2
Saham Toney 23 D4
Saighdinis 46 B1
St. Abbs 35 E1
St. Agnes 3 E3
St. Albans 16 A3

St. Andrews 39 E4
St. Asaph 19 D1
  (Llanelwy)
St. Athan 7 D2
St. Austell 4 A3
St. Bees 29 D3
St. Briavels 14 A3
St. Brides Major 7 D2
St. Buryan 3 D4
St. Clears 12 A4
St. Columb Major 3 F2
St. Combs 43 F2
St. Cyrus 39 F2
St. David's 12 A1
St. Day 3 E3
St. Dennis 3 F2
St. Dogmaels 12 A3
St. Endellion 4 A2
St. Enoder 3 F2
St. Fergus 43 F2
St. Fillans 38 A3
St. Germans 4 B2
St. Helens Mersey. 25 D4
St. Ishmael 6 B1
St. Ive 4 B2
St. Ives Cambs. 16 A1
St. Ives Cornw. 3 D3
St. John's Chapel 30 B2
St. John's Town 28 C1
  of Dalry
St. Just 3 D3
St. Just in 3 F3
  Roseland
St. Keverne 3 F4
St. Leonards 8 C3
St. Margaret's at 11 F2
  Cliffe
St. Margaret's 49 E4
  Hope
St. Martin's 19 E3
St. Mary Bourne 9 D1
St. Mary's 49 E3
St. Mary's Bay 11 E3
St. Mawes 3 F3
St. Merryn 3 F2
St. Monans 39 E4
St. Neots 16 A1
St. Osyth 17 E3
St. Peter's 11 F1
St. Stephen 3 F2
St. Teath 4 A2
Salcombe 4 C3
Sale 25 E4
Salen Arg. & B. 36 C3
Salen High. 37 D2
Salford Gt.Man. 25 E4
Salfords 10 B2
Salhouse 23 E3
Saline 34 A1
Salisbury 8 C2
Salsburgh 34 A2
Saltash 4 B2
Saltburn-by- 31 E3
  the-Sea
Saltcoats 33 E3
Saltdean 10 B4
Saltford 8 A1
Saltney 19 E2
Sanaigmore 32 A1
Sandbach 20 A1
Sandgarth 49 E3
Sandhead 28 A2
Sandhurst 9 F1
Sandiacre 21 D2
Sandness 48 A3
Sandown 9 E4
Sandplace 4 B3
Sandridge 16 A3
Sandsend 31 F3
Sandwich 11 F2
Sandwick 48 B4
Sandy 16 A2
Sandygate 24 B2
Sanquhar 34 A4

Place	Page	Grid
Sapcote	21	D4
Sarre	11	F2
Satley	30	C2
Saundersfoot	6	A1
Sawbridgeworth	16	B3
Sawston	16	B2
Sawtry	16	A1
Saxilby	21	F1
Saxmundham	17	F1
Saxthorpe	23	E3
Scalasaig	36	B4
Scalby	31	F4
Scalloway	48	B3
Scampton	21	F1
Scapa	49	E3
Scarborough	27	D1
Scarcliffe	21	D1
Scarinish	36	A3
Scarisbrick	24	C3
Scleddau	12	B1
Scole	17	E1
Sconser	40	B3
Scorton	30	C4
Scotch Corner	30	C4
Scotter	26	C4
Scotton	30	C4
Scourie	44	A2
Scousburgh	48	B4
Scrabster	45	E1
Scraptoft	21	E3
Scremerston	35	E2
Scunthorpe	26	C3
Seaford	10	C4
Seaham	31	D2
Seahouses	35	F3
Seamer N.Yorks.	26	C1
Seamill	33	E2
Seascale	29	E4
Seaton Cumb.	29	E3
Seaton Devon	5	E1
Seaton Delaval	31	D1
Seaton Sluice	31	D1
Sedbergh	30	A4
Sedgebrook	21	F2
Sedgefield	31	D3
Sedgley	20	B4
Seend	8	B1
Seghill	31	D1
Seighford	20	B3
Selattyn	19	E3
Selby	26	B3
Selkirk	34	C3
Sellafield	29	E4
Sellafirth	48	C1
Sellindge	11	E3
Selsey	9	F4
Selston	21	D2
Send	10	A2
Sennen	3	D4
Sennybridge	13	D4
Setter	48	B3
Settle	25	E1
Seven Sisters	7	D1
Sevenoaks	10	C2
Severn Beach	7	F2
Sgiogarstaigh	47	F1
Shaftesbury	8	B2
Shalfleet	9	D4
Shalford	10	A2
Shanklin	9	E4
Shap	30	A3
Sharpness	14	A3
Shavington	20	A2
Shaw	25	E3
Sheering	16	B3
Sheerness	11	D1
Sheffield	26	A4
Sheffield City Airport	26	A4
Shefford	16	A2
Shelf	25	F3
Shenstone Staffs.	20	C3
Shepley	25	F3
Shepperton	10	A2
Shepshed	21	D3
Shepton Mallet	8	A2
Sherborne	8	A3
Sherborne St. John	9	E1
Sherburn	31	D2
Sherburn in Elmet	26	A2
Shere	10	A2
Sheriff Hutton	26	B1
Sheriffhales	20	A3
Sheringham	23	E2
Sherston	14	B4
Shevington	25	D3
Shiel Bridge	41	D4
Shieldaig	40	C2
Shifnal	20	A3
Shilbottle	35	F4
Shildon	30	C3
Shinfield	9	F1
Shinness Lodge	44	C3
Shiplake	15	E4
Shipley W.Yorks.	25	F2
Shipston on Stour	14	C2
Shipton N.Yorks.	26	B1
Shipton Shrop.	20	A4
Shipton-under Wychwood	14	C3
Shirebrook	21	D1
Shiremoor	31	D1
Shirenewton	7	F1
Shirland	21	D1
Shoeburyness	11	E1
Shoreham Kent	10	C2
Shoreham-by-Sea	10	B4
Shotley Gate	17	E2
Shotton Flints.	19	E2
Shotts	34	A2
Shrewsbury	13	F1
Shrewton	8	C2
Shrivenham	14	C4
Siabost	47	E1
Sible Hedingham	16	C2
Sibsey	22	B2
Sidbury	5	E1
Sidcup	10	C1
Sidford	5	E1
Sidley	11	D4
Sidmouth	5	E1
Sigglesthorne	27	D2
Sileby	21	E3
Silloth	29	E2
Silsden	25	F2
Silverdale Lancs.	24	C1
Silverstone	15	E2
Silverton	5	D1
Simonsbath	6	C3
Sittingbourne	11	D2
Siulaisiadar	47	F2
Skaill (East Coast) Ork.	49	F3
Skaill (West Coast) Ork.	49	D3
Skaw	48	C2
Skegness	22	B1
Skelmersdale	24	C3
Skelmorlie	33	E2
Skelton	31	E3
Skelwick	49	E2
Skenfrith	13	F4
Skerray	44	C1
Skipness	32	C2
Skipsea	27	D2
Skipton	25	E2
Slaidburn	25	D2
Slaithwaite	25	F3
Slamannan	34	A1
Sleaford	21	F2
Sledmere	26	C1
Sleights	31	F4
Sligachan	40	B3
Slinfold	10	A3
Slough	10	A1
Smailholm	35	D3
Smalley	21	D2
Smeeth	11	E3
Smethwick	20	B4
Snainton	26	C1
Snaith	26	B3
Snettisham	22	C3
Snitterfield	14	C1
Snodland	11	D2
Soham	16	B1
Solas	46	B1
Solihull	20	C4
Solva	12	A1
Somercotes	21	D2
Somersham	16	B1
Somerton	7	F4
Sompting	10	B4
Sonning Common	15	E4
Sorbie	28	B2
Sorisdale	36	B2
Sorn	33	F3
South Anston	26	B4
South Bank	31	E3
South Benfleet	11	D1
South Brent	4	C2
South Cave	26	C3
South Chard	5	F1
South Harting	9	F2
South Hetton	31	D2
South Kelsey	27	D4
South Kirkby	26	A3
South Leverton	26	C4
South Lopham	17	D1
South Molton	6	C4
South Normanton	21	D1
South Ockendon	10	C1
South Oxhey	10	A1
South Petherton	7	F4
South Queensferry	34	B1
South Shields	31	D1
South Skirlaugh	27	D2
South Woodham Ferrers	16	C4
South Wootton	22	C3
Southam	15	D1
Southampton	9	E3
Southampton International Airport	9	D3
Southborough	10	C3
Southbourne W.Suss.	9	F3
Southdean	35	D4
Southend Arg. & B.	32	C4
Southend-on-Sea	11	D1
Southery	22	C4
Southgate Gt.Lon.	10	B1
Southminster	17	D4
Southport	24	C3
Southwell	21	E2
Southwick Wilts.	8	B1
Southwold	17	F1
Sowerby	26	A1
Sowerby Bridge	25	F3
Spalding	22	A3
Spean Bridge	37	F1
Speen	9	D1
Spennymoor	31	D3
Spey Bay	42	C2
Spilsby	22	B1
Spinningdale	42	A1
Spittal	45	E2
Spittal of Glenshee	38	C2
Spixworth	23	E3
Spofforth	26	A2
Springholm	29	D1
Springside	33	E3
Sproatley	27	D2
Sprowston	23	E3
Sproxton	26	B1
Stadhampton	15	E3
Stadhlaigearraidh	46	A2
Staffin	40	B2
Stafford	20	B3
Staindrop	30	C3
Staines	10	A1
Stainforth N.Yorks.	25	E1
Stainforth S.Yorks.	26	B3
Staintondale	31	F4
Stalbridge	8	B3
Stalham	23	F3
Stalling Busk	30	B4
Stalybridge	25	E4
Stamford	21	F3
Stamfordham	30	C1
Standish	25	D3
Standon	16	B3
Stane	34	A2
Stanford-le-Hope	11	D1
Stanhoe	22	C2
Stanhope	30	B2
Stanley Dur.	30	C2
Stanley P. & K.	38	C3
Stanley W.Yorks.	26	A3
Stannington Northumb.	30	C1
Stansted Airport	16	B3
Stansted Mountfitchet	16	B3
Stanton	17	D1
Stanway	17	D3
Stapleford Notts.	21	D2
Staplehurst	11	D2
Starcross	5	D2
Startforth	30	C3
Staunton	14	A2
Staveley	21	D1
Staxton	27	D1
Steeple Claydon	15	E2
Steeton	25	F2
Stenhousemuir	34	A1
Stenness	48	A2
Stenton	35	D1
Stevenage	16	A3
Stevenston	33	E3
Stewarton	33	E2
Steyning	10	B4
Stibb Cross	6	B4
Stichill	35	D3
Stickney	22	B2
Stillington N.Yorks.	26	B1
Stilton	22	A4
Stirling	34	A1
Stobo	34	B3
Stock	16	C4
Stockbridge	9	D2
Stockport	25	E4
Stocksbridge	26	A4
Stocksfield	30	C2
Stockton Heath	19	F1
Stockton-on-Tees	31	D3
Stoer	44	A3
Stoke Albany	21	E4
Stoke Ash	17	E1
Stoke Holy Cross	23	E4
Stoke Mandeville	15	F3
Stoke Poges	10	A1
Stoke Prior Worcs.	14	B1
Stoke-by-Nayland	17	D2
Stoke-on-Trent	20	B2
Stokenchurch	15	E4
Stokenham	5	D3
Stokesay	13	F2
Stokesley	31	E4
Stone Glos.	14	A4
Stone Kent	10	C1
Stone Staffs.	20	B2
Stonehaven	39	F1
Stonehouse Glos.	14	A3
Stonehouse S.Lan.	34	A2
Stoneykirk	28	A2
Stony Stratford	15	E2
Stornoway	47	F2
Storrington	10	A4
Stotfold	16	A2
Stourbridge	20	B4
Stourport-on-Severn	14	A1
Stow	34	C2
Stow-on-the-Wold	14	C2
Stowmarket	17	D2
Strachan	39	E1
Strachur	37	E4
Stradbroke	17	E1
Stradishall	16	C2
Stradsett	22	C4
Straloch	38	C2
Stranraer	28	A2
Stratford-upon-Avon	14	C1
Strathaven	33	F2
Strathblane	33	F1
Strathdon	42	C4
Strathmiglo	38	C4
Strathpeffer	41	F2
Strathy	45	D1
Strathyre	38	A4
Stratton	4	B1
Stratton St. Margaret	14	C4
Streatley	15	E4
Street	7	F4
Strensall	26	B1
Stretford	25	E4
Stretham	16	B1
Stretton (Burton upon Trent) Staffs.	20	C3
Strichen	43	F2
Stromeferry	40	C3
Stromness	49	D3
Stronachlachar	37	F4
Strone	33	E1
Strontian	37	D2
Stroud	14	B3
Stuartfield	43	F3
Studley Warks.	14	C1
Sturminster Newton	8	B3
Sturry	11	E2
Sturton le Steeple	26	C4
Sudbury Derbys.	20	C2
Sudbury Suff.	17	D2
Sully	7	E2
Sumburgh	48	B4
Summer Bridge	25	F1
Sunbury	10	A1
Sunderland	31	D2
Sunninghill	9	F1
Surfleet	22	A3
Sutterton	22	A3
Sutton (Ely) Cambs.	16	B1
Sutton Bridge	22	B3
Sutton Coldfield	20	C4
Sutton Courtenay	15	D4
Sutton in Ashfield	21	D1
Sutton on Trent	21	E1
Sutton Valence	11	D2
Sutton-on-the-Forest	26	B1
Swadlincote	20	C3
Swaffham	22	C4
Swanage	8	C4
Swanland	26	C3
Swanley	10	C2
Swanscombe	10	C1
Swansea	6	C1
Swanton Morley	23	D3
Sway	9	D3
Swindon Swin.	14	C4
Swindon Village	14	B2
Swinefleet	26	C3
Swinton Gt.Man.	25	E4
Swinton Sc.Bord.	35	E2
Swinton S.Yorks.	26	A4
Symbister	48	C3
Symington S.Ayr.	33	E3
Symington S.Lan.	34	A2
Synod Inn	12	B3
Syre	44	C2
Syston	21	E3

T

Tabost	47	F1
Tadcaster	26	A2
Tadley	9	E1
Taffs Well	7	E2
Tain	42	A1
Takeley	16	B3
Talgarreg	12	B3
Talgarth	13	E4
Taliesin	12	C2
Talisker	40	A3
Talladale	41	D2
Tamworth	20	C3
Tannadice	39	E2
Tansley	21	D1
Taobh Tuath	47	D3
Tarbert (Jura)	32	B1
Arg. & B.		
Tarbert (Kintyre)	32	C2
Arg. & B.		
Tarbet	37	F4
Tarbolton	33	F3
Tarfside	39	E1
Tarleton	24	C3
Tarporley	19	F2
Tarrel	42	B1
Tarves	43	E3
Tarvin	19	F2
Tattershall	22	A2
Taunton	7	E4
Taverham	23	E3
Tavistock	4	C2
Tayinloan	32	C2
Taynuilt	37	E3
Tayport	39	D3
Tayvallich	32	C1
Teangue	40	C4
Tebay	30	A4
Teesside	31	D3
International Airport		
Teignmouth	5	D2
Telford	20	A3
Temple Bar	12	B3
Temple Sowerby	30	A3
Templeton	6	A1
Tenbury Wells	14	A1
Tenby	6	A1
Tenterden	11	D3
Terrington	26	B1
Terrington St.	22	B3
Clement		
Tetbury	14	B4
Tetford	22	A1
Tetney	27	E4
Teviothead	34	C4
Tewkesbury	14	B2
Teynham	11	E2
Thame	15	E3
Thatcham	9	E1
Thaxted	16	C3
The Mumbles	6	C2
The Stocks	11	D3
Theale	15	E4
Thetford	17	D1
Thirsk	26	A1
Thornaby-on-Tees	31	D3
Thornbury	14	A4
Thorne	26	B3
Thorney *Peter.*	22	A4
Thorngumbald	27	D3
Thornhill *D. & G.*	34	A4
Thornhill *Stir.*	38	A4
Thornley	31	D2
Thornton *Fife*	39	D4
Thornton *Lancs.*	24	C2
Thornton *Mersey.*	24	C4
Thornton Dale	26	C1
Thorpe Market	23	E2
Thorpe on the Hill	21	F1
Lincs.		
Thorpe St. Andrew	23	E4
Thorpe-le-Soken	17	E3
Thorpeness	17	F1
Thrapston	21	F4

Threlkeld	29	F3
Threshfield	25	E1
Thropton	35	E4
Thrumster	45	F2
Thrupp	14	B3
Thrybergh	26	A4
Thundersley	11	D1
Thurcroft	26	A4
Thurlby	22	A3
Thurmaston	21	E3
Thurnscoe	26	A4
Thursby	29	F2
Thurso	45	E1
Thurton	23	E4
Thwaite	30	B4
Tibbermore	38	C3
Tibshelf	21	D1
Ticehurst	11	D3
Tickhill	26	B4
Ticknall	21	D3
Tidenham	14	A4
Tideswell	20	C1
Tighnabruaich	33	D1
Tilbury	10	C1
Tilehurst	15	E4
Tillicoultry	38	B4
Tillyfourie	43	D4
Tilston	19	F2
Timsbury	8	A1
Timsgearraidh	47	D2
Tingewick	15	E2
Tingwall	49	E3
Tintagel	4	A1
Tintern Parva	7	F1
Tiptree	17	D3
Tisbury	8	B2
Tiverton	7	D4
Toab	48	B4
Tobermory	36	C2
Toberonochy	37	D4
Toddington *Beds.*	15	F2
Toddington *Glos.*	14	B2
Todmorden	25	E3
Toft	48	B2
Togston	35	F4
Tolastadh	47	E2
a'Chaolais		
Tolastadh Ur	47	F1
Toll of Birness	43	F3
Tollesbury	17	D3
Tolleshunt D'Arcy	17	D3
Tomatin	42	A3
Tomich	42	A2
Tomintoul	42	C4
Tomnavoulin	42	C3
Tonbridge	10	C2
Tongland	28	C2
Tongue	44	C2
Tonna	6	C1
Tonyrefail	7	D2
Topcliffe	26	A1
Topsham	5	D1
Tore	41	F2
Tormore	32	C3
Torphichen	34	A1
Torphins	43	D4
Torpoint	4	B3
Torquay	5	D2
Torrance	33	F1
Torridon	41	D2
Torrin	40	B4
Torthorwald	29	E1
Torver	29	F4
Toscaig	40	C3
Tosside	25	E2
Totland	9	D4
Totnes	5	D2
Tottington	25	E3
Totton	9	D3
Tow Law	30	C2
Towcester	15	E2
Town Yetholm	35	E3
Townhead of	29	D1
Greenlaw		

Towyn	19	D1
Tranent	34	C1
Trawsfynydd	18	C3
Trecastle	13	D4
Tredegar	7	E1
Tredington	14	C2
Treeton	26	A4
Trefaldwyn	13	E1
(Montgomery)		
Trefeglwys	13	D2
Trefriw	18	C2
Trefynwy	7	F1
(Monmouth)		
Tregaron	12	C3
Tregony	3	F3
Tregynon	13	E1
Treharris	7	E1
Treherbert	7	D1
Trelech	12	A4
Trelleck	7	F1
Tremadog	18	B3
Trenance	3	F2
Treorchy	7	D1
Tressait	38	B2
Tretower	13	E4
Trimdon	31	D3
Trimsaran	6	B1
Tring	15	F3
Trinity	39	E2
Trochry	38	C3
Troedyrhiw	7	E1
Troon	33	E3
Troutbeck	29	F4
Troutbeck Bridge	29	F4
Trowbridge	8	B1
Trumpington	16	B2
Truro	3	F3
Tudweiloig	18	A3
Tummel Bridge	38	B2
Tunga	47	F2
Tunstall *Suff.*	17	F2
Turnberry	33	E4
Turners Hill	10	B3
Turriff	43	E2
Tutbury	20	C3
Tutshill	7	F1
Tuxford	21	E1
Twatt	49	D3
Twechar	33	F1
Tweedmouth	35	E2
Tweedsmuir	34	B3
Twyford *W'ham*	15	E4
Twyford *Hants.*	9	E2
Twynholm	28	C2
Twyning	14	B2
Tyndrum	37	F3
Tynemouth	31	D1
Tythegston	7	D2
Tywardreath	4	A3
Tywyn	12	C1

U

Uachdar	46	B2
Uckfield	10	C3
Uddingston	33	F2
Uddington	34	A3
Uffculme	7	E4
Uig	40	D1
Ulbster	45	F2
Ulceby	27	D3
Ulgham	35	F4
Ullapool	41	D1
Ulleskelf	26	B2
Ulpha	29	E4
Ulsta	48	B2
Ulverston	24	C1
Umberleigh	6	C4
Unapool	44	B2
Undy	7	F2
Unstone	21	D1
Up Holland	25	D4
Upavon	8	C1
Uplyme	5	F1

Upper Clatford	9	D2
Upper Heyford	15	D2
Upper Knockando	42	C3
Upper Tean	20	B2
Uppingham	21	F4
Upton *Ches.*	19	F2
Upton *Dorset*	8	C3
Upton St. Leonards	14	B3
Upton on Severn	14	B2
Urafirth	48	B2
Urmston	25	D4
Ushaw Moor	30	C2
Usk	7	F1
Uttoxeter	20	C2
Uxbridge	10	A1
Uyeasound	48	C1

V

Valley	18	A1
Valsgarth	48	C1
Veensgarth	48	B3
Ventnor	9	E4
Verwood	8	C3
Vickerstown	24	B1
Vidlin	48	C2
Viewpark	33	F2
Virginia Water	10	A2
Voe	48	B2

W

Waddesdon	15	E3
Waddington	21	F1
Wadebridge	4	A2
Wadhurst	10	C3
Wainfleet All	22	B2
Saints		
Wainhouse Corner	4	A1
Wakefield	26	A3
Walberswick	17	F1
Walderslade	11	D2
Wales	26	A4
Wallasey	19	E1
Wallingford	15	E4
Walls	48	B3
Wallsend	31	D1
Walmer	11	F2
Walsall	20	B4
Waltham	27	D4
Waltham Abbey	16	B4
Waltham on the	21	E3
Wolds		
Walton on the	17	E3
Naze		
Walton-le-Dale	25	D3
Walton-on-Thames	10	A2
Wantage	15	D4
Warboys	16	A1
Warcop	30	A3
Wardington	15	D2
Ware	16	B3
Wareham	8	B4
Wargrave	15	E4
Wark	30	B1
Warkworth	35	F4
Warlingham	10	B2
Warmington	15	D2
Warminster	8	B1
Warrington	19	F1
Warslow	20	C1
Warsop	21	D1
Warton (Carnforth)	24	C1
Lancs.		
Warwick	14	C1
Warwick Bridge	29	F2
Wasbister	49	E2
Washington	31	D2
T. & W.		
Wass	26	B1
Watchet	7	E3
Watchgate	30	A4
Water Orton	20	C4
Waterbeach	16	B1

Waterbeck	29	F1
Waterlooville	9	E3
Watford *Herts.*	16	A4
Wath upon Dearne	26	A4
Watlington	15	E4
Watten	45	F2
Watton	23	D4
Watton-at-Stone	16	A3
Weaverham	19	F1
Wedmore	7	F3
Wednesbury	20	B4
Weedon Bec	15	E1
Weem	38	B2
Weldon	21	F4
Wellesbourne	14	C1
Wellingborough	15	F1
Wellington	20	A3
Tel. & W.		
Wellington *Som.*	7	E4
Wells	7	F3
Wells-next-the-Sea	23	D2
Welney	22	B4
Welshpool	13	E1
Welton *Lincs.*	21	F1
Welwyn	16	A3
Welwyn Garden	16	A3
City		
Wem	19	F3
Wembdon	7	E3
Wemyss Bay	33	E1
Wendens Ambo	16	B2
Wendover	15	F3
Wendron	3	E3
Wensley	30	C4
Wentworth	26	A4
S. Yorks.		
Weobley	13	F3
Wereham	22	C4
West Auckland	30	C3
West Bergholt	17	D3
West Bridgford	21	E2
West Bromwich	20	B4
West Calder	34	A2
West Coker	7	F4
West Grinstead	10	B3
West Haddon	15	E1
West Harptree	7	F3
West Hill	5	E1
West Kilbride	33	E2
West Kirby	19	E1
West Knapton	26	C1
West Lavington	8	C1
West Linton	34	B2
West Lulworth	8	B4
West Malling	11	D2
West Meon	9	E2
West Mersea	17	D3
West Monkton	7	E4
West Moors	8	C3
West Somerton	23	F3
West Tarbert	32	C2
West Winch	22	C3
West Wycombe	15	E4
West Yell	48	B2
Westbury	8	B1
Westcott	10	A2
Westerdale	45	E2
Westergate	9	F3
Westerham	10	C2
Westfield	11	D4
Westgate	30	B2
Westhill	43	E4
Westleton	17	F1
Westness	49	E2
Westnewton	29	E2
Weston *Dorset*	8	A4
Weston *Staffs.*	20	B3
Weston-super-Mare	7	F3
Westonzoyland	7	F4
Westruther	35	D2
Westward Ho!	6	B4
Wetheral	29	F2
Wetherby	26	A2
Weybridge	10	A2

Weymouth	8	A4	Wickford	11	D1	Winkleigh	4	C1	Wooburn	10	A1	Wymondham *Leics.*	21	F3

Weymouth 8 A4
Whaley Bridge 25 F4
Whalton 30 C1
Whaplode 22 A3
Whauphill 28 B2
Wheatley Hill 31 D2
Wheaton Aston 20 B3
Wheddon Cross 7 D3
Wherwell 9 D2
Whickham 30 C2
Whiddon Down 4 C1
Whimple 5 E1
Whiston *S.Yorks.* 26 A4
Whitburn *W.Loth.* 34 A2
Whitby *N.Yorks.* 31 F3
Whitchurch *Bucks.* 15 E3
Whitchurch *Cardiff* 7 E2
Whitchurch *Hants.* 9 E1
Whitchurch *Shrop.* 19 F3
Whitecraig 34 C1
Whitehall 49 F2
Whitehaven 29 D3
Whitehill 9 F2
Whitehills 43 E2
Whiterashes 43 E4
Whitfield 11 F2
Whithorn 28 B2
Whiting Bay 33 D3
Whitland 12 A4
Whitley Bay 31 D1
Whitnash 15 D1
Whitstable 11 E2
Whittingham 35 E4
Whittington *Shrop.* 19 E3
Whittlesey 22 A4
Whitworth 25 E3
Wick *High.* 45 F2
Wick *S.Glos.* 14 A4
Wick *V. of Glam.* 7 D2
Wick *W.Suss.* 10 A4
Wickersley 26 A4

Wickford 11 D1
Wickham *Hants.* 9 E3
Wickham Market 17 E2
Wickwar 14 A4
Widecombe in 4 C2
  the Moor
Widford 16 B3
Widnes 19 F1
Wigan 25 D3
Wigmore 13 F2
Wigston 21 E4
Wigton 29 F2
Wigtown 28 B2
Willaston (Wirral) 19 E1
  Ches.
Willingdon 10 C4
Willingham 16 B1
Willington *Dur.* 30 C3
Willington 20 C2
  Derbys.
Williton 7 E3
Willoughby 22 B1
Wilmington *Kent* 10 C1
Wilmslow 25 E4
Wilton *Wilts.* 8 C2
Wimblington 22 B4
Wimborne Minster 8 C3
Wincanton 8 B2
Winchburgh 34 B1
Winchcombe 14 B2
Winchelsea 11 D3
Winchester 9 E2
Windermere 29 F4
Windsor 10 A1
Windygates 39 D4
Winford 7 F2
Wing 15 F3
Wingate 31 D2
Wingerworth 21 D1
Wingham 11 F2
Winkfield 10 A1

Winkleigh 4 C1
Winnersh 9 F1
Winscombe 7 F3
Winsford *Ches.* 19 F2
Winsley 8 B1
Winslow 15 E2
Winston 30 C3
Winterbourne 14 A4
Winterbourne 8 A4
  Abbas
Winterton 26 C3
Winton 30 B3
Winwick *Cambs.* 16 A1
Wirksworth 20 C2
Wisbech 22 B3
Wishaw *N.Lan.* 34 A2
Wistanstow 13 F2
Wistaston 20 A2
Witham 16 C3
Witheridge 7 D4
Withernsea 27 E3
Witley 9 F2
Witney 15 D3
Wittering 21 F3
Witton Gilbert 30 C2
Wiveliscombe 7 E4
Wivenhoe 17 D3
Woburn 15 F2
Woburn Sands 15 F2
Woking 10 A2
Wokingham 9 F1
Wold Newton 27 D1
Wollaston 15 F1
  Northants.
Wolsingham 30 C2
Wolston 15 D1
Wolverhampton 20 B4
Wolverley *Worcs.* 20 B4
Wolverton *M.K.* 15 E2
Wombourne 20 B4
Wombwell 26 A4

Wooburn 10 A1
Woodborough 21 E2
Woodbridge 17 E2
Woodcote 15 E4
Woodhall Spa 22 A1
Woodingdean 10 B4
Woodland 30 C3
Woodley 15 E4
Woodmansey 27 D2
Woodplumpton 25 D2
Woodstock 15 D3
Woodton 23 E4
Woodville 20 C3
Wool 8 B4
Woolacombe 6 B3
Wooler 35 E3
Woolston *Warr.* 19 F1
Wootton 15 F2
Wootton Bassett 14 C4
Worcester 14 B1
Worfield 20 A4
Workington 29 E3
Worksop 21 E1
Wormit 39 D3
Worplesdon 10 A2
Worth 10 B3
Worthing 10 A4
Wotton-under-Edge 14 A4
Woughton on 15 F2
  the Green
Wragby 22 A1
Wrangle 22 B2
Wrea Green 24 C3
Wrelton 31 F4
Wrexham 19 E2
Wrington 7 F2
Writtle 16 C4
Wroughton 14 C4
Wyberton 22 A2
Wye 11 E2
Wylye 8 C2

Wymondham 21 F3
  Leics.
Wymondham 23 E4
  Norf.
Wyre Piddle 14 B2
Wythall 14 C1

Y

Y Drenewydd 13 E2
  (Newtown) *Powys*
Yapton 10 A4
Yarm 31 D3
Yarmouth 9 D4
Yarnton 15 D3
Yarrow 34 C3
Yate 14 A4
Yateley 9 F1
Yatton 7 F2
Yaxley 22 A4
Yeadon 25 F2
Yealmpton 4 C3
Yeovil 7 F4
Yeovilton 7 F4
Yetts o' Muckhart 38 C4
Ynysddu 7 E1
York 26 B2
Youlgreave 20 C1
Yoxall 20 C3
Yoxford 17 F1
Ysbyty Ystwyth 12 C2
Ystalyfera 6 C1
Ystrad 7 D1
Ystradgynlais 6 C1

Z

Zennor 3 D3

DISTANCE IN KILOMETRES

DISTANCE IN MILES